Nothing Like Work
or
Right in the D'Oyly Carte

A memoir of the D'Oyly Carte Opera Company
in its final years 1975–1982

David Mackie

GHP
Grosvenor House
Publishing Limited

This book is published by
Grosvenor House Publishing Ltd
Link House
140 The Broadway, Tolworth, Surrey, KT6 7HT.
www.grosvenorhousepublishing.co.uk

A CIP record for this book
is available from the British Library

ISBN 978-1-78623-316-5

Giorgio: That, I think, will meet the case. But you must work hard – stick to it – nothing like work.
W.S. Gilbert – *The Gondoliers*

Bloodnok: Surely you don't suspect this man – why, we were together in the same company during that terrible disaster.
Seagoon: What company was that?
Bloodnok: Desert Song 1933.
Seagoon: Were you both in the D'Oyly Carte?
Bloodnok: Right in the D'Oyly Carte.
Spike Milligan – 'The Dreaded Batter Pudding Hurler (of Bexhill-on-Sea)', *The Goon Show*

The Operas

Theatrical impresario Richard D'Oyly Carte (1844–1901) famously brought together the dramatist William Schwenck Gilbert (1836–1911) and composer Arthur Sullivan (1842–1900) and established the D'Oyly Carte Opera Company to present Gilbert & Sullivan operas.

See below for the abbreviated titles of the operas cited in this text. All works are by W.S. Gilbert and Arthur Sullivan, except *Cox and Box*, which is a collaboration between Sullivan and librettist Francis Cowley Burnand (1836–1917).

Cox – *Cox and Box, or The Long-lost Brothers* (1866)
Thespis – *Thespis, or The Gods Grown Old* (1871)
Trial – *Trial by Jury* (1875)
Sorcerer – *The Sorcerer* (1877)
Pinafore – *HMS Pinafore, or The Lass that Loved a Sailor* (1878)
Pirates – *The Pirates of Penzance, or The Slave of Duty* (1879)
Patience – *Patience, or Bunthorne's Bride* (1881)
Iolanthe – *Iolanthe, or The Peer and the Peri* (1882)
Ida – *Princess Ida, or Castle Adamant* (1884)
Mikado – *The Mikado, or The Town of Titipu* (1885)
Ruddigore – *Ruddigore, or The Witch's Curse* (1887)
Yeomen – *The Yeomen of the Guard, or The Merryman and his Maid* (1888)
Gondoliers – *The Gondoliers, or The King of Barataria* (1889)
Utopia – *Utopia Limited, or The Flowers of Progress* (1893)
Grand Duke – *The Grand Duke, or The Statutory Duel* (1896)

Acknowledgements

I have to thank a number of people who in various ways have contributed to this memoir. First of all, I owe a debt of gratitude to Tim Hurst-Brown for encouraging me to write an account of my time in D'Oyly Carte. While the deaths of many of my colleagues in recent years finally prompted me to set pen to paper before it was too late, I might not have had the impetus to begin without Tim's endless prompting – "Have you started yet?" I'm particularly grateful to Peter Riley, who has kindly read the manuscript and made numerous helpful suggestions, and also to Christine Airey who has reminded me of so many happy days in the best theatrical digs I ever had. I must also thank Norma Farnes for permission to quote from *The Goon Show*'s – 'The Dreaded Batter Pudding Hurler (of Bexhill-on-Sea)'. I thank Ken McAllister for his recollections of the orchestra, Walter Paul, who reminded me of his parents' enthusiasm for G&S and their hospitality in Glasgow, Paul Seeley for many helpful reminders and confirmations, Overton and Suzette Shelmire for elucidating certain facts about the 1978 tour of North America, Tony Joseph, John MacLeod, Allan Morrison and Robert Todd for further help and encouragement; and the following D'Oyly Carte colleagues: Margaret Bowden, Jane Button, Andrea Cawston, Barry Clark, Julia Goss, Fraser Goulding, Bruce and Caroline Graham, Peter Hamburger, Bob Lever, Cynthia Morey, Suzanne Taylor, Lorraine Patient, Ken Robertson-Scott, Billy Strachan and Vivian Woodrow. Finally, my thanks to Tamsin Rush and Becky Banning and all at Grosvenor House Publishing. To anyone I have omitted to thank I offer my apologies. Any mistakes, inaccuracies and other shortcomings are entirely my own.

Preface

This is not an official history. It is simply a personal account of my time with the D'Oyly Carte Opera Company from August 1975 until its closure in February 1982. I began this memoir in March 1977, took it up again in the summer of 1982 and returned to it many years later when I started to compile from my diary entries a list of all the places I had visited with the Company. I added subsequent recollections and further information from letters, programmes, memorabilia of various sorts, Company call sheets and other sources. This account may well contain mistakes and inaccuracies, but it is an honest attempt to describe those years, and hopefully it may add something to the story of this world-famous opera company of which I was privileged to be a member. It was a unique experience.

Introduction

I was born in Greenock in Scotland on November 25, 1943 and was educated at Greenock Academy. I grew up in a musical environment – my father played the violin and my mother the piano. I started to have piano lessons at around the age of seven and while I was not a child prodigy, I soon found that I could read music quickly and with comparative ease. This was perhaps because I had been an avid reader from an early age, becoming a member of two local libraries while still at school. I believe that the ability to read easily, either words or music, is a facility that some people are born with, just as some have an ability to draw and paint, are good at sport, or have other skills. Greenock Public Library had quite a large music section and this was a great opportunity to improve my sight-reading and to get to know all kinds of music. I clearly remember hearing Act I of *The Gondoliers*, which was broadcast during Coronation week in 1953, and sometime later I got the vocal score from the library to play through at home.

At secondary school our music teacher, Dr Percy Elton, dutifully produced school choirs for end of term concerts, but he was a DMus (more common for a musician in those days than a PhD), and his musical interests lay elsewhere, particularly with church music. He was an organist and had composed a setting of the Lord's Prayer, which we used to sing at our morning assemblies. Then the school appointed a new music teacher, Donald B. Miller, immediately nicknamed 'Minty' as his surname, with slightly different spelling, is that of a well-known Scottish confectionary manufacturer. Already in his early sixties, and despite having an artificial leg, he travelled to Greenock every day from his home on the island of Bute in the Firth of Clyde, a journey that involved him getting up at the crack of dawn to catch a steamer from Rothesay to Wemyss Bay and a bus from Wemyss Bay to Greenock, with the reverse journey at the end of the day. He was made of stern stuff. Minty Miller was more interested in stage work – he had conducted an early performance in the UK of Shostakovich's *Lady Macbeth of the Mtsensk District* – and he decided that the school should tackle some Gilbert and Sullivan. The first opera chosen was *HMS Pinafore*, and this was produced in June 1958. Minty was spared his daily journey from Rothesay during the week of the opera performances as he stayed with the headmaster in Greenock.

As I knew some of the G&S operas from my perusal of Greenock Public Library's vocal scores, I wanted to be in this production, but my voice had not yet broken, and Minty decided that he couldn't let me sing in the chorus. But my sight-reading skills were put to good use at rehearsals and when the opera finally went on at the Arts Guild Theatre, Greenock, I was given the job of call-boy. I was thus closely involved in the production from the very beginning. It was a great success and the first of many – in the early days all the productions were of G&S. Sir Joseph Porter was played by Peter Morrison, later to become a well-known singer, while Captain Corcoran was played by Ian McCrorie, also well known in the musical world in Scotland. Ian was later awarded an MBE.

I have written very little original music, but throughout my life I have made many arrangements of existing music. Appropriately, as it turned out, my very first arrangement was the overture to *The Mikado* – a reduction for piano solo from the piano duet version in the Chappell vocal score. The impulse for my arrangement almost certainly came from Minty's choice of *The Mikado* for the school's second production of a G&S opera in 1959.

As my voice had now broken, I was allowed to take part. At last I was in the actual production, but only in the chorus. The following year, as previous luminaries such as Peter and Ian had left school, I was offered a principal role. The opera for 1960 was *The Pirates of Penzance* and I found myself playing Major-General Stanley. Luckily I had almost a year to learn that extremely difficult patter song, 'I am the very model of a modern Major-General'. I must have proved equal to the task as I was then offered the role of the Lord Chancellor in *Iolanthe*, the opera we put on in 1961. *Iolanthe* has an even more difficult patter song, 'When you're lying awake with a dismal headache', which is generally known as 'The Nightmare Song'. The operas' copyright did not expire until the end of 1961, fifty years after Gilbert's death, and these early school productions simply followed those of the D'Oyly Carte Opera Company. We also made two visits to Glasgow to see the Company perform.

Pre-D'Oyly Carte – as Major-General Stanley (*The Pirates of Penzance*), Arts Guild Theatre, Greenock, June 1960.

I left school in 1961 and spent the summer as an assistant purser on the paddle steamer *Waverley* (happily still with us), before entering the Royal Scottish Academy of Music and Drama (RSAMD), now the Royal Conservatoire of Scotland, with the intention of becoming a school music teacher and hopefully getting involved in more productions of G&S. I had greatly enjoyed taking part in my own school's productions, but never dreamed that one day I would be working for D'Oyly Carte, and even conducting performances. At the RSAMD we were supposed to be studying 'serious' music and were not exactly encouraged to consort with light opera or 'light' anything – an attitude which has happily changed everywhere since those days – and so I was not much involved with G&S during my time there. But any students who were asked to sing at church concerts or at other functions invariably included 'forbidden' items such as G&S or Lehar in their programmes and I sometimes accompanied them on these occasions.

I graduated from the RSAMD in 1964 and after two terms at Jordanhill College of Education, entered the teaching profession. But even at Jordanhill I knew that teaching was not for me. As a trainee student I was sent to a comprehensive school, Glenwood, in Castlemilk in south Glasgow. It was a world away from the grammar school that I had attended in Greenock and I hoped that I would be given a post elsewhere. But I was sent back to Glenwood on Mondays, Wednesdays and Fridays. On Tuesdays and Thursdays I was at a boys' grammar school, Allan Glen's, in the centre of Glasgow, where they had a good orchestra for which I made numerous arrangements. There was music at Glenwood too, of course, and I also made some arrangements for the pupils there, mainly for smaller groups. The head of music, Iain Turpie, had written an operetta called *Highwayman's Inn*, which I orchestrated, and which was put on by the school in the Couper Institute in Glasgow. Iain had also founded the Glasgow Arts Centre for schoolchildren in the city. It had choirs, an orchestra and drama groups, and I was drafted in to help with the musical side, mainly as an accompanist. I also made orchestral arrangements, some of these for an early BBC *Songs of Praise*. I certainly enjoyed all of this, but most of it took place outside school hours, and my heart was still not in teaching. Iain persuaded me to stay on at Glenwood, but I think this was because I was of more use to him in the Arts Centre as an accompanist and arranger than I was as a teacher.

After four years I decided to leave teaching, and managed to get a place at Glasgow University, where I enrolled in a BMus. During the course, I chose to study the period 1680–1890 in depth and to write a short thesis on settings of lyrics in Shakespeare's plays. While researching this topic, I discovered that Arthur Sullivan had written much more besides his operas with W.S. Gilbert, including, among other Shakespearean music, his incidental music for *The Tempest* – his opus 1. I already knew that he had written the famous song 'The Lost Chord', the tune which he named 'St Gertrude', for the hymn 'Onward, Christian soldiers', and the orchestral *Overture di ballo*. And so, after a lapse of some years, I was working again with Sullivan's music, if not with Gilbert's words.

After graduating BMus in 1972, I was awarded a research grant. Having written on settings of Shakespeare, I wondered if I might study something along those lines and I was eventually accepted at Birmingham University as a research student. My field was nineteenth-century English song. I arrived at Birmingham in the autumn of 1972 and for the first term I simply turned up each week with lists of song composers – many of whom, such as Mrs Ann Bartholomew (née Mounsey), are hardly known today – until my tutor, Dr John Drummond, eventually said, "This isn't getting anywhere. We need to find someone of stature who has written a decent number of songs that haven't yet been studied seriously". It didn't take long to settle on Sullivan, who had written approximately one hundred songs. My research had to avoid the operas, but it did include three songs with words by Gilbert: 'The Distant Shore', 'The Love That Loves Me Not', and 'Sweethearts'.

I graduated MA in 1974, my thesis having the somewhat cumbersome title *The Songs of Arthur Sullivan: a Catalogue and Commentary*. I still had a year's money from the Scottish Education Department (I wonder if such largesse would be as readily available today) and I continued with my research while beginning to look for a job. I had now been a full-time student for nigh on ten years and I thought that with extra qualifications I might be able to get a job in higher education. I would have preferred this to school teaching. I had also done some extramural lecturing which I *did* enjoy, but in that last year (1974–75) there was an economic squeeze and many academic posts were frozen. With fewer jobs I was competing with a greater number of applicants and many of them, with doctorates, were ahead of me in the queue. I then began to wonder if it might be possible to become a repetiteur. Over the years I had acquired much experience as an accompanist and I also now had an ARCM (accompanist) diploma. I wrote to all the major companies: Covent Garden, English National Opera, Scottish Opera, Welsh Opera, the now defunct Kent Opera – and the D'Oyly Carte Opera Company. I had spent the last three years immersed in Sullivan's music and I thought that my thesis might interest them. One by one the replies came back with essentially the same message: "We have no vacancies at the moment, but we will put your name on our list". This wasn't very encouraging, but at least they had all replied, all, that is, except D'Oyly Carte.

By the end of July 1975 I still had no job and my grant would soon be finished. I had to find something soon. On the afternoon of Friday August 1, along with some other students, I was in the music library of the Barber Institute of Fine Arts (home to the university's music department) trying to do some work. It was a hot day and most of us were finding it hard to concentrate. I heard the phone ringing in the librarian's inner office. He went through to answer it, came back, and said, "It's for you". This was surprising. No one ever phoned me there. I picked up the phone and a voice said, "Hello, this is Royston Nash of the D'Oyly Carte Opera Company. We have your letter here and are in need of a repetiteur". That woke me up! He then said, "You did write to us some time ago, but we didn't reply as we didn't have any vacancies. But the post of repetiteur has now come up unexpectedly. Are you still interested?" By this time my heart was beginning to thump, but I managed to say, "Yes indeed", to which he replied "Can you come down to London for an interview?" I said, "Yes", and he said, "We are performing at the Royal Festival Hall. Could you come down next Wednesday? That is our matinee day and we could see you between shows, say at around six?" Again I said, "Yes", thanked him for phoning, and went back into the library, scarcely believing that I might just possibly have a job.

I duly turned up at the Royal Festival Hall the following Wednesday, and was interviewed in a dressing room by Royston Nash, D'Oyly Carte's musical director, and Glyn Hale, the chorus master and associate conductor. Glyn had just been conducting the matinee performance of *The Yeomen of the Guard*. Jimmie Marsland, the assistant producer, was also present. They gave me a vocal score of *Iolanthe* and asked me to play the opening chorus and sing whatever parts I could. I'm not a singer (and it's the ladies' chorus!), but I did know the opera, as we had done it at school, and I managed to do this. They also told me something about the job, including the payment: £50, being a salary of £32 plus a touring allowance of £18. Royston later told me that I said, "Is that a week or a month?" It was, of course, a week, but having been a student for the last six years I had become used to living on very little money and had rather lost track of wages in the real world. I realised later that even in 1975 the sum of £50 per week wasn't exactly a fortune. In my first year with the Company the rate being offered to orchestra principals for the London season was £73, with £71 for rank and file, and the Musicians' Union was demanding even more: £86 and £78 respectively. I also remember being told that touring was not for everyone. The Company was on the road all the time. Did I think I could cope with that? I had had no experience of touring, but I needed a job fairly soon, enjoyed travelling, and said that I didn't think it would be a problem at all. Then they said, "Go back to Birmingham and think about it. We also have to see someone else". My heart almost stopped at that. I might not get the job after all. "We'll phone you again tomorrow".

The interview was quite short as Royston had to conduct the evening performance of *Yeomen*. I was invited to attend this, but instead had a drink in the bar with Glyn Hale and Jimmie Marsland and was introduced to several people, including chorister Gillian Burrows, Glyn's girlfriend. I then went back to Birmingham, having already decided that I would take the job if it was offered, and spent an anxious, rather sleepless night. Royston phoned the following morning and said that no one else had turned up, and they would be happy to have me. Could I start on Monday? I said that I could, at the same time wondering where I was going to stay in London. Luckily I had friends there, and over the next few days I was able to find some temporary accommodation. I also phoned the Scottish Education Department to inform them of my new employment and terminated my research facility at Birmingham. After the false start in teaching, the extra years of study, and particularly the frustration of the previous year, I could hardly believe that my luck had changed. I had now found a job that, hopefully, I could do competently and also enjoy.

There did seem to be an Ariadne thread of Sullivan's music in my life: my school performances in the G&S operas, my first piano arrangement (the overture to *The Mikado*), my BMus essay which included the settings from *The Tempest*, my recent research into Sullivan's songs, and now this. It was almost as if I was being led along a path by an unseen hand. I was, in fact, joining D'Oyly Carte in its centenary year, although initially I hadn't been aware of this milestone. When I eventually learned what had happened earlier in 1975 I was sorry that I had missed the centenary performances at the Savoy Theatre. If I had been taken on when I first wrote to the Company late in 1974 I would have experienced what must have been a wonderful season – a truly unique event. But that is perhaps the only regret that I have from those days. The most memorable phase of my working life was about to begin.

Chapter 1: 1975–1976

I

It is difficult to be precise about things that happened forty years ago, such as when I first heard that the Company would be going to North America in 1976. Royston may have mentioned this at my interview, and may also have said that it would be unlikely that I would be able to go with them; this would certainly appear to be confirmed by my first contract with D'Oyly Carte, dated August 7, 1975, the day after my audition, which stated that my engagement as music assistant/repetiteur would terminate "about March/April 1976". Perhaps this new job would be a very short one, but at least I did have a job, and half a loaf was better than no bread. If I was to be made redundant in March or April I would cross that bridge when I came to it. And so I turned up at Sadler's Wells Theatre in Rosebery Avenue, London at 10.30am on Monday August 11, 1975.

The next four weeks consisted of rehearsals for the new choristers in the ballet rehearsal room, which overlooked Arlington Way. The Company would shortly be back on the road with five operas. With a schedule of eight performances a week for forty-eight weeks of the year there was little time for rehearsals on tour. The new choristers had to know their work thoroughly – not just the music, but the stage movement as well – to be able to fit in with members of the Company who had been performing these operas for at least one year and in some cases, for many years. Over and above our eight performances each week, we usually had a further three sessions on Tuesday, Thursday and Friday mornings, which were used mainly for principal or understudy calls. There were never any Monday morning sessions, partly because the previous day was often a travelling day, but an exception might be made for an understudy who had to go on at very short notice. Individual Company members would seldom be asked to appear at more than two of these calls, but staff members were usually involved in all three. Some of the operas, *Pinafore*, *Pirates* and particularly *Mikado*, were done so often that they worked like clockwork, but if we were about to do one that was performed less frequently, such as *The Sorcerer*, *Patience, Princess Ida* or *Ruddigore*, we could use one of those three sessions for the full Company to remind everyone of words, music and moves.

Contracts at D'Oyly Carte were usually issued for a year, renewable if it suited both performers and management. While it was possible that no one would leave at the end of each year, invariably some did. Sometimes there were just one or two departures, but often there were more than that. At the risk of forgetting someone, the intake for the 1975–76 tour consisted of sopranos Patricia Elliott (later known as Patricia Rea), Helen Moulder, Suzanne O'Keefe, Andrea Phillips, Glynis Prendergast and Vivian Tierney, and alto Elise McDougall who came from Paisley near my home town of Greenock. Lorraine Daniels (mezzo) joined later that season. The men were tenor William 'Billy' Strachan (another fellow Scot) and basses Paul Burrows and Kevin West (later Michael Westbury). Billy Strachan had actually joined the Company earlier in the year and, as he told me, had been thrown into the extra performances of *Utopia Limited* at the Royal Festival Hall in July, one of which I might have seen if my audition had been a few weeks earlier. The principals who joined at that time were soprano Barbara Lilley, mezzo Jane Metcalfe and tenor Geoffrey Shovelton.

I didn't do much playing during the first week as I had been told to stand by the piano and watch the work being done by

Stewart Nash (no relation to Royston), a freelance pianist who knew all the tempi and the traditional way of doing things that marked D'Oyly Carte's productions. This traditional approach had long been attacked by critics who felt that the Company was stuck in its ways. Many people have since suggested that D'Oyly Carte's eventual closure was due to its unwillingness to update its productions. That may have been a factor, but it is by no means the whole story. Much has been written on the subject, but this is not the place to discuss it or to begin to defend the Company's position. I had just joined D'Oyly Carte and was being paid to help present these operas in a particular way. I could only try to do this to the best of my ability.

During the first weeks I got to know the new choristers. I also got to know Jimmie Marsland whom I had met at my audition. Jimmie was one of the Company's great characters. He had joined as a chorister in 1949 and had played the small parts of the Solicitor (*Patience*) and Annibale (*The Gondoliers*). When the post of assistant producer became vacant in 1966, he took it so that he could remain in the Company that was so dear to his heart. He was still there in the same job when we closed in 1982 – *The Slave of Duty* indeed. Stories about Jimmie abound, although it is always difficult to know which are true and which are apocryphal. One concerns a time when he was still onstage himself. In one opera the men were lined up along the back of the stage. Somehow, over a period of time, the line gradually moved forwards – all of the men, that is, except Jimmie, who stayed exactly where he had been told to stand, muttering to the others, "You're doin' it all wrong".

True or not, that does sound like Jimmie and epitomises his attention to what was required of him. He knew where everyone, principals and chorus alike, should be at any given moment, and no one was better qualified to get new choristers into shape in one brief rehearsal period. During rehearsals he preferred to address the choristers as Miss Phillips, Mr West and so on, as indeed that is how they were always designated on Company call sheets. "You're doin' it all wrong" was certainly one of Jimmie's treasured remarks, but another favourite one was "Send for Billy Morgan", a reference to C. William 'Billy' Morgan, another former chorister who also later joined the staff. When Jimmie joined the Company in 1949, Billy was assistant stage manager; he too loved the operas, had an encyclopaedic knowledge of every note and every move, and was a useful person to have around in an emergency. Billy had been in the Company when the legendary J.M. Gordon, who had trained under Gilbert, was stage director. Gordon was a notorious stickler for tradition in the presentation of the operas and Billy almost certainly picked that up from him. Jimmie would have picked it up from Billy and was thus the last link in that unbroken chain of tradition, which stretched from Gilbert himself right through to the Company's closure in 1982.

One day during my first weeks with the Company I was sitting in the canteen at Sadler's Wells on a coffee break, when I heard a rather gruff voice at my elbow say, "I hear you're from Greenock". I turned round and found myself face to face with Gordon MacKenzie, who was also from Greenock, and whose real name was Michael Lynch. Like Jimmie Marsland he had been in the Company for many years, initially as a chorister (under his own name) from 1954 to 1956. He then left to pursue other interests, singing with the famous Scottish tenor Robert Wilson who had been in D'Oyly Carte from 1931 to 1937, (Robert Wilson's son, Carey, had been a fellow-student with me at the RSAMD), and touring with him as part of his White Heather group, forerunner of the television programme *The White Heather Club*. Michael also made several recordings, including a duet with Robert – 'Two Highland Lads'. Robert had planned that Michael would eventually take over from him, but he thought that Michael Lynch wasn't the best name for the lead singer in a Scottish variety show and suggested Gordon MacKenzie. Michael told me that he thought that Robert Wilson had coined the name from 'A Gordon for Me', a song that he had written himself. (The 'Gordon' refers to the Gordon

Highlanders.) It contains the line "My kilt is MacKenzie o' the HLI", which stands for Highland Light Infantry – and hence Gordon MacKenzie. By the early 1960s, however, it was obvious that variety was on the wane and Michael returned to D'Oyly Carte, appearing this time under his new stage name. But he continued to be known as Michael, usually shortened to Mike, and there was always confusion about his real name, particularly among the new choristers, as he was invariably referred to as Mike MacKenzie. Like Jimmie Marsland he forsook the stage, becoming assistant business manager to Stanley Knight in 1969, then assistant company manager in 1970 to Herbert 'Bert' Newby – another great character with a similar Company career. He founded the group known as D'Oyly Carte in Concert, which performed on occasional Sunday evenings at selected venues throughout the country, with principals from the Company being supported by a local amateur chorus or occasionally by our own chorus. He toyed with the idea of television appearances for the group, but nothing came of this. Michael stayed with the Company until its closure in 1982.

After four weeks of rehearsing the new intake it was almost time to begin the autumn tour. Before this, at the Wigmore Hall on September 7, I saw the celebrated comic duo Hinge and Bracket who sang a range of numbers from Verdi to 'Dear Ivor' (Novello). G&S was invariably included in their programmes, especially a spectacular rendering of 'Poor wandering one' (*The Pirates of Penzance*) by Dame Hilda Bracket, (actually Patrick Fyffe, whose sister Jane had been in D'Oyly Carte from 1956 to 1959), and they had even appeared at the Last Night of the Company's 1975 London season at Sadler's Wells. Next day I met the full Company for the first time as they assembled after their annual break for a week's rehearsal of the operas we would be performing on the tour. There was a run-through each morning with piano followed by a full rehearsal onstage in the afternoon with the orchestra, the sequence being *Pirates* (Monday), *Iolanthe* (Tuesday),

Mikado (Wednesday), *Ruddigore* (Thursday) and *Yeomen* (Friday). We were now ready to go out on the road.

The autumn tour that year took us to Oxford, Glasgow, Billingham, Edinburgh, Newcastle upon Tyne and Liverpool; after this we were in London for a long season at Sadler's Wells. My first experience of being on tour was the two weeks at the New Theatre, Oxford. As repetiteur, I was primarily there to play for rehearsals, although I also had other duties. One of my first tasks was to rearrange orchestral parts (wind parts in *Iolanthe* and brass parts in *Yeomen*) for our small touring orchestra, led at that time by Ivan Fox, which even in 1975 was not up to full strength; I did this in our somewhat dreary dressing room. Oxford was also my first experience of having to find accommodation and, while I can't honestly remember, I may have stayed with some fellow students from Birmingham who were now living there.

After Oxford I drove up to Greenock to stay with my parents while the Company performed in Glasgow for two weeks. I had by this time acquired a travelling companion in Andrea Phillips, one of that year's new choristers. As well as our touring allowance, everyone in the Company was given either a train ticket from one town to the next or the equivalent in cash. Not everyone had a car, but for those who did drive it made sense to share the cost and have company on the journeys. We played at the King's Theatre in Glasgow, often to pretty poor houses. One reason for this was that although the theatre had just been re-decorated the job wasn't quite finished and there was still no box office. Tickets were available from a kiosk in the city centre, but this unsatisfactory arrangement left us with not a few empty seats. The opening night almost didn't happen as the train bringing some of the orchestra up from London was delayed and didn't get into Glasgow until 7.20pm. I volunteered to drive down to Central Station to meet them and then had a nightmare journey to the theatre, going through at least one set of red lights. Luckily the performance was only held up for about five minutes, which wasn't too bad. Principal baritone Kenneth

Sandford had digs in Glasgow with a couple, Jimmy and Chrissie Paul, who were great fans of D'Oyly Carte, and on Friday October 3 they gave a party for the Company. Jimmy had a homemade instrument that he called a Zonkatina. It consisted of a five-foot long stick, a string, bottle tops, a boot at the bottom and a couple of tin lids. Unlikely as it may seem, Jimmy could really make this contraption come alive, particularly if he was playing along with a piano. Many years later, on returning to Scotland, I worked with Jimmy and Chrissie's son Walter, a producer and compere.

We then moved to Billingham on Teesside for two weeks and it was here that I first became aware of the need to book digs well in advance. Andrea, my travelling companion, had arranged to stay with a Mrs Walford in the nearby village of Norton, but I hadn't arranged anything. I must have thought, naïvely, that I would easily find a B&B somewhere. By the time we got to Andrea's digs it had finally dawned on me that I had nowhere to stay. I told her to go in, announce herself, and ask Mrs Walford if she knew of any place where I might find accommodation. Mrs Walford, who had "never done this sort of thing before", immediately said that she had plenty of room and would be happy to take me as well. Helen Moulder, another of our new choristers, was also staying there. The house, at 108 High Street, dated from *c.*1700 and was mentioned in Sir Nikolaus Pevsner's famous *The Buildings of England* series; among several other houses in the High Street it was even singled out as being of special interest. Mrs Walford had a daughter, Ruth, aged about twelve, who had Down syndrome. She was quite a handful and consequently the house was always in a mess. It also had a lot of mice and there was one memorable night when I had to remove about six from a trap in quick succession. Despite, or perhaps because of, all of this, it was great fun being there.

Billingham itself, seemingly nothing but a huge industrial area dominated then by ICI, was not very interesting. The Forum Theatre was part of a sports complex that included an ice rink and a swimming pool. We took advantage of the latter when it was kept open for half an hour after one of our performances, solely for the Company's benefit; I believe there are photographs of the occasion. Although the theatre was not large we didn't play to full houses, possibly again due to bad publicity as in Glasgow. It was here that Julia Goss, one of our principal sopranos, had one of her rare bouts of absenteeism. She had fallen down the stairs in her digs and sprained her ankle. Glynis Prendergast, who had only just joined the Company, then had a busy week of understudy work as Mabel (*Pirates*), Yum-Yum (*Mikado)* and Rose Maybud (*Ruddigore*). In a situation like that Jimmie Marsland's expertise was crucial.

From Billingham we went north again for three weeks, this time to Edinburgh. Although it is a smaller city than Glasgow we seemed to do better business there. Long-standing members of the Company said that had always been the case. I stayed with an old school friend, Allan McEwan, and his family. They had once lived in Edinburgh's prestigious New Town, but had shifted east of the city to North Berwick. This meant a twenty-mile journey each way each day, but it was very pleasant, particularly on the coast road; it was also good to catch up with Allan again. During our second week I took the opportunity to catch up with other friends and, to give Allan and Jean a break, I spent two nights with one of them, Bruce Ogilvie, in the Corstorphine area of the city near the Zoo, and a further night with another, Norman Adam, who lived some miles west of Edinburgh. In the light of later experiences, with freezing cold digs and unfriendly landladies, this first tour was certainly an easing-in to the old-style touring life. It was not always to be so pleasant.

The venue in Edinburgh was the King's Theatre in Leven Street. Just beside it was a public house, Bennets [sic] Bar, which had wonderful wood panelling behind the bar. In those days pubs in Scotland closed at 10pm (the English ones at 10.30pm) and it was almost impossible to get to a pub after the show, as most of the operas finished at around 10pm (*Iolanthe)* or later

(*Mikado*, *Ruddigore* and *Yeomen*). Only with *Pirates*, which usually finished at around 9.40pm, was there any possibility of getting to a pub after the show and the pub had to be literally next door as in Edinburgh. During the curtain calls for *Pirates* the hardened drinkers could be seen loosening their costumes for a quick change in order to get at least one pint down before closing time. (In some towns it was possible for drinks to be brought into the theatre if there was a pub nearby, although not every pub, or every theatre, sanctioned this practice.)

Other recollections of Edinburgh on that tour include one memorable, if potentially disastrous, occasion. Jane Metcalfe and Barbara Lilley were sharing a flat and I was invited round one evening for a meal. Geoffrey Shovelton was there too, so this must have been on the night of a *Ruddigore* performance as that was the one opera that all four of us were not involved in. (None of those three principals was in *Pirates*, but one of my duties was to conduct offstage choruses, and if it had been *Pirates* I would have been in the theatre conducting the ladies' 'Climbing over rocky mountain' in Act I and the men's 'A rollicking band of pirates we' in Act II.) We were having lasagne and to accompany this we had a large bottle of Valpolicella that I was asked to open with a compressed-air opener that we had found in a drawer in the kitchen. It hadn't occurred to me that you should never use this type of opener on a bottle that has shoulders. I was pumping air into the bottle, but the stopper seemed reluctant to come out, and it had just begun to dawn on me that something wasn't quite right when the bottle exploded, giving us all quite a shock. We eventually cleared up the mess and got another bottle of wine (one without shoulders), which we managed to open successfully. (There were very few screw-tops in those days.) Another memory of Edinburgh on that tour was climbing Arthur's Seat in Holyrood Park, again with Jane and Barbara.

We moved from Edinburgh to Newcastle upon Tyne, playing at the lovely old Theatre Royal in Grey Street for two weeks. There was a very nice Italian restaurant just by the stage door and it was much frequented during our stay. My digs here were with other fellow students from Birmingham, Frank and Ruth Bowler. Frank had recently brewed some beer and one Friday night I had half a pint of this, followed, I have to admit, by a whisky chaser. Was I ill! Next day, Saturday, we were doing *Pirates* twice, which meant that I had to conduct four off-stage choruses. Even when we started at 2.30pm I hadn't recovered properly. I spent most of the afternoon lying on a skip in our very small dressing room, only getting up to rush down to the stage, conduct a chorus and rush back to the dressing room to be violently sick. I have been wary of home brewing ever since.

It was in Newcastle that the chorus master, Glyn Hale, went down with an attack of shingles. He wasn't able to do his share of the conducting, essentially the two matinees each week, and this meant that Royston had to do all of the performances. It was frustrating for me not being able to help, but it was not part of my job to conduct (I didn't know the operas well enough anyway). This highlighted the lack of personnel in most departments and how easily the workings of the Company could be disrupted. At least Glyn was in a form of isolation. He and Gill had solved the accommodation problem by touring in a caravan. Along with a couple in the orchestra, trumpeter Roy Ramsbottom and his flautist wife Jenny, they were the last of many – often referred to as the Tinkers' Club – who had toured this way. My birthday fell during the second week that we were there and I went out to the caravan for a birthday tea with them. Glyn certainly wasn't looking too well.

We then moved to Liverpool on a miserable, cold, wet Sunday where our venue was the Royal Court Theatre. For our two-week sojourn I stayed in Birkenhead with a family who were quite interested in the theatre world. I also remember buying a bottle of whisky so that I could have a wee dram to warm me up when I came back each evening. I seldom drove my car into Liverpool, but instead took a bus down to the pier and crossed the Mersey on the ferry. It was quite invigorating at that time of year and to someone who came from the Clyde area it was almost like being at home. The centre of Liverpool actually reminded me very much of the centre of Glasgow. We often rehearsed in the theatre itself; sometimes we used a space under the stage, but this was usually for understudy calls with smaller groups.

As it was the Company's centenary year, there were receptions in several of the cities that we played in. Oxford (in the Town Hall with Mayor Bill Fagg), Glasgow (with Lord Provost McCann and his wife – this included a tour of the Municipal Buildings) and Edinburgh (in the City Chambers in the High Street); our final reception was in Liverpool Town Hall on December 2. I don't recall much about that particular reception, but I do vividly remember a return visit to the Town Hall the following week on the occasion of the Lord Mayor's Christmas party for underprivileged children. At the reception the previous week several members of the Company including Julia Goss, Michael Rayner (principal baritone) and myself had agreed to come to this event to entertain the children and help look after them. We duly prepared a programme, but, needless to say, we didn't get through half of it. We then turned our attention to trying to stop the children from bursting balloons, climbing the walls and potentially wrecking a beautiful Georgian building that should never have been used for such an event. The Lord Mayor himself seemed oblivious to the possible damage to his priceless heritage and merely smiled benignly on it all. The afternoon rapidly got out of hand; some children began crying for their parents and others started the food-throwing that invariably happens at these functions. We left in the midst of this melee and were walking up the street when we heard a fire engine coming. "It'll be for the Town Hall", said Michael Rayner jokingly. We stopped to watch: it was! We never found out what had happened, but assumed that one of the children had set off an alarm that had summoned the fire brigade. That was certainly a day to remember.

We were often invited to Arts Clubs in Edinburgh, Liverpool and London; we would go along after the show and sing for our supper, with drinks usually provided as well. Similar events also took place at local golf clubs. Over the years golfers in the Company had arranged to use certain courses in return for a 'sing for your supper' evening. While we were in Liverpool we had one such evening at Heswall Golf Club in Wirrall. Gordon MacKenzie, a keen golfer himself, introduced our musical offerings. Pre-empting Hyacinth Bucket (sorry, Bou-quet), the menu listed this event as a Candlelight Dinner.

As well as playing for rehearsals and conducting offstage choruses I was also drafted in to help with walk-on parts (known as 'supers') along with other members of the touring staff, one of whom, John Carnegie, latterly the wardrobe master, took the part of the priest who was to attend the execution of Colonel Fairfax in *Yeomen*. Dressed in a monk's habit with a cowl, and with his head bowed and his hands clasped in the folds of the habit, John was virtually unrecognisable. It could have been anyone standing there, and I was told that occasionally, in previous performances, it *had* been someone else - sometimes even a lady! I took three of these walk-on parts: the Sergeant of Marines in *HMS Pinafore*, the Lord Chancellor's train-bearer in *Iolanthe* and – unlikely as it may seem to anyone who knows me – a soldier in *The Yeomen of the Guard*. The costume for *Yeomen* was ill-fitting. It included a breastplate which reminded me of the cuirass mentioned in *Princess Ida*. This dug into my shoulders and was extremely uncomfortable, but supers' costumes were never altered to suit individuals – you just had to wear them and bear them. The costume for the Sergeant of Marines, however, was a much better fit. Wearing it I looked like the soldier on the packaging of a well-known chocolate assortment. These walk-on parts, without which the stage would have looked somewhat underdressed, were taken by staff members; withdrawing people from the chorus to play them would have diminished its ranks, and the Company wasn't prepared to pay extras who would only appear occasionally. It was a system that worked well until the actors' union Equity, in its wisdom, decided that we were taking work away from its members. Given the circumstances of touring and the Company's limited budget (no public funding for us), this was patently absurd, but eventually most of the staff, not being Equity members, were denied these roles. In some cases the roles simply disappeared, one such being the Lord Chancellor's train-bearer in *Iolanthe*.

D'Oyly Carte – as the Sergeant of Marines (*HMS Pinafore*), Sadler's Wells Theatre, London, January 1976.

There were two marines in *HMS Pinafore,* one of the operas that we would soon be performing in London. In preparation for our appearance we rehearsed under the stage of the Royal Court Theatre, using umbrellas instead of rifles, with the production director Michael Heyland. We marched on to the ship's deck just before Sir Joseph Porter's entrance in Act I; although the supers were not supposed to say anything onstage, I had to shout, "Shoulder arms!", which we then proceeded to do (or try to do). The second marine was the property master Frank Coghill, an Irishman with a very thick accent who always appeared to be under the influence even if he wasn't. Poor Frank just couldn't get the hang of it; his marching and rifle drill were never quite right.

And so ended the first part of my first tour. The journey from Liverpool to London was another miserable one, on a foggy December Sunday, and my car, a Morris 1100, was not behaving itself. It had deteriorated somewhat during the tour, possibly due to the combined weight of Andrea Phillips's luggage and my own, and there was an alarming clanking sound coming from somewhere in the vicinity of the steering column. It was, in fact, on its last legs, but it did get me into London, minus Andrea who had travelled back with Lyndsie Holland (principal contralto) after Saturday evening's performance. We were still officially on tour when we played in London, but it never felt like part of the tour. The Christmas seasons were long ones and there was always a more settled feeling when we were there. Many of the Company lived in London, or within easy reach of it, and the Company office was there too, as was the Savoy Theatre which had been built by Richard D'Oyly Carte as part of his plan to establish a school of English comic opera. We played a fourteen-week season at Sadler's Wells Theatre from December 15, 1975 to March 20, 1976.

II

The second part of my first year with the Company was spent entirely in London, although initially I had no idea that this was going to happen. First of all I had to find somewhere to stay. An old college friend from Glasgow, the tenor Alexander 'Sandy' Oliver, was now living in Hampstead and he managed to persuade his neighbours Michael and Antoinette Pernetta, whom I had already met, to take me in. They were very kind, but they were in the middle of decorating and they put me in a room that was piled high with furniture from the other rooms so that I could hardly move. Early in the New Year I was shunted off to a friend of Antoinette's, a Swedish lady with a heart of gold, but also a fetish for cleanliness and tidiness. If I was making a cup of instant coffee she would hover at my elbow. I would take the lid off the jar and put it down and as I put the granules in the cup she would pick up the lid, put it back on the jar, and have the jar back in the cupboard before I had time to add the hot water. This was somewhat unnerving. She also had a country cottage and once invited Antoinette to stay there with her. Waking up early one morning, Antoinette thought that she would make herself a cup of tea. She went into the kitchen, made the tea, and tiptoed back to her room so as not to wake her friend. When she got back to her room she found that her bed had already been made! I could only take so much of this fetish and eventually moved one Sunday to 3A Heather Park Parade, Wembley, which was to be my home for some time. It was a four-bedroomed flat above a betting shop and I shared it with three other musicians. Our trombone player Les Baxter had just vacated my room, a second room was occupied by another trombonist, Paul Barrett, who was with us for the London season, and a third by trumpeter Chris Blood who later joined the orchestra and married our oboist Tina Cumming. I don't recall the fourth musician.

The London season opened with a double bill of *HMS Pinafore* preceded by the short one-act *Trial by Jury*. The principal parts in *Trial* were played by our choristers, giving them a chance to create roles rather than simply be understudies. Jon Ellison was the Learned Judge, Barry Clark was the Defendant and Glynis Prendergast was the Plaintiff. I knew the music of *Trial* quite well, but I had never seen it performed professionally. On the opening night, after watching it from the wings – where I often stood to familiarise myself with the music and the productions – it was time for my first appearance as the Sergeant of Marines in *Pinafore*. I knew Sadler's Wells as we had rehearsed there during my first weeks with the Company, but there was definitely something special about walking onto a London stage for the first time.

There were several differences between the London performances and the rest of the year's touring. First of all, the orchestra was larger, thirty-seven (or thirty-nine in *Yeomen* and *Gondoliers*, which have a second bassoon and third trombone) rather than a mere twenty-one on tour. Our touring string section then was 3-2-2-2-1, later 4-2-2-2-1, and we had just one horn and one trombone. The extra numbers were mainly in the strings and this gave a much richer sound – something that I particularly noticed when I was onstage for the first time. We also stopped performing a different opera each day and generally played one for a week at a time, but rather than play it continuously from Monday to Saturday we usually played Thursday, Friday, Saturday, and then Monday, Tuesday, Wednesday, the Sunday break helping to keep the later performances fresh. (To do this, of course, we would have to open the season with a half-week of one opera, and (usually) end it with a half-week of another.) One further difference was that for once the Company *did* employ extras, although they only appeared in *The Gondoliers*, perhaps the least traditional of our offerings.

The production of *The Gondoliers*, dating from 1968, was by Anthony Besch, and the extras were 'tourists'. The opera was now set in Edwardian times (updated from Gilbert's 1750) and one of the tourists carried an old-fashioned camera. Besch also added the infamous 'spaghetti scene' in Act I. During Don Alhambra's song 'I stole the Prince', the refrain of which ("No possible doubt whatever") is sung by the Duke, the Duchess, Casilda and Luiz, the Duke was served with a bowl of spaghetti by Company stalwart Jon Ellison as the waiter. This extra stage business was something of a departure from traditional D'Oyly Carte productions and had originally invoked bristling indignation from some quarters. The scene was sometimes enlivened for the performers by the presence of an additional item, such as a glass eye, a spider (or worse), in the spaghetti itself. The cast never knew what to expect. How they kept straight faces during this number will forever be a mystery. On a provincial tour the spaghetti could sometimes be obtained from a local restaurant, but otherwise had to be of the tinned variety which would be heated up in the wings. If the sauce was too pungent the smell pervaded the auditorium. Sometimes, during the song, even the orchestra could be seen casting glances up at the stage if the aroma was particularly strong. This scene certainly spiced up an otherwise somewhat perfunctory number whose purpose is simply to carry the plot forward.

Sadler's Wells was to be our home for all of the remaining London seasons except one: our very last season (1981–82) was at the Royal Adelphi Theatre in the Strand. In my first six years, however, coming in to Sadler's Wells really did seem like coming home after touring in the provinces. The dressing rooms were at the front of the theatre and looked out on to Rosebery Avenue. Our very small music department room was at the top of a flight of stairs about as far from the stage door in Arlington Way as it was possible to be. In my early days at the Wells there was a canteen backstage, run by a lady who, as I recall, was rather vague. One evening during a performance she was standing in the wings. She then started to wander onstage to get a better view of what was happening. Luckily there was someone on hand to restrain her, or she would almost certainly have been seen by the audience. Another character in the theatre at that time was the stage door keeper.

He had a strong London accent and would put out calls for Company members in his own inimitable way, ("Kenny Sandford wanted at stage door"), which is almost impossible to convey in print. Inevitably he was the butt of practical jokes and had been known to announce, "Henry Lytton wanted at stage door", this being greeted with howls of laughter in the dressing rooms as Sir Henry Lytton, former star of the Company, had died in 1936.

The area was well served with pubs, two of them being virtually at the stage door. Directly across the street was the Shakespeare's Head, which was favoured by many of the Company. On the same side as the stage door, and just a few yards along, was the Harlequin. Company members also frequented it, but it was the particular favourite of the orchestra and for that reason I tended to use it myself. For a pub fairly close to the centre of London it had an almost rural, certainly suburban, atmosphere. Intimate and cosy, with coloured lights round the bar, it was run by an amiable Irishman called Con Rea, whose son worked for the Company as a dresser, and it was there that I really acquired a taste for Guinness. I had tried it elsewhere on numerous occasions and had always found it rather bitter, but one night our bass player Sandra Hill persuaded me to try Con's Guinness, and I was hooked. Another pub that was used by some Company members was the Empress of Russia. It was on the other side of the theatre in a cul-de-sac off St John Street.

There was a bell in the Harlequin, which informed everyone that the show, or Act II, was about to begin. This was very useful, particularly for the orchestra. Being so close to the stage door, and as they were very familiar with the music, some of them – usually the brass players, who only played in certain numbers – would often stay in the pub long after Act II had begun, having timed almost to the second when they needed to be back in the pit. Often, perilously close to the start of a number, they would still not be there. Then, as if by magic, they would suddenly appear, pick up their instruments and play. This system worked well enough so long as nothing happened to disrupt the routine, but on rare occasions they might be caught out. Sometimes an expected encore to a number wasn't given, with the result that the next number in which they were playing came just a little sooner than they had anticipated. They could also be caught out if someone onstage (often an understudy) forgot his or her dialogue and jumped several lines. If that happened the conductor might also be seen to spring up hurriedly in readiness for the next musical number.

During the run of *Yeomen* in December, Pamela Field, former principal soprano, returned briefly to sing Elsie. The performance schedule was slightly different every year, depending on which day Christmas and New Year's Day fell. Christmas Eve and Christmas Day that year were both free, but we did a matinee on Boxing Day. When we performed on New Year's Eve we sang 'Auld Lang Syne' at the end of the performance, the cast coming down from the sides of the stage to join hands with the audience. The orchestra had a very basic arrangement of this and I decided that if I was still with the Company the following year I would make a more elaborate arrangement. I was well aware that 'Sassenachs', and many Scots too, often had difficulty with Burns's words and so I thought that I might also put up a notice with the proper text and some hints as to pronunciation of the more difficult words and phrases such as "a right guid-willie waught".

And so into 1976. As I got to know the principals I would occasionally be asked to play for them at other concerts – that January I played for Geoffrey Shovelton at his church in Pinner. A few days later, I auditioned for a repetiteur's job at English National Opera. It wasn't that I was unhappy at D'Oyly Carte, but my position regarding employment after April was still not clear and I had to think of the future. Fortunately for me, in the light of my later time with the Company, I didn't get the job, but the audition was rather more formal than my interview for D'Oyly Carte. It made me aware of my limitations and also that I was very lucky to be where I was. I could only hope that somehow I might be able to stay on. After this I had no more thoughts of auditioning for anything else, particularly after the 1976–77 season – for obvious reasons, as will soon become apparent.

Whatever was going to happen, I was now in 'the business' and I needed an accountant. Several members of the Company were with John Kennedy Melling, who operated from a tiny, rather cluttered flat at the head of a long flight of stairs at an address in Mayfair. I went to see him on January 21 and became another of his D'Oyly Carte clients. John was another character; apart from accountancy, his interests included theatre and the circus, and he had published a short guide to heraldry. If anything went wrong with your tax affairs he was a very good barrier between you and the taxman. He would write letters on behalf of his clients, proclaiming indignantly that they were "sensitive artists who should not be harassed in this way".

The London season continued with two operas that we had not performed in the provinces: *Patience* and *The Gondoliers*. On February 25, Her Majesty the Queen attended a performance of the latter. What she thought of the spaghetti scene has never been divulged and may forever remain a state secret! Afterwards there was the usual presentation onstage, with principals and heads of departments on the front row. Lesser mortals, such as myself, were in the second row and were not presented. But we were close enough. I was standing behind Bert Newby, and heard him say, reverentially, as he bent almost double, "Your gracious Majesty".

I enjoyed my walk-on parts, particularly the Sergeant of Marines (*Pinafore*) with its splendid uniform. I am short-sighted, but unlike Charles Hawtrey in the *Carry On* films, I couldn't wear spectacles every time I appeared. *Pinafore* wasn't too bad, but I once had a problem with *Yeomen*. In Act I the Lieutenant says, "Clear the rabble", and the soldiers – there were two of us with heavy arquebuses – would then push the chorus back into the wings. One night I found myself in a different position, this time on a rostrum. But I had forgotten where I was and without my glasses I couldn't see clearly. On the word of command I rushed forward as usual – and promptly fell off the rostrum, adding an uncalled-for touch of hilarity to the scene. Those were the days! Another of my duties was to sound the offstage bell in the Act I finale of *Yeomen*, but more of that later.

After the evening performance on March 4 several members of the Company went to the Arts Club in Dover Street to entertain and to be wined and dined. In the years that I was in the Company there were several visits to the club. The man who organised these, Andre Eldon-Erdington, was a friend of Michael and Antoinette Pernetta, who had offered me accommodation when I came to London in December; he later ran the Connaught Rooms in Great Queen Street. We were always well looked after at the Arts Club. On one occasion, while we were having our meal, we were given a Russian drink, which we were told to down in one. We all tried to do this although it was quite fiery.

The forthcoming North American tour had been finalised and any hope that I had entertained of being allowed to go had been well and truly dashed. But it was nearing the end of the London season and I still wasn't sure what was going to happen to me. On March 10 I had an interview with the general manager, Frederic 'Freddie' Lloyd OBE, who said, "I'm afraid we can't let you go. You wouldn't have much to do and it would be like a paid holiday". Was this to be the end of my all-too-brief time with D'Oyly Carte? Then he said, "But we would like you to come back for the next season, and we are prepared to offer you some work in the office. Would that be acceptable to you?" Naturally I said, "Yes", and breathed a sigh of relief. I might not be going to America, but at least my job was secure and I would be back in harness for the 1976–77 season.

The next major event was my first experience of a recording session. Having joined the Company in its centenary year, 1975, I knew that there had been a centenary recording of *Trial by Jury* coupled with some other interesting music by Sullivan – the overture *Macbeth* (1888) and two movements from the incidental music to Shakespeare's *Henry VIII* (1877).

I also knew that during the centenary season the Company had performed *Utopia Limited*, the first professional performance in the UK since the original run in 1893, and had given a concert performance of *The Grand Duke*, which had not had a professional performance since *its* initial run in 1896. Over a three-day period in March, we recorded *The Grand Duke* at Decca's studios in West Hampstead (now Lilian Baylis House, English National Opera's rehearsal studios), with the Royal Philharmonic Orchestra conducted by Royston Nash. It had long been Company policy to record one opera every year, but the centenary recording of *Trial by Jury* was actually made in 1974, the same year as the earlier recording of *Iolanthe*. (Photographs of the recording of *Trial* appeared in the September 1974 edition of *The Savoyard*, the magazine issued by the D'Oyly Carte Opera Trust Limited.) Presumably *Utopia Limited* had been recorded in the normal 1975 slot early in the year. It had certainly been done before I joined in August, although the recording says 'Copyright 1976' as does that of *The Grand Duke*.

As the junior on the staff I simply went along to the studio to help with the band parts, which were poor photocopies of the handwritten originals in the Company archives. They were full of mistakes, and although some of these were obvious to the players others were not. As we identified them I rushed around the studio during breaks in the recording sessions trying to correct the individual parts, but we didn't get all of them. At one point I was halfway towards one desk when the red light went on for a 'take', and I had to freeze. That particular mistake is almost certainly in the recording and I'm sure there must be other wrong notes too and probably some in *Utopia* as well. But it was still a fascinating experience for me. We made four recordings during my time with the Company. On the Monday and Tuesday, after the daytime sessions, the Company was back at Sadler's Wells for the evening performances; on the Wednesday Royston and I went back to the studio, collected the band parts, and took them in a taxi to the Company office.

Later that week, we finished our season at Sadler's Wells, and I experienced another 'first' – my first D'Oyly Carte Last Night. The last night of the London season had developed over many years into something very different, with an air of mystery in that the audience would not be told beforehand what they were about to see. As the overture would doubtless give it away to most people, it had been decided that after an overture had been played the curtain would go up to reveal the set of a different opera. Then perhaps only the first act of this opera might be given, with the second act of another opera after the interval. I believe that in earlier days the performances were played more or less straight, but eventually it became very much a case of 'anything goes' with, for instance, characters appearing in different costumes, the inclusion of songs from other operas in order to give all the principals a chance to sing, and many other changes.

The Last Night became so popular that tickets eventually had to be acquired by ballot. It was always greatly enjoyed by the audiences who were invariably fans of the Company and often of individual performers. They delighted in seeing their heroes and heroines sending up particular numbers, or other famous stars and personalities, and generally letting their hair down, before going back on the road to perform the operas properly as if nothing out of the ordinary had happened. The following is a typical example of what could be expected. In Act II of *Patience*, Lady Angela says, "But we don't know the fable of the Magnet and the Churn", to which Grosvenor replies, "Don't you? Then I will sing it to you". In 1975's Last Night, after Lady Angela's line, the ladies' chorus chimed in with, "Oh yes we do!", the audience responding with, "Oh no you don't!", in the best pantomime tradition. The ladies' chorus then proceeded to read newspapers, file their nails and pay no attention whatever while Kenneth Sandford, as Grosvenor, tried to sing the song against howls of laughter from the audience. This was just the sort of inspired clowning that a Last Night audience, most of whom were aficionados and knew the operas backwards, wanted to see.

After our season at Sadler's Wells we did one more week, this time at the Wimbledon Theatre. Since we were moving from one theatre to another, the procedure was that we had to be given a train ticket or the equivalent in cash, even though we were still in London, and so it was with some amusement that I recall being given something like 30p for the journey. We opened with *Yeomen* on Monday March 22, followed by *Ruddigore* on Tuesday and three performances of *Gondoliers* on Wednesday and Thursday, the latter, unusually, being matinee day. During the week, along with other members of staff and management, I paid another visit to Decca to hear the recording of *The Grand Duke*. There were also auditions on the Wednesday, held in the Royal Adelphi Theatre, where six years later we would play our last season. Among those we heard were Susan Cochrane and Suzanne Sloane, both of whom would join us as choristers in 1977.

The week ended with three performances of *Iolanthe*, and here I played the Lord Chancellor's train-bearer. I came on with John Reed and simply had to hold the train and follow him around. But during the first song, at the refrain "A pleasant occupation", John gave a little jump on the first syllable of "*plea*-sant", and I had to time this and jump with him. I have a photograph of John and me taken backstage, and have written on it, "The second of the two occasions on which I played the train-bearer". The photograph was presumably taken during the Saturday evening performance, implying that I also did the matinee and I think I was standing in for whoever normally took this role. And so the first part of my time with the Company came to an end. For the rest of the summer I would be working in the Company office. But before that, on April 3, I went down to the Savoy Hotel to see the Company off on the North American tour. I then walked along by the river to Tower Bridge and went on board the cruiser HMS *Belfast*.

My temporary job started on Monday April 5, 1976. The Company office was then in the east side of the main river block of the Savoy Hotel, which had been built, like the Savoy Theatre, by Richard D'Oyly Carte. The Company's address was 1 Savoy Hill. Savoy Hill was also the location of the original premises of the BBC – the British Broadcasting *Company* as it was then. When I joined D'Oyly Carte I gave 1 Savoy Hill to my bank as my address. I had lived in temporary accommodation for years and, other than my parents' home in Greenock, had no permanent home of my own. (I often wondered if the bank gave any thought to how someone with no funds and a comparatively small salary was living at such a prestigious address.) Although I could have entered the office via the door at 1 Savoy Hill, I usually went into the hotel through the River Entrance and made my way through corridors decorated with scenes from G&S operas into the office itself. This was partly because I used to come in from Wembley on the Underground, get off at Embankment and walk through Victoria Embankment Gardens, past the Sullivan memorial. The first entrance I came to was the River Entrance. It did give one a sense of belonging to something rather special. I wasn't in the office all the time as I was occasionally sent over to the Company store and wardrobe department in Walworth on some errand or other. Later I would be used again in my original capacity as the repetiteur. But I enjoyed my time at Savoy Hill and got to know the staff quite well. I became particularly friendly with Margaret Bowden who, almost alone among the staff, had a genuine interest in G&S outside office hours. Her husband, Ken, a West Ham supporter, was more interested in football, but he had to put up with numerous home visits from me and other G&S buffs, the conversation invariably coming round to the operas and D'Oyly Carte.

My job in the office was in the library. It consisted of helping Wilfred 'Wilf' Hambleton to prepare the sets of band parts, which, with an annotated vocal score, were sent out to the numerous schools and amateur operatic societies that were putting on productions of G&S (including my old school Greenock Academy which was doing its third *Pirates* that year). I became an expert packer under Wilf's guidance. He had been a very fine clarinettist and had played in one of the top London orchestras, but he had contracted cancer and had to have his larynx removed. (I think the actor Jack Hawkins had the same operation.) This meant that Wilf had to give up playing, but he took up the cello so that he could continue to make music and he also found this day job with the Company. His speaking technique consisted of barking out sounds on the breath and at first I found it very difficult to understand him. But I gradually got used to it. Also in the library with us was Frankie Doll, a former actress. We got on very well together, sharing the same sense of humour and often going into fits of giggles over nothing at all. Frankie dealt with the associate members of the D'Oyly Carte Opera Trust and was always sending out hundreds of envelopes containing information of interest to the faithful. Frankie was not really one of the faithful and consequently she found the job pretty boring. This probably accounted for the fact that she and I spent a lot of time laughing at anything even remotely amusing.

The library was in a room that opened off a corridor parallel with Savoy Hill, but it was on the inside of the building, and had no windows; we had lights on all day and an old fan whirring constantly. (Now I knew what Hitler's bunker must have been like.) The space had been part of an entrance in some distant history of the hotel and a stairway inside the room led up to a little landing, which now ended in a blank wall. It was here that Bill Hart worked. Bill, then approaching eighty, usually worked at home, but occasionally he came in to the office. His job was to copy all the orchestral cues into the vocal scores in red ink so that the conductor would know what was happening in the orchestra, there being no full scores available. He was effectively copying these cues from older scores that someone else had annotated and invariably he made mistakes, such as putting the cue – 'strings', 'wind', 'brass', or whatever – either before or after where it should have been. When I started to conduct I sometimes found that I was giving orchestral cues too early or actually missing them, although eventually I adjusted any that were not quite right. In fairness this may have been because the scores that Bill was copying from were themselves not very clearly marked. One classic mistake, perhaps committed by a previous copyist, concerned the cues from the libretti, which were also put in so that the conductor would know when to start the music. In Act II of *The Yeomen of the Guard*, the cue line before the quartet 'When a wooer goes a-wooing' is "Go thou, and apply it elsewhere!" Whoever had prepared my score of *Yeomen* had absentmindedly written, "Go thou, and do likewise". This, however, had been corrected by someone – possibly Bill.

The library had a sliding door that was always open to help the ventilation. Directly across the passage was the office of Joan Robertson, secretary to the Company's general manager Freddie Lloyd, whose office was next door. Freddie was also secretary of the D'Oyly Carte Opera Trust. Joan's office looked out on to Savoy Hill and, as *her* door was always open, some natural light filtered through to us. Joan, who had been at Savoy Hill for more than twenty years, was yet another great character – my little world seemed full of them. She retired in 1977 and died suddenly in November 1981, being spared the closure of the Company just three months later. On her retirement, Joan was replaced by Anne Anderson. The others who worked in the main office were Jill Evans, Frances Jones and Margaret Jones, who was the Company's accountant. Margaret Bowden, who was her assistant, was originally part-time, but soon became full-time. Albert Truelove, a somewhat Dickensian character who held various positions, including that of private secretary to Dame Bridget D'Oyly Carte, was also in this office. (There was always a vast amount of correspondence on Albert's desk, seemingly in total disorder, but there was also a sign that read, "A cluttered desk is a sign of genius".) These offices had been fashioned out of existing spaces, and were consequently of various shapes and sizes. It was all a bit of a hotchpotch, but fascinating nevertheless. I spent most of the day in the library, but we had tea in the main office.

Dame Bridget, the granddaughter of Richard D'Oyly Carte, who became DBE in 1975, the Company's centenary year, would occasionally come in for tea, or to ask about something or other. She was never averse to lending a helping hand and I remember one particular day when we had to take large numbers of *The Savoyard* from the office, via a flight of stairs, to the main door in Savoy Hill. The magazines were in mailbags and the procedure was for someone to throw a bag from the top of the stairs to the bottom; whoever was at the bottom dragged the bag to the door. I was at the foot of the stairs, and coming back from having dragged one bag to the door I found myself at the receiving end of another bag – thrown by Dame Bridget!

Over many years the library had acquired an accumulation of old band parts, newspaper cuttings, original designs for costumes and so on. One day, when I was looking through the contents of a drawer, I came across an old leader's (first violin) band part from *Pinafore*, which included a number that was not in the vocal score. It was a duet, presumably between Josephine and Captain Corcoran as it came between Josephine's Act I aria 'Sorry her lot' and the chorus's 'Over the bright blue sea'. There was no melody in the part, just an accompaniment of chords on the second and third beats of the 'um *cha cha*, um *cha cha*' variety, and rather more, in fact, like a typical second violin part. There were no words to it, and at that time I could find no reference to any duet at this point in the opera. Some years later Dr Percy Young, who had been the external examiner for my MA thesis on Sullivan's songs, became the editor of a critical edition of *Pinafore*, and identified this duet as 'Reflect my child'. I made a copy of the part while I was in the library and it was just as well that I did. When the office moved to another part of the building this rare item disappeared.

On April 9 I was sent to Norman Punt, one of the Company's specialist consultants, to have my hearing tested.

After the test he said, "You have a deficiency in the upper registers, but you'll be pleased to know that your ears are very well balanced". (That was something!) I think this visit was to do with the fact that Glyn Hale, the chorus master, would be leaving the Company after the American tour, and I was to be offered his job; the management obviously wanted to find out just what my hearing deficiencies were. I still can't remember exactly when I was told that I was to be promoted. It may have been before this, or the management may have delayed telling me until I had had the test, but whichever way round it was, I got the job.

My old Morris 1100 had now finally expired and later that month I acquired another car for the princely sum of £315 from Freddie Williams, a famous speedway rider in his day (world champion 1950–53), who was now a car dealer at a showroom near Wembley Stadium. My new car was a rather unusual two-door estate-type Austin 1300. It was dark green and quite stylish, but its one disadvantage was that it had no proper boot and anything left in the back could be seen; this later resulted in the car being broken into while we were on tour.

My diary entry for May 10 says "Holiday", and there are no further entries for the next three weeks apart from "Bring back some 'Castle' rock"; this suggests that I went back to Scotland and had been told by the office staff to get some Ross's Edinburgh Castle Rock – dry sticks of confectionary (unlike the Blackpool or Brighton variety) which perhaps they couldn't find in London. While I was away on holiday in Scotland, I received a letter from Joan Robertson about plans for the next season. She mentioned that work was being done in preparation for a move to another part of the hotel complex at the carriage entrance just off the Strand. Albert Truelove was already giving guided tours, but the new address, 2 Savoy Court, didn't have quite the same ring as 1 Savoy Hill. I was back in London at the beginning of June, where I played for auditions at the Savoy Theatre.

There were always people writing in for auditions and it was useful to have details of potential choristers, or even principals, on whom we could call when singers left the Company. We invariably took on some of the people we heard, but there were always ones who might as well not have bothered. One habitual auditionee would walk onto the stage, remove his toupee, and shout into the stalls, "Do you want it with or without the wig?" There were other considerations too, apart from a good voice. We wanted the Company to look good as well as sound good, and if we knew which singers were leaving we would try to find replacements who would fit their costumes without too many costly, time-consuming alterations, although this wasn't always possible. After hearing the candidates the selection process was sometimes peppered with bizarre comments. Albert Truelove, who was often on the panel, once remarked, "He won't do. He's wearing a brown suit".

Another auditionee had travelled a long way to sing 'Take a pair of sparkling eyes' from *The Gondoliers* for his audition, but he seemed very nervous. I played the introduction and he started – in the wrong key. He meandered about vocally, trying to find the right key, "Take a pair... take a pair... take a pair... ", while I repeatedly vamped the opening chords, but to no avail. "Start again" came the imperious direction from Freddie Lloyd, or maybe Albert Truelove, in the stalls.

Me: Introduction...

Auditionee (even more nervous): "Take a pair... take a pair... take a pair..."

Voice from the stalls: "Just relax and try again".

Me: Introduction...

Auditionee (a nervous wreck by now): "Take a pair... take a pair... take..."

Voice from the stalls: "Thank you".

End of audition.

That was an extreme case, but how disappointing for him, after a very long journey, for it to end like that.

Being once again in a nine-to-five job I found that I had free evenings and was able to catch up on some social life. I saw some of my old friends from Birmingham University whose families either lived in London or who, themselves, had found employment there, or were furthering their studies at one or other of the music colleges. I had also begun to make new friends, some of them fans of the Company. During the London season Royston had introduced me to Sarah Lenton and Dilys Jones who shared a flat at Barons Court, and I saw them several times during this five-month period. Sarah was a talented cartoonist and she produced many clever drawings with witty captions, often of Royston and myself. One of these took the form of a lengthy strip cartoon in which I woke up one morning to find that I had grown considerably during the night. I now towered over Royston who was forced to grovel and to comply with my every demand. (This delightful piece of nonsense was produced after I became chorus master and associate conductor.)

I started to rehearse the intake of new choristers at Sadler's Wells on June 28 – music only, no movement. As well as the ballet rehearsal room there was also an opera rehearsal room and a further rehearsal room on the opposite side of the building, but we didn't use any of these. Rehearsals were held in the theatre's upper circle bar where there happened to be a piano. There was also tap water and an ice machine, both of which we were able to use – a godsend as the summer of 1976 was the hottest since records began. Soft drinks with lots of ice helped us through the rehearsal period. During breaks we would go out into Arlington Way and sit on the pavement with our drinks. The new choristers that year were Sara Mousley (soprano), Linda Brindley (later D'Arcy), Jane Guy and Madeleine Hudson (altos), Richard Braebrook and Michael Farran-Lee (tenors) and Richard Mitchell and Patrick Wilkes (basses). For various reasons, however, not all of them were able to attend all of these rehearsals. A number of others – Gillian Swankie and Alison West (sopranos), Susan

Cochrane, Elizabeth Denham and Hélène Witcombe (altos) and Bryan Secombe (bass) – joined during the first half of 1977. On July 1 we rehearsed in the morning at Finsbury Library and in the afternoon we were at Islington Town Hall where I had to enquire about extra rehearsal rooms. We were back at Sadler's Wells on July 12, this time in the ballet rehearsal room, and the music calls finished on July 16.

The Company returned from the North American tour on July 19 and the annual month's holiday began. During this week the new choristers had to go for wig and costume fittings. The full complement of choristers was essentially thirty-two – eight each of soprano, alto, tenor and bass – although the numbers varied slightly from time to time for one reason or another. Many choristers, such as Jon Ellison, were regular small-part players, while others were understudies.

Royston and I auditioned Simon Vout who became our only horn player, until the following year, when we hired another. He married one of the orchestra's violinists, Janice White, whose sister Pam also played with us regularly. Simon later gave up playing the horn and opened a recording studio. The following Monday, July 26, saw the start of three weeks of production rehearsals for the new choristers; and that was the end of my first year with D'Oyly Carte. In the following week I would start my second year – not as repetiteur but as chorus master and associate conductor.

Chapter 2: 1976–1977

I

My second year with D'Oyly Carte began on Monday August 16, 1976. I was now chorus master and associate conductor and my salary had gone up to £54 per week, with a subsistence of £23 per week. I also had to be kitted out for my professional duties. I already possessed a standard dinner jacket and trousers, but now had to get a set of tails, white waistcoat, white shirt and white tie for any evening performances I might have to do, and a black jacket, striped trousers, white shirt and grey tie for matinees. Even in 1976 this latter outfit seemed very staid, if not downright old-fashioned (I looked more like an undertaker's assistant than a musician), but this was in keeping with D'Oyly Carte's very traditional approach. I was given a special dress allowance of £65 in the form of a cheque from Coutts Bank, signed by Dame Bridget herself -- "The Aristocrat who banks with Coutts". If I had been well off I would have kept the cheque and framed it! I went to Moss Bros in Covent Garden, as I knew that they sold off hired formal dress, but they suggested that I go to a shop nearby in Henrietta Street and it was there that I got everything that I needed. It was also at this time that the Company office moved to 2 Savoy Court.

Promotion after just a year seemed like the archetypal meteoric rise to fame, but I think I was retained during the 1976 North American tour because the management thought that I was 'right' for the Company and wanted me to stay on.

That was nothing to do with exceptional ability, but more to do with attitude: I did what I was told, and didn't ask awkward questions. I also think that Royston Nash had a hand in this. I knew that Royston and Glyn Hale didn't always see eye to eye, and I think that Royston felt that he could work with me as his assistant – we got on well together, and shared the same sense of humour. He knew that I had never conducted an opera, but he *had* seen me conduct. When we were on tour we always had a short band call in each new venue to let the players get the feel of the theatre – it surprised me just how different the music could sound in different venues. The band call consisted of a play-through of the overture to the opera we were doing that evening. Royston usually took these calls, but occasionally during my first year as repetiteur, he would ask me to conduct. It never occurred to me at the time, but presumably he did this deliberately to see if I *could* conduct. When I was a student in Birmingham I had conducted the university's wind band, so I wasn't a complete novice, and I must have made some favourable impression. But apart from these Monday band calls the management had no idea of my ability, or otherwise, to get through an entire show – a touching faith indeed as my new post would entail conducting the two matinees each week and possibly evening performances if Royston was absent on Company business.

My successor as repetiteur was Paul Seeley, a graduate of the University of Wales and of Edinburgh University. One of the repetiteur's duties was to deal with the orchestra, particularly with deputies. It was something that I had found rather irksome, but Paul seemed to take to it, and he made a much better job of it. Like me, he was very interested in the operas and the history of D'Oyly Carte, and that, along with the general uncertainty of the music business, was a factor in both of us remaining with the Company until it closed.

We had our customary week of rehearsals before the tour started, most of them in Islington Town Hall and I had my first experience of taking a full chorus rehearsal on my own.

One of the problems of promotion in the same company is that your fellow workers are used to you in a certain position, often one, such as the repetiteur, without very much clout. And then overnight you are in a different position and have to show a bit more authority. This can be difficult, and that first chorus rehearsal was, I must admit, far from successful. It was in the afternoon and a number of the men had been imbibing during the lunch hour, the inevitable result being that some of them just wouldn't settle down. This was particularly unnerving to someone taking a rehearsal for the very first time. It would be charitable to say only that some of the behaviour was less than professional, and, to their credit, some of the ladies were acutely embarrassed. This situation was the inevitable result of promotion within the Company, but I had to live with that if I wanted to stay in D'Oyly Carte. Just being part of the Company was compensation for any such problems. But it is still easier to come to a new position from elsewhere.

The tour began with a two-week season in Brighton and it was there in the Theatre Royal that I conducted my first performance, a matinee of *The Mikado*. I had had an afternoon session with Royston to have the awkward passages pointed out to me, but playing through the operas at rehearsals was one thing – actually conducting them was going to be quite another. You can practice playing the piano at home, but you can't just practice conducting in front of a mirror. You need to have the performers in front of you to see if what you are doing actually works. Royston had said to me, "We'll give you *Mikado* first. It's the one we do most often, so even if you do anything untoward it will probably keep going". It still amazes me, forty years later, that as late as 1976 a professional opera company could take on a conductor of no proven ability and entrust him with the direction of a performance without giving him even one rehearsal, but, incredible as it may seem, that is exactly what happened. I simply went into the pit, lifted my baton and conducted *The Mikado*, never having conducted an opera before – never even having rehearsed one. That's how it was in D'Oyly Carte; it's all part of the legend.

Another complication was the orchestra pit in the Theatre Royal, probably the most difficult of all the many pits that I conducted in – and this one had to be the first! The problem was that the pit was very deep, and much of it was under the stage. If you stood on a normal podium the members of the orchestra who were at the back (under the stage) could see you, but you could barely see on to the stage. Even Royston, who was tall, couldn't see properly. There was a high podium, which raised you up to enable you to see the stage, but in that position the players at the back of the pit (brass and wind) couldn't see the beat and therefore you had to conduct the stage with your left hand at one level, while conducting the orchestra with your right hand at a lower level. This situation was enough to tax an experienced conductor, but here I was, with virtually no experience, conducting my first opera under these conditions. Geoffrey Shovelton suggested an ingenious solution to the problem in one of his cartoons, which showed Royston's successor, Fraser Goulding, conducting the orchestra, while I sat on his shoulders conducting the stage. The cartoon was published in Tony Joseph's *The D'Oyly Carte Opera Company 1875–1982*.

My debut wasn't exactly a brilliant performance, but somehow I got through it without any major mishaps. I must have had the right ideas or it could have been an unmitigated disaster. Before the performance I went into a pub to fortify myself for "the fearful ordeal", but although I had something to drink I was so nervous that I could hardly eat anything. I didn't realise it at the time, but *The Mikado* is not particularly difficult to conduct, the worst part being the 'O ni! bikkuri shakkuri to!' in the Act I finale. I had dreaded this section, although it seemed to go fairly well, but I remember that by that time I thought that I wasn't going to make it to the interval as my arms felt as if they were about to drop off. But I made it. The ladies of the Company had given me a good luck card and one of the Peanuts booklets – *Charlie Brown's Reflections* – inscribed, "Good luck, from all the ladies of the Company", and I seem to recall that there was a bottle of champagne afterwards. And that was my conducting debut. It was certainly rough at the edges, but it was a miracle that it had happened at all. I could only hope to get better with subsequent performances, and there would eventually be at least two of these each week.

The fact that a new conductor (with or without experience) had to conduct his first performance without any rehearsal was simply due to the lack of money and rehearsal time, but while such an operating procedure might appear ludicrously behind the times in 1976, it did give me an opportunity to show that having been thrown in at the deep end I could actually swim. Over the next few years I proved that I could do the job, although I admit that it was a slow grind. It was more like a long traditional apprenticeship, but it was ironic that D'Oyly Carte had to close just as I felt that I had completed it. I did, however, vindicate their faith in me by being entrusted with the last complete performance of an opera that the Company gave. But that is for a later chapter.

It was also in Brighton that I had another unnerving experience. When I became chorus master I gave up my walk-on parts, although I was available to do one again if someone was ill. Paul took on his share of these, as well as conducting the offstage choruses, but there was one other duty that the repetiteur performed and that was 'the bell' ("Hear it not, Duncan…"). This is the sounding of the funeral bell, representing the bell of St Peter ad Vincula in the Tower of London, rung during executions, which is heard tolling during the Act I finale of *Yeomen* in the section beginning 'The prisoner comes to meet his doom'. At one time this had been a heavy bell in the wings, but because of the difficulties of co-ordination it had been decided to use a tubular C bell, which could be played by the timpanist in the orchestra pit. By the time I joined the Company, the bell was now back in the wings, suspended from a frame, and played by the repetiteur. In our production there were thirty-two strokes in all – originally there were a few more – one on the first beat of every second bar. As Paul was going to take over this duty, I said that I would do it one more time to show him what was required. There was no TV monitor to enable you to see the conductor. You just had to listen to the orchestra and strike the bell fractionally before the beat. As a musician I didn't find this particularly difficult, but it does have to be strictly in time.

The bell itself had two holes at the top, and a leather thong passed through these and was tied to the top of the frame. It was a Heath Robinson contraption if ever there was one. In all the times that I had done this I had never had any problems and to this day I don't know how it happened, but about halfway through what was supposed to be my last performance, the bell suddenly came away from the frame and crashed to the ground – at perhaps the most solemn moment in all the Savoy operas. The effect this had, particularly on the Company who were all onstage at the time trying to look serious, can only be imagined. But imagine, too, the effect on the poor chorus master. The departure of the Company earlier in the year for North America had not ended my time at D'Oyly Carte, but I really thought that this incident might well result in instant dismissal. At the interval Royston said, rather grimly, "Well, what happened?" I could only say that the bell had unaccountably come away from the frame – in darker moments I did suspect sabotage – and, like Elsie who sings during this scene, pleaded, "Oh, Mercy". I didn't lose my job and it became just another Company tale. But I was still glad to be relieved of this duty.

Bells featured in several of the operas and were something of a headache for the property department. As well as the C bell in *Yeomen* we had another C bell for *Cox and Box* and *Princess Ida*, and both A and D bells for *The Sorcerer*. *Trial by Jury* ought to have had a B bell, but Royston had said that one of the C bells would have to do, and an A flat bell was also required for *Ruddigore*. On August 18, just two days after this 1976–77 season had begun, Peter Riley, the technical and stage director, sent a memo on the subject to Royston stating that Frank Coghill, the property master and second marine in *Pinafore*, had actually "lost a few", and that he (Peter) wanted to avoid any last-minute panics when we came in to London in December. A week later Peter sent Royston another memo (stamped RUSH!!) in which he said, "I have found a solution to the bell problem. We need an A flat bell for *Ruddigore* – so I have spent all afternoon hammering the "Sorcerer" A bell, and although we don't have an A flat bell, we do have a flat A bell – do you think this will do – it makes a sound like a ruptured peacock when struck (with a vicuña-tipped hammer of course)". Memos of this sort, which always raised a smile, were a regular feature of life in the Company.

An altogether more pleasant experience while we were in Brighton was meeting the legendary Isidore Godfrey, born in 1900, the year that Sullivan died. Known as Goddie, he had spent over forty years with D'Oyly Carte, as musical director from 1929. He had been awarded the OBE in 1965 and retired in 1968. Living nearby, in West Sussex, he came in to the theatre one day. He was then almost seventy-six and the famous shock of red hair was now grey. He was also in poor health and he died the following year. I'm glad that I did have an opportunity to meet him, if only briefly.

From Brighton we moved to Bristol for two weeks, opening at the Hippodrome on September 6 with *Yeomen*, which was preceded by the usual band call at 4.30pm. Apart from getting used to the acoustic in another theatre, these band calls, which at one time were a full three hours, were as much for the seating arrangements as for the music. Opera companies with large orchestras, and large budgets, could take out several rows of front stalls, but we had to make do with pits as they existed and there was often very little room, even for our small orchestra. Many of the venues that we played in had been built as variety theatres and didn't have the sort of orchestral accommodation that Wagner had designed for his operas at Bayreuth. The pit at the Hippodrome was better than the one at Brighton's Theatre Royal in that it did not extend under the stage, but it was long and thin, and wasn't big enough for the orchestra. Consequently we had to have the double bass in a box, stage right, and the timpanist in the corresponding box, stage left.

A new timpanist, Harry Smaile (yet another character), had just joined us in Bristol. Lacking a van, Harry toured his timpani with the sets and costumes. Each drum had a black wooden cover on which he had written in large white letters his name and that of the Company, but he had spelled the latter D'Oly [sic] Carte. When the scenery was being unloaded at each theatre Harry's timpani would often be left on the pavement, proclaiming to passers-by that the D'Oly Carte was back in town – not really the best advertisement. Sometime later, after a performance of *Pinafore*, he said to me, in reference to one particular section, "I hope you didn't mind, but I hurried you along there. I thought it was too slow". So much for my carefully prepared individual interpretation. Harry's spelling variation – D'Oly Carte – was by no means unique, the name being rather an unusual one. During my time in the Company I received a letter which was addressed to me c/o Budget D'Oyle Carte, and circulars once arrived at the office for Dame Doyley Carter and Doyly Carte Dame B.

I conducted my second *Mikado* at the mid-week matinee in Bristol and my first *Gondoliers* on the following Saturday. As the players were stretched out in a thin line some of the music came at you with a slight delay, particularly from the double bass and the timpani in the boxes at opposite ends. This wasn't very helpful for my technique or my confidence, but the constant change of venue, and consequent change of sound, was something I eventually got used to. It was, in fact, the sort of work experience that money can't buy, and was extremely useful. A week later I did my first evening performance – yet another *Mikado*. Royston might have given me this one to see how I coped with it, or it might have been that he was away on

Company business and I just had to do it. I soon learned that evening performances were invariably different from matinees. Cast, orchestra and audiences alike all seemed to be much livelier. With the best will in the world it was sometimes difficult for artists to give of their best in the afternoons, particularly at the mid-week matinees. These usually had smaller audiences, which often consisted largely of pensioners, and as many of them would fall asleep during the performances there was invariably a corresponding lack of response and applause. Audiences don't always realise just how much the level of their response can make or mar a performance.

Encores should really only be given if the audience demands them. They were usually dispensed with at mid-week matinees, although they were sometimes given during Saturday matinees as these usually attracted larger and more enthusiastic audiences. On a really good Saturday, for instance, Julia Goss, as Mabel (*Pirates*), would have to sing 'Poor wandering one' not only twice but with an encore for each. Luckily the encore was a shortened version, but it still included the difficult coloratura section with the piccolo. Before going into the pit to conduct mid-week matinees I would often find principal bass-baritone John Ayldon at my elbow saying, in his wonderfully distinctive voice, "No encores please". I was once ticked off by a fan for not giving an encore at a matinee. "We clapped and clapped", she said in a wounded tone. But the fans often failed to realise that there really had to be an appreciable volume of applause from the *entire* audience before it became evident that an encore was justified – particularly at mid-week matinees.

The Hippodrome at Bristol, like so many of the older theatres, did not have air conditioning, but the roof had a segmented circular section in the middle that could be opened on very hot days. We must have had some of these as I can distinctly recall the roof being opened. Another memory of Bristol was a very good Indian Restaurant, the Rajdoot, at the top of Park Street. As we were more or less permanently away from home, eating out was an essential part of the job rather than a once a week luxury, and economy was necessary for much of the time. But it was good to splash out every so often, and the Rajdoot was a favourite haunt.

My other non-musical memory of that first visit was the worst digs that I had yet encountered, and possibly the worst of all during my seven years on the road. It was quite common for a number of people to share digs and on this occasion several of us took what we thought would be an interesting house in the Clifton district of the city. It was part of a Georgian terrace and it looked all right from the outside, but we soon discovered its negative qualities. The communal lounge on the first floor had the standard two single windows with wooden shutters, with a short stretch of wall between, but the wall bulged out into the room, and if you leant on it, the window shutters on either side would pop out. This in itself was quite amusing, but it was nothing to the other problems which included a substantial amount of water coming through the roof, which damaged clothing, books and a cassette tape recorder, bites from bed bugs, no lighting in my upstairs back bedroom, even after putting money in a meter, and a really filthy bathroom, which we had to clean before we could use it. Even some of the 'beds' were only mattresses on the floor. The end result was that we drafted a letter to the landlady saying that we were only prepared to pay half of what was being asked and this is what we did. We never heard another word from her.

From Bristol we moved to Birmingham for a week. I knew the city well, having been at university there, and was able to stay with some friends who were still in student accommodation, although this was almost as bad as the digs we had just left in Bristol. We were at the Alexandra Theatre and once again I had to get used to a different pit. In fact it wasn't really a pit at all, simply a space at the foot of the stalls with a rudimentary curtain round it. We played *Mikado* on the Wednesday and I did both shows. I was rapidly becoming familiar with it. We had auditions on the Friday, hearing two young men who were both just eighteen, and on the Saturday we played *Pinafore*. I hadn't conducted it yet and this time Royston did both shows.

The next port of call was Nottingham where we played at the Theatre Royal for a week, and here I did conduct my first *Pinafore* at the matinee on Wednesday September 29. We heard another eighteen-year-old on Friday October 1, and held more auditions on Saturday. Nottingham was another city that was new to me. With all the touring that we did I gradually got to know most of the large English cities, one exception being Sheffield. We never played there during my time with the Company.

Many of the theatres that we played were Victorian and in the mid to late 1970s few of these had been upgraded to any noticeable degree. The Theatre Royal, Nottingham was certainly in need of some attention. There had once been another theatre next door, the Empire Palace of Varieties, and stories are told that they shared dressing room accommodation and, more importantly, passages leading to their respective stages, with the result that people had been known to appear in the wrong show. I don't know if this ever happened, but the Empire had certainly gone by 1976. The complex now includes the Concert Hall, and as the ground was then being prepared for it the area around the stage door was a bit of a mess and could be a quagmire on rainy days.

I soon realised that any money that was available for theatres would invariably be spent on the front of the house rather than on the backstage area. In the Theatre Royal this showed itself in two distinct ways. First of all there was the pit – yet another variation on a basic design. This one was certainly lower than the auditorium, but only by about the height of a chair leg, and there was no rail or curtain to separate it from the front row of the stalls. It was also quite small, like so many of the pits that we had to use, but previous musicians had devised an ingenious, if somewhat unorthodox, way of making some more room. This consisted of sawing the legs off chairs (the two left ones or the two right ones for either side of the conductor) so that you could put them on the edge of the pit. This gave the string players, now effectively sitting on the floor of the auditorium, much-needed extra arm room. It was, however, rather odd to see these two-legged chairs lying around forlornly in the space under the stage. The band room, as so often, was also under the stage, with little in the way of amenities.

The other victim of this lack of modernisation was the dressing room accommodation. Some of this may have been part of the Empire Palace of Varieties, or formed out of other adjacent buildings, but the result was a bewildering complex of rooms and interconnecting corridors and stairways. Some of the dressing rooms were a long way from the stage and the whole backstage area of the theatre had a reputation as one of the worst in the country. Artists are supposed to make sure that they are on time for their appearances without relying on calls, although calls are invariably given. In Nottingham's Theatre Royal the tannoy system, certainly in those days, was essential, and when it broke down one night there was a most embarrassing, if unintentionally hilarious, outcome.

We were doing *Pirates*, with James Conroy-Ward as Major-General Stanley. Towards the end of Act I there is a chorus ('With cat-like tread') for the pirates and police, with a solo ('Here's your crowbar') for Samuel. After this Frederic enters, singing, 'Hush, hush, not a word! I see a light inside! The Major-General comes, so quickly hide!' The pirates sing, 'Yes, yes, the Major-General comes!', and this is echoed an octave lower by the police. The sequence is then topped off by the appearance of the Major-General with 'Yes, yes, the Major-General comes!' – the classic big build-up. I was standing at the back of the balcony that night and I watched the sequence unfold. All went well until the Major-General's entrance. Silence. No Major-General! Unfortunately at this point in the opera there is virtually no music to cover any such eventuality, just a few chords under the vocal lines. There is also a break before the Major-General continues with 'Tormented with the anguish dread' and if there is no Major-General, there is no action. A crowd scene, with a dose of spontaneous 'rhubarbing', might have eased the situation, but in our production the pirates were sitting cross-legged on the stage facing the audience and they had to try to keep straight faces when they realised that the Major-General had failed to arrive. No prizes for guessing that this was almost impossible and that heads went down and shoulders started to heave. For anyone in the audience who didn't know the opera it might have taken a while to realise that something had gone wrong. I realised immediately, and a silence of even a few seconds can seem interminable.

At first the stage manager was not aware that the tannoy system had broken down, but when James didn't appear someone had quickly been sent to fetch him. The panic backstage was probably punctuated by some fairly blue language, and who knows what might have been heard in the front row of the stalls. But even at the back of the balcony, as I watched with mounting apprehension the complete inaction on stage, you could hear a pre-entry clattering and banging before James rushed on in a somewhat undignified way finally to deliver his line. The orchestra, who couldn't always hear the singers, were only just beginning to realise that something untoward had happened. Some of them had already played all the underlying chords and were a bar or two ahead of James when he finally came in, and it took a while for this to sort itself out. Mercifully the introduction to the next number ('Sighing softly to the river') gave everyone the chance to synchronise again and the performance finally returned to some semblance of normality.

Something similar happened to Geoffrey Shovelton during a performance of *Yeomen* in Brighton. The tannoy system had broken down, or there might not even have been one, and the theatre was using the old call-boy system. Geoffrey played Colonel Fairfax, who has an entrance just before the Act I finale, and he was sharing a dressing room with Michael

Rayner (the Lieutenant) and Meston Reid (Leonard Meryll) who are not on until later. Geoffrey and Meston were deep in conversation about something when the call-boy came round shouting, "Finale, Act I". Michael said, "Thank you", and went on reading his paper, unaware that Geoffrey hadn't heard the call. Onstage the dialogue before the finale was proceeding apace. John Ayldon, as Sergeant Meryll, delivered the lines, which include, "But the Colonel comes", after which Fairfax enters – but no Geoffrey. John then added some dialogue of his own along the lines of, "I thought I saw him. Wait, is that him now? Why has he gone into that room?" and so on. As with the *Pirates* situation at Nottingham Geoffrey was quickly summoned and could be heard running down the stairs to make a similarly undignified entrance with his line "My good and kind friend" – a highly appropriate one as John Ayldon was one of the best ad-libbers in a situation like that. But very occasionally he did forget his own lines. At one performance of *Iolanthe*, just before the Act I finale, he suddenly had a complete blank at his short dialogue beginning, "Well, now that the Peers are to be recruited entirely from persons of intelligence"; he then walked upstage and, to the great amusement of the entire cast, went off into some fanciful concoction of his own. Geoffrey Shovelton (as Tolloller) was waiting for his cue "I really don't see what use *we* are, down here, do you, Tolloller?" to give his reply "None whatever". It just didn't come, and Royston quickly started the finale to put them both out of their misery.

From Nottingham we moved to Eastbourne for a week, playing at the comparatively modern Congress Theatre. I took to Eastbourne immediately, particularly as it was by the sea, and later bought my first house there. I continued to conduct matinee performances of the operas that I had already done – all good experience. A mid-week matinee was usually on a Wednesday, but occasionally, as here, it was on a Thursday. There was also at least one venue where it was on a Tuesday, and an announcement would have to be made over the tannoy during the Monday performance (with a notice on the board as well) to remind everyone to come in the following afternoon. If the matinee was on a Thursday the announcement would be made on the Tuesday to say "Don't come in tomorrow afternoon, just the evening", with usually another announcement during Wednesday's performance: "Remember there's a matinee tomorrow!" If you missed the Tuesday announcement (for whatever reason) and came in for a matinee on Wednesday you would simply have wasted a journey, and would have to remember to come in for Thursday's matinee. But if you missed the reminder on a Monday that there was a Tuesday matinee you could miss the show itself – no second chance! This occasionally happened with principals who might not be in the Monday show, and understudies were sometimes hurriedly made ready for an unexpected performance. I had to be particularly careful myself about any deviation from the norm as I would soon be conducting virtually all the mid-week matinees – Tuesday, Wednesday or Thursday.

After Eastbourne we were in Bournemouth for two weeks, playing at another old theatre, the Pavilion. Like the Hippodrome in Bristol it had no air conditioning, although unlike the Hippodrome it had no opening roof for hot days. But we were now into October and I don't recall that really hot days were a problem on that visit. There were, in fact, some really stormy days, one of them the occasion of an amusing incident. We sometimes used the theatre on the end of the pier for rehearsals and I had to play there one morning for the new ladies in the chorus in preparation for the forthcoming performances of *Ruddigore* in London. (Paul was concurrently playing for a *Mikado* understudy call at the YMCA.) It was a pretty wild day when we arrived. We went through the gate and onto the pier, watched by a slightly bemused attendant who was obviously wondering why anyone would want to be there in such weather. We did tell him that we were working in the theatre. We rehearsed all morning and even inside the building it was obvious that the weather was getting worse, the storm causing the entire structure to shake quite noticeably – this seemed very appropriate for *Ruddigore* whose subtitle is *The Witch's Curse*. Eventually we finished the rehearsal and started to make our way back to the head of the pier – but with some difficulty as it was now blowing a gale. When we got to the gate we found that it was locked. The attendant had forgotten that we were in the theatre and the pier had been closed as it was now considered too dangerous to be on it. His face was quite a study when he saw us, but he duly let us out. I related this story to Joan Robertson in the London office and received a typical reply: "We're sending you to some very choice places next year – Hull, Hell and Halifax in fact! – but not to Wigan, so it's no use thinking you can rehearse Ruddigore on the end of Wigan Pier". Of those four we only ever got to Hull, although several other places did seem like Hell at times.

Following yet another session with Royston, but again no actual rehearsal, I conducted my first *Pirates* in Bournemouth. I eventually conducted all of the operas in our repertoire and the first time for each was always the same: no rehearsal – just go into the pit, raise your baton and hope for the best. That must surely be some kind of record. *Pirates* is one of the most operatic of the series in that much of it consists of one musical number played 'segue' after another, and it is therefore quite tiring for the conductor and players. It also took me longer to master some of its technical intricacies, but by now I was beginning to get into my stride. If I had had to conduct *Pirates* as my first show it would probably have been a disaster. On October 15 I had to play for Geoffrey Shovelton and Julia Goss at a concert for the Shaftesbury Society, with a lunch beforehand. As this was a Friday I missed one of the highlights of a visit to Bournemouth: tea with Mrs Yorke Batley. (I made up for this on later visits.) During the second week the principals and I received a letter from Freddie Lloyd to the effect that parties for sponsors, which had apparently been instigated on the recent tour of North America, would probably have to be continued, and artists who sang at these events should be properly compensated. It seems a trifling amount now, but a fee of £10 per performance had been agreed. It was also proposed that there should be two teams, A and B. Several people – John Reed, Kenneth Sandford, Lyndsie Holland and myself – were common to both. John Ayldon, Meston Reid, Julia Goss and Patricia Leonard made up the remainder of team A and Michael Rayner, Geoffrey Shovelton, Barbara Lilley and Jane Metcalfe completed team B. Two such forthcoming events were mentioned in this letter.

After Bournemouth we were in Oxford again for another two weeks. This was the first return visit I had experienced and there were to be quite a number of these. There were also several places that we played only once during those years, one of them being Billingham. As on my first visit I found myself in the same dreary old dressing room doing more rewriting of parts, this time a reallocation of the vocal lines at the end of the Act I finale of *Princess Ida*. I had to turn the SATB into an all-male TTBB in preparation for our performances of *Ida* in the coming London season. In the afternoon of Friday October 29 there was the first of the sponsor-driven functions mentioned in Freddie Lloyd's letter. This was held at the home, near Henley, of Colonel Kenneth Osborne, with team A performing. No current sponsors were present, but among the guests were Sir Geoffrey Tuttle, vice-chairman of the British Aircraft Corporation, and Lord Black, a former chairman of British Leyland. Support was clearly being sought from big business. Also present were Dr Robin Wilson, son of Sir Harold, both of whom were keen lovers of G&S, the actor Robert Morley and his wife, and Freddie Lloyd – who arrived from London by helicopter!

The second week was a particularly busy one for me. I had to be in London on the Monday, calling in at the new office at 2 Savoy Court, then return to Oxford to conduct *Mikado* twice on the Wednesday, and twice again on the Saturday, and I also had to play for rehearsals. On the Thursday, after the evening performance of *Pinafore,* we had a 'sing for your supper' at Oxford Cricket Club. Cricket, like golf, was an interest of many of the men; the Company had at one time fielded a side. An article on the subject by Tony Joseph, along with a photograph of the team in the late 1950s, appeared in the September 1978 edition of *The Savoyard*. On the following day, November 5, there was a champagne party onstage for John Reed who was celebrating twenty-five years with the Company. Two fans from Trowbridge had also presented him with a large cake and he was photographed with it in his dressing room. After this we had one more day in Oxford. My digs here had been with a strange, somewhat aggressive lady and I was glad to be moving on.

We were now into November and the next stop was Manchester where we played for three weeks. It was yet another new city for me and yet another old theatre, the Opera House in Quay Street, a rather drab building at that time. On our first day there was another party for John Reed, this time at the Midland Hotel, given jointly by D'Oyly Carte and Decca, the latter presenting John with an especially cut silver disc of the 'patter' songs that he had recorded for them. At that time he was the only person who had made commercial recordings of all the comedy roles in the complete series from *Trial by Jury* to *The Grand Duke*. A single album of excerpts from all thirteen operas was issued under the title *I have a song to sing O* to celebrate his 25th anniversary. A signed copy of it is still in my possession – one of many treasures from those days.

It was in Manchester that I did my fifth 'new' opera, *Patience*, which has always been one of my favourites. The Company also enjoyed doing it. Like *Sorcerer*, *Ida* and *Ruddigore*, it was performed less often and these four were always a welcome change from a surfeit of *Pirates* and *Mikado*. *Patience* seems to me to be the first of the operas to arrive at a true balance of words and music. In the earlier operas Gilbert had provided Sullivan with operatic-style libretti. They have many recitatives and little dialogue – the opening section of

Pirates, the previous opera, was originally to have been sung throughout. With *Patience* one can almost hear him saying, "Sullivan, it's time my words were heard on their own", and so the format now becomes effectively a play with musical items at regular intervals. They have finally arrived at their own G&S style.

This format, of course, is just another variant of the English ballad opera, for example John Gay's *The Beggar's Opera*, the German singspiel (Mozart's *Die Zauberflöte*), the French opéra comique (the original version of Bizet's *Carmen* with its spoken dialogue), or the many less well-known Spanish zarzuelas. *Patience*, with more dialogue, is a good twenty minutes longer than the three previous full-length operas which came after *Trial by Jury*. It is a delight from start to finish, but that didn't stop me being nervous again as I stepped into the pit for yet another excursion into the unknown. But they are never quite so bad once you have got through that first nerve-wracking performance. I had now conducted all of the five operas that we had on tour – *Mikado, Gondoliers, Pinafore, Pirates* and *Patience*.

Three weeks in Manchester meant that I had plenty of time to get to know the city. I have always been interested in architecture, having once considered it as a profession, and there were plenty of wonderful buildings such as the Town Hall (the competition-winning design of Alfred Waterhouse) to feast one's eyes on. Much later I was even able to see inside this masterpiece as the Manchester branch of the Gilbert and Sullivan Society temporarily held meetings there. But it wasn't just the towns and cities themselves that were appealing; on free afternoons I often explored the surrounding country to see other places of interest. It could take some time to get out of a large conurbation like the Greater Manchester area, but from Nottingham, for instance, you could easily get to Chatsworth and Hardwick Hall, and Harewood House is just a few miles outside Leeds. Driving from, say, London would have added to the expense of seeing all of these places. It was also useful if you happened to be a member of the National Trust or English Heritage; you certainly got your money's worth by being able to visit many of their properties. An interest like this was not only fun but a way of helping to pass any spare time that we had. It was all part of a life that was being lived almost permanently away from home (although as yet I had no permanent home), a way of life that didn't always suit everyone. On wet days you could go to the cinema. As members of Equity the Company could get in free, at least in the afternoons. I was not a member of Equity, but I would occasionally tag along with a group, although I stayed at the end of the queue. The cashier would usually look at a few Equity cards and then say, "All right, in you go". I was never caught!

Manchester also had the Press Club which was open all night and to which we had access during our stay. It was a favourite haunt of the orchestra and the consequences of this were sometimes noticeable at the mid-week matinees when some of the players appeared to have just woken up, having seemingly been at the club most of the night, with very some strange noises emanating from the pit. In return for the Press Club's hospitality the orchestra would often give impromptu jam sessions, and as there was a piano in the bar I would sometimes join them in numbers like 'Tiger Rag', a particular favourite of our trumpeter Allan Wilson. My digs in Manchester were in the Cheetham Hill district, courtesy of Stuart Levington who had quite a few properties to let. Several Company members had recommended them as being cheap and cheerful. I had written to him a few weeks before we were due in the city; he had replied saying that I was "a bit late", but he would try to fit me in which he duly did.

At the end of November we moved to the Grand Theatre, Leeds (also new to me) for a week. A favourite eating place here was just across the road from the theatre: Nash's Fish Restaurant (again, no relation to Royston). A number of people had digs in the famous Ivor Novello House; ours were with a lady who went out early, leaving us to make our own breakfast. We would have a good old fry-up with sausages, bacon and eggs, although we always made sure that we cleaned the pan properly before putting it away. On the Saturday, as she wasn't working, we finally got a chance to talk to our landlady, and suddenly realised that she was Jewish. "I hope you haven't had any bacon in that frying pan", she said. "I would have to throw it out if you had". I don't know if our faces displayed any reaction to the contrary as we said (lying through our teeth) that we hadn't. We were glad to get away the following morning.

Leeds was followed by a week in Liverpool. I think there had been a fire at the Royal Court Theatre; it certainly wasn't available, and we played at the Empire next to Lime Street Station, a great barn of a place which had opened in 1925. With a seating capacity in excess of two thousand it was really far too big for us. The pit here, although large enough, was another nightmare. The floor consisted of four wooden rostra which didn't quite fit together. The wood must have warped as each section moved up and down independently – just one more problem that we had to deal with.

It was a busy week. We had another invitation to the Arts Club after the Monday performance and were invited to Heswall Golf Club for another Candlelight Dinner after the Wednesday evening performance. The entertainment was again introduced by Gordon MacKenzie who would always contribute songs on these occasions. Among his favourites were 'The Wee Cock Sparra', made famous by the Scottish actor Duncan Macrae, and a version of 'Galway Bay' which included the lines, "On her back she had tattooed a map of Ireland/ And when she took her bath each Christmas Day/ You could watch the soap suds falling over Claddagh/ And see the sun go down on Galway Bay". He always accompanied himself in these gems. Other featured members of the Company during our entertainment that night were Beti Lloyd-Jones and Suzanne O'Keefe, who were both local girls, Beti from Crosby and Suzanne from Liverpool, John Ayldon and Meston Reid;

I played for most of the items. Earlier, on the Wednesday morning, I had to play for auditions. We often held these in the provinces to save people from the north having to travel to London. Also on that day (December 8) Freddie Lloyd wrote to me to say that my salary, which had earlier been fixed at £54 per week, was going to be increased to £60, backdated to November 15 – almost twice what I had received the previous year as the repetiteur. Things were looking up.

We then had a week in Blackpool, another place I had not yet been to. We played at the Opera House, an enormous theatre with a seating capacity of almost three thousand. Ironically the pit here was so small that we could hardly fit our orchestra into it. They had to enter from under the stage via a door at one side, and once they were all in there was no room for anyone else to come through. The conductor had to go into the auditorium via the pass door, walk along the front of the stalls and then literally slide over a broad catwalk onto the podium. Very dignified! Without the catwalk we would have had more room in the pit. There was also a lift backstage which brought artists from the dressing rooms to the stage level, and although I don't recall it sticking I did hear tales of principals missing entries when it had stuck on previous visits. Coming to Blackpool out of season should have helped in finding accommodation, but there was not much of this available anyway as many of the lodging houses – there seemed to be whole streets of them – closed for the winter. Presumably the owners were enjoying the fruits of their summer takings in warmer climes. It was here that I had possibly the dampest digs that I ever stayed in. There was a mist hovering in the hallway as you went in, and damp sheets too. I don't know how we survived some of these experiences. Another memory of Blackpool was a Yates's Wine Lodge in the centre of town where we would often enjoy a session of people watching. But our tour of the provinces had once again come to an end and on Monday December 20 we were back in London for another season at Sadler's Wells.

II

My digs in London were rather more pleasant than some I had encountered. I was staying at the home of chorister Madeleine Hudson, known by her first Christian name of Caroline. We were now in a relationship, which lasted throughout most of the time that we were together in the Company. The subject of relationships is one that needs careful handling, but it is something that has to be mentioned, if only briefly. In any working environment it is inevitable that people will get together, and it was no different in D'Oyly Carte. Many indeed were the marriages made there between numerous combinations of principals, choristers, orchestra, staff and management – to say nothing of other relationships. The biggest problem was that if a relationship foundered, for whatever reason, you couldn't really get away from your ex-partner. We were on the road all the time, doing eight performances a week, and there was effectively no place to hide. Even when the relationship was working it was extremely difficult to pursue any individuality in your life. I also found it awkward that Caroline was on one side of the fence as a performing member of the Company and I was on the other as a member of the staff. A relationship is subjective, but when you are sitting on a panel for Company auditions and have to be objective about your partner, it is quite another matter. My predecessor, Glyn Hale, was in a similar position with chorister Gillian Burrows, but while they may not have experienced these problems they had both now left the Company. They were married at the Savoy Chapel in December 1976. Caroline and I decided to stay on and the relationship did survive after a fashion, but eventually it came to an end.

I had now been conducting the operas for almost five months, and was about to make my London debut, but with a significantly larger orchestra. The sound, with the extra strings, was a revelation. No matter how good the individual players are you need numbers to get 'string sound'. We opened with a half week of *Yeomen*, but I didn't conduct the Wednesday matinee as Royston wisely felt that I should ease my way in with some of the operas I had already conducted before attempting a new opera with the extra players who hadn't yet played under me. We followed *Yeomen* with *Pinafore* (minus *Trial*) which we played on December 23 and 24. Christmas that year was on a Saturday and we had a welcome three-day break, returning to *Pinafore* on the Tuesday. But we had to "'make up' for lost time" and so there were two performances on the Tuesday which Royston conducted and a further two on the Wednesday which I conducted. We were also busy at this time with rehearsals.

On December 30 I played for an understudy call in the opera rehearsal room, while Paul played for one in the ballet rehearsal room, and even on New Year's Eve we were kept at it, this time switching venues, with Paul playing for a full chorus rehearsal of *Ruddigore* and *Iolanthe* while I played for a call with Geoffrey Shovelton (as Box) in *Cox and Box*. We were now playing *Patience* and after the performance on New Year's Eve we sang 'Auld Lang Syne' in a new arrangement that I had made for the orchestra. I found out later that in the audience that night was HRH Princess Alice, Countess of Athlone, Queen Victoria's last surviving grandchild, who had come to the theatre incognito with a companion. Born in February 1883, she was an interesting link with Gilbert and Sullivan's own times.

Patience was followed by a week of *Mikado* and I conducted my quota of these. The extra London players had now got used to me and it was time for me to do my first *Yeomen*. Of all the Savoy operas it is the closest to the grand opera that Sullivan always wanted to write, and eventually did, with *Ivanhoe* (1891), but it isn't as difficult to conduct as some of the earlier operas. The format is still that of a play with musical numbers, with correspondingly less recitative than in, say, *The Sorcerer*, that was established in *Patience* – and

I didn't have to play that wretched bell! The extra strings were particularly welcome given those cascading triplets and semiquavers in the overture – a nightmare for a small orchestra on tour. We followed *Yeomen* with *Ruddigore* and I conducted my first performance of it on January 22. *Ruddigore* was followed by a week of *Gondoliers*. *Gondoliers* was also the opera that we recorded in 1977 along with a filler: Sullivan's then unpublished, and virtually unknown, concert overture *Marmion* (1867), albeit in a much shortened version.

On Sunday January 30, between the two half weeks of *Gondoliers*, several of the principals – Julia Goss, Jane Metcalfe, John Ayldon, Michael Rayner, Geoffrey Shovelton – and I went down to Berkshire to give a concert at St Michael's Church in Bray; this became an annual event. Michael Heyland, who had lived in Bray as a child, and who had organised the concert, was also with us. The programme was mainly G&S, but it included some operatic items and an arrangement I had made of the famous old song 'The Vicar of Bray'. At the rehearsals it proved to be too complicated and we eventually performed it in a modified version. It was on this first visit to Bray that I met Charles (also known as Peter) Goulding and his wife Tina. Charles was the son of Charles Goulding, a principal tenor with D'Oyly Carte in the 1920s and 1930s. I visited Charles and Tina on a number of occasions, and kept in touch with them for many years. The vicar at Bray in 1977 was a nephew of the composer Herbert Howells, then in his mid-eighties, who died in 1983 at the age of ninety.

Back in London we moved on to *Iolanthe* and I conducted my first performance of it on Saturday February 5. This was the old production, which was to be superseded later in the year by Michael Heyland's new production. On February 10 we began a week of *Cox and Box* and *Pirates*; these were the last performances of *Cox* that the Company gave. Although shorter than *Trial*, in our truncated version, it is still a tricky little piece to conduct and Royston felt that it would be better to wait until I had seen the first six performances before being sent in to conduct it for the first time. On Sunday February 13, after the first four performances of *Cox* and *Pirates*, there was a D'Oyly Carte Gala Evening at the Savoy Hotel in aid of both the Cancer Research Campaign and the D'Oyly Carte Opera Trust. It was given in the presence of the Duke and Duchess of Gloucester, the Duke being president of the Cancer Research Campaign. Again we had to provide the entertainment. This was given by the B team as outlined in Freddie Lloyd's letter of the previous October, but with Patricia Leonard replacing Lyndsie Holland. Michael Heyland was also present, and he introduced the items in the fifty-minute programme. It happened to be John Reed's birthday and at the end of the evening he was presented with, of all things at a performance partly in aid of cancer research, a cigarette case – truly a sign of former times.

During the following week we received letters from Freddie Lloyd thanking us for our hard work; photographs of the event appeared in the May 1977 edition of *The Savoyard*. The fact that the evening was not just in aid of cancer research also highlighted the Company's precarious financial position. This had even been mentioned in the January 1975 edition of *The Savoyard*, before I joined D'Oyly Carte in August, and in retrospect I'm amazed that I was in the Company at all. It might so easily have closed after the centenary celebrations earlier in the year.

After the Gala Evening at the Savoy it was back to the final four performances of *Cox* and *Pirates*, and I conducted the matinee. I survived the experience and I'm glad that I had an opportunity to conduct *Cox*, if only once. The idea of playing *Cox* with *Pirates* was simply to give a longer evening's entertainment, although this only happened in London, at least in my time. When I joined the Company in 1975, *Trial by Jury* was also in the repertoire, played as a curtain-raiser to *HMS Pinafore* and likewise making a longer evening – *Pinafore* being a little shorter even than *Pirates*; again this only happened in London. Unfortunately these two combinations each lasted for just under three hours and as there was often a delay in starting the performance, and sometimes delays after each interval, it was inevitable that the evening would overrun, if only by a few minutes. Technically we would then be in overtime, but overtime was never paid as the official running time was under three hours. It was just 'unfortunate' that the evening had overrun because of these 'unavoidable delays'.

But the problem wouldn't go away – the Musicians' Union was particularly insistent that overtime must be paid if this happened – and something had to be done. Our management, perpetually short of money, decided that the obvious solution was to remove the curtain-raisers: *Trial by Jury* had been the first to go and now it was the turn of *Cox and Box*. I used to watch *Trial* during my first London season in 1975, but I didn't finally conduct a performance of it until 1987, five years after D'Oyly Carte had closed. That performance took place at London's Mansion House during the Lord Mayor's year of office, and while the bulk of the performers were ex-D'Oyly Carte, the Learned Judge was played by the Lord Mayor himself, Sir David Rowe-Ham. Sir David was a great lover of G&S and it had always been an ambition of his to play the Learned Judge – and, "to do him justice" he "did it very well".

After *Cox* and *Pirates* we began a week's run of *Princess Ida*, re-staged by Leonard Osborn who had taken over as production director from Michael Heyland, and on the Saturday I was due to conduct the opera for the first time. At some point during the morning we heard that Meston Reid, who played Hilarion, had lost his voice and couldn't sing. This was quite a problem – the understudy, Richard Braebrook, had only recently started to learn the role and wasn't ready to go on. Hilarion had previously been understudied by Jeffrey Cresswell who had left the Company after the centenary season and was now in the chorus of the recently renamed English National Opera (formerly the old Sadler's Wells Opera

Company) which was playing at the Coliseum. It was then decided to ask if Jeffrey might be released for the day to cover these two performances and this was agreed. Under the circumstances, as the matinee was going to be my first *Ida* and Jeff's first for some time – I didn't even know how often he had played the part as an understudy – Royston offered to conduct it, but I decided to do it anyway, going in at the deep end as usual. I didn't think that having a previous member of the Company singing a major role would really make it any more difficult for me. In fact it went off very well and Jeff was easy to work with. He went back to the Coliseum, but I met up with him again after 1982 and we did many concerts together.

But if Saturday's performances were unusual, this was nothing to what followed on Wednesday February 23, 1977 – the last night of the *Ida* run. In all my time with D'Oyly Carte I was in the theatre almost every night, very often in the wings during the performance, but every so often I would have a night off, and this happened to be one of them. I found that when I did have a night off something untoward would invariably happen – and this was one of the most untoward in all my seven years there. I can't remember now what I was doing, but as I was staying with Caroline Hudson I said that I would come back to the theatre to pick her up. I walked into the theatre at around 10pm expecting to hear the closing strains of the Act III finale: 'With joy abiding, Together gliding'. As I walked through the passageway from the stage door, I realised that what I was hearing was one of the famous 'string of pearls' numbers from the middle of Act II. This was somewhat disorientating. Had I arrived far too early? I looked at my watch. No, it was 10pm. Had my watch gone awry? Why were we only halfway through the opera? I soon found out: there had been a bomb scare.

The story has been told elsewhere, but is worth repeating. The curtain had come down after Blanche's dialogue, "This sounds involved. It's not. It's right enough", and everyone had to evacuate the theatre while it was searched. Eventually it was decided that the phone call had been a hoax, and the performance was allowed to continue. In the opera Blanche's dialogue is followed by her aria 'Come, mighty Must!', but this aria had been cut, and the next number, following directly on, is the trio for Hilarion, Cyril and Florian. Aficionados in the audience knew what was coming and when the first line of the trio came, 'Gently, gently, Evidently/ We are safe so far', the roar from the auditorium might have been heard at the Savoy. It was several minutes before the opera could get going again. This was certainly one of the most unusual events of the Company's last years – and I missed it by having a night off.

The cast, with no time to change, had had to join everyone else – management, orchestra, stage crew and audience – outside, and the *Princess Ida* costumes were rather unusual, to say the least. Geoffrey Shovelton, as Cyril, wore a grey tunic that was quartered with black and white *fleurs-de-lis* markings. He was also in tights, had knee-length white boots, sported a wig, and had some rather exotic eye make-up. Geoffrey was a born raconteur and often told the story that as he stood in Arlington Way he found himself talking to a lady from New Zealand. After a while the conversation flagged. The lady then eyed him up and down with a puzzled look, and said, "Are you in this opera?" We followed *Ida* with three more performances of *Mikado* before another entertaining Last Night on February 26 at the end of our ten-week season. During these last two weeks we also recorded *The Gondoliers* and Sullivan's *Marmion* overture for Decca. We then set off on what was now my third provincial tour.

The first date on this tour was Stratford-upon-Avon. We were there for one week and played at the Royal Shakespeare Theatre, one of the most prestigious cultural icons in the country. I knew Stratford from my days in Birmingham, and had already been to the theatre, but it was certainly one of the more unusual venues for D'Oyly Carte, and only possible because the Royal Shakespeare Company's season ran from

March to January. Our three visits to Stratford in 1977, 1978 and 1981 were at the end of February, immediately after our winter season in London. There was one night when there nearly wasn't a performance because the heating system had broken down. It was extremely cold – so cold that after an Equity meeting the Company refused to perform unless something could be done. We managed to get a number of large square heaters placed at various points around the theatre and I remember seeing two in the wings and thinking how potentially dangerous they were. This, of course, was before the days of Health and Safety. Across the road from the theatre there was a row of cottages, some of which served as accommodation for Company members, and further along the road was a pub, the White Swan, usually referred to as the Dirty Duck. I was in there one night and was amazed to see a man with a pet lion cub on a leash. It certainly attracted a lot of attention.

After Stratford we had two weeks in Birmingham and this time I stayed with Harold and Hazel Oakley who lived in a wonderful Georgian rectory (1799) in the picturesque village of Appleby Magna, some twenty miles north-east of Birmingham. Harold wasn't particularly interested in G&S, but Hazel was an associate member of the D'Oyly Carte Opera Trust and received its magazine, *The Savoyard*. In the latest edition (January 1977) there had been mention in the editorial of the Company's difficulties in finding suitable accommodation, with a plea for any assistance that associate members could offer. The Oakleys had two grown-up children who were both living away from home and as there was now plenty of spare room in this very large house Hazel persuaded her husband that they might offer accommodation to members of the Company.

People who had been touring for some time had often found suitable places in a particular town and always tried to stay there each time they returned, but if you were still fairly new to finding accommodation there was a system operating within the Company itself. On the Monday preceding a move to the next venue letters from prospective landlords, or individuals, would be available in the theatre before the show. You simply turned up and formed a queue. Whoever was at the head of the queue read through whatever was available, picked out a letter that appealed and handed the sheaf of letters to the next person, and so on down the line. On our one and only Monday in Stratford I joined the queue and eventually received a pile of letters. Among these was one whose heading, The Old Rectory, Appleby Magna, immediately caught my eye. It was from Hazel Oakley. I had already experienced some pretty poor accommodation on tour, but this sounded very much better. Hazel had no less than four rooms available, but pointed out that a car would be essential as Appleby Magna was some twenty miles from Birmingham. She also said that if four people came, each with a car, there was plenty of room for parking. Four of us did take up this offer and for me it was the start of a lifelong friendship. Hazel pointed out that the house was equidistant from five cities – Birmingham, Nottingham, Derby, Leicester and Coventry – and that we could stay in Appleby if we also played any of the other four. We had already played Nottingham and would play there, and Birmingham, again, but later we did also play both Leicester and Coventry – just once each. Derby was the only one that we didn't play in those last seven years. The other Company members who came this time didn't always stay again with the Oakleys, but I usually did. I also stayed with them many times after the Company closed, if I was working in the Midlands.

After Birmingham we had another week in Oxford, my third visit in two years. We always seemed to do well there, possibly because it is a university town, and universities invariably have (or had) G&S societies. Think of the film *Chariots of Fire*, set partly in Cambridge, where there is a strong element of G&S, beloved by the athlete Harold Abrahams. *Chariots of Fire* also has a D'Oyly Carte connection which I will come to later. From Oxford we moved to Wolverhampton for two weeks. This was another city that I didn't really know, although during my time at Birmingham University I had given extramural lectures there. A few things stand out from this visit, including yet more digs we were happy to get away from. Our rather slatternly landlady had several young children who were running riot most of the time and each room had at least three different patterns of wallpaper; some of the rolls had not been put on straight, so that it looked as if the floor wasn't level – somewhat disorientating! Then there was the theatre itself, the Grand. Like the Theatre Royal in Nottingham the Grand hadn't yet received a make-over, as they would say today, and so it was yet another set of shabby dressing rooms, and the potential for anything to happen – and it did, twice, once with *Yeomen* and once with *Gondoliers*, the former incident being potentially the more disastrous.

I was watching *Yeomen* from the back of the balcony and the performance was going well enough. We were halfway through the Act I finale when suddenly all the lights in the pit went out. The lights onstage were fine and at first I don't think that anyone noticed what had happened in the pit. The orchestra obviously knew the piece pretty well and kept going for a while with whatever light was being cast from the stage, but orchestral players seldom play without music, and when you can't see the music properly, and can't remember exactly what you are supposed to be playing, then things will eventually start to go a bit awry. This was gradually being noticed onstage, and several surreptitious glances were made in the direction of the pit. But still the orchestra ploughed on, with the music beginning to sound more like Schönberg than Sullivan. At the same time, as I learned later, there was frantic activity backstage to try to sort out the problem.

First of all they had to find the theatre electrician. When he was told what had happened, he said, "One of your players must have moved his chair on to a cable". This wasn't too surprising. Orchestra pits, certainly in those days, were invariably a mass of cables to enable each music stand to have a light clamped on to it. (Modern stands have built-in lights that dispense with much of this cabling.) The electrician couldn't find a screwdriver and our stage crew had to provide one; only then did he begin to deal with the problem. I was now watching the performance with mounting horror. Then, just when I thought that it would all grind to a complete standstill, one light came back on – it happened to be the oboist's – and this was quickly followed by the others. Gradually the music got back to what it should sound like and the act finished more or less as normal. Phew!

The *Gondoliers* incident was somewhat different, if a little less dramatic. Again I happened to be in the auditorium and again the performance had been going along perfectly well until it came to the end of Act I, where Gilbert's stage direction reads "The girls wave a farewell to the men as the curtain falls". Curtains (tabs) in the theatre are of two types: those that do indeed rise and fall, and those that open and close from each side. The Grand had the latter. We were right at the end of the act, with the ladies bidding their tearful farewells as the tabs started to come in – then the tabs stuck. As the playout was finishing the ladies were left standing onstage wondering what to do. An audible hiss came from the corner, "Walk off. Clear the stage". Eventually they did this, with the inevitable giggles which always accompanied any such happening. Never a dull moment.

Wolverhampton was followed by no less than five weeks in Manchester where I had a busier than usual schedule of performances, including several evening ones, as Royston had to be away. It was all good practice. During term time the mid-week matinees here were often made up largely of school parties. At the interval there was always a great demand for ice cream, popcorn and soft drinks and it was often difficult to get the children to go back to their seats. This was a particular problem as the conductor had to enter the pit at the Opera House directly from the auditorium. From backstage you had to go through the pass door (stage right), walk along the front row of the stalls and go through a little gate into the pit. Even after a good quarter of an hour's break at the interval you could hear the noise out front as the little darlings had still not all been served. Ken Robertson, the assistant stage director, would say to me, "Right, out you go", and I would say, "I can't go out yet. Listen to that racket". He would then say, "Can't help that, have to keep to schedule. Out you go". So I had to go out, fight my way through a horde of very noisy children, and attempt to get into the pit to start Act II. When we had school parties there would often be sweets thrown into the pit and if these were hard they made quite a noise as they hit the floor. Sometimes they also hit the conductor, who couldn't do much about it, and sometimes they hit members of the orchestra who, at the first opportunity, would pick them up and throw them back. All this during the performance! So much for a cultural afternoon.

When I first learned that we were coming back to Manchester I thought again of Stuart Levington for digs and decided to write in plenty of time as I had left it a bit late before. Shortly afterwards my letter was returned with a note scribbled across the top: "Far too early. Contact me later". Such is life. I did stay in one of his flats, but on subsequent occasions found alternative accommodation as he didn't always play fair with us.

For our rehearsals in Manchester we often used rooms in the premises of the long-established Forsyth Brothers – today one of the few family-owned music shops still operating – but we also used the GPO Club. In other towns we would use church halls which sometimes had dreadful old pianos. There was one in Bristol in such a state that the keys wouldn't come back up once they had been depressed. This meant that you were playing and trying to push up keys at the same time – to say nothing of the resulting cacophony. Not easy.

As well as getting to know all these English towns and cities I was also getting used to finding my way around the country.

As each year wore on into summer it was usually quite pleasant driving from one town to another on a Sunday afternoon. Some people preferred to drive as quickly as possible to the next place, using the motorways if they could, but it was all still quite new to me, and I would usually work out a quieter, if longer, route to wherever we were going (I still had Andrea Phillips as my travelling companion). I would also try to find yet another National Trust property, or other place of interest, along the way, or simply enjoy the scenery. I could scarcely believe that my job allowed me to do all this – "too much happiness!" indeed, and certainly "nothing like work".

We had *Princess Ida* with us on this tour and Leonard Osborn – our new production director, and formerly one of D'Oyly Carte's most charismatic tenors – had decided to reinstate 'Come, mighty Must!' which had been cut from previous performances. This had occasioned the unintentional humour of 'Gently, gently, Evidently/ We are safe so far' after the bomb scare in February. It was sung a few times before word of this got back to London, at which point we were told in no uncertain terms to take it out again – immediately! But at least I did get the opportunity to conduct it.

After Manchester we were in Cardiff for two weeks. This was my first visit to Wales. We played at the New Theatre and it was there that I had one of my few altercations with a member of the Company. I was conducting *Gondoliers* and there was a problem with Don Alhambra's song 'I stole the Prince, and I brought him here' sung by Ken Sandford during the infamous 'spaghetti scene'. It is a fairly straightforward number – a four-verse strophic setting in 6/8, essentially a simple two-in-a-bar, which even a fledgling conductor should be able to manage without too much difficulty. The first two verses didn't present any problems, but in verses three and four Ken paused halfway through and not at the same place each time: after "dropp'd a Grand Inquisitor's tear" in verse three, when he put a finger to his cheek to indicate the tear, and after "one of the two (who will soon be here)" in verse four. I don't know if these pauses were his own idea, or if they had been suggested by Anthony Besch, but from the orchestra's point of view they are rather awkward and they are just as awkward for the conductor. They are not so difficult if you have had a lot of experience, but of course I hadn't yet had that experience and was still finding my feet. I had played for many *Gondoliers* rehearsals, and hadn't had any difficulty in following him, but that was as an accompanist. I had even conducted several performances of *Gondoliers*, and so far there hadn't been any real problems with that particular number. But there certainly was a problem that night. It was all over the place at these pauses.

I went round to see him at the interval. He was not at all pleased, saying that I had ruined his song, and a fairly stormy scene followed. It may have been my fault that the number was a mess (or perhaps he had been distracted by something particularly nasty in the spaghetti), but, ironically, this probably came about because I *was* trying to follow him. You can do this easily enough as a pianist, but it is not so easy when you are conducting. The conductor is there to set a tempo and give a clear beat to the orchestra, or the result can be very scrappy. If a singer doesn't like the tempo that is set, or there are problems with interpolated pauses that are not indicated in the original score, then the singer can speak to the conductor afterwards, although preferably that should be done *before* the performance. Of course, as well as my inexperience, it all came down to a lack of rehearsal time. In any other opera company there would probably have been a morning's rehearsal on that one number alone, to make sure that conductor and singer knew exactly what tempo was expected, and where any pauses might come. Conducting that number in Cardiff was one of my least successful efforts so far, but it was all part of the learning curve. The experience might even have been called "a useful discipline" – a phrase that Ken Sandford himself had uttered, literally thousands of times, as Pooh-Bah (*Mikado*).

A more pleasant recollection of Cardiff – a real eye-opener, or should I say ear-opener? – was the way in which the entire audience rose to sing not just the national anthem but the Welsh anthem too; we had to play both there. I was quite taken aback when I heard this for the first time. I can't recall another audience, anywhere, making such an impact, particularly with 'Land of My Fathers'. We had a fairly perfunctory arrangement of the Welsh anthem and I always intended making another one for the orchestra, but never got around to it. Paul Seeley did eventually make one; as a graduate of the University of Wales this was entirely appropriate. The Welsh, of course, have always been great singers, which accounts for the continuation of so many male voice choirs in Wales when they have ceased to function elsewhere throughout the country, and singing is also very evident at rugby internationals in Cardiff. The playing of the national anthem was something that varied from venue to venue and was entirely dependent on what each theatre manager wanted. If he wanted it played at each performance then we played it, although that didn't happen very often. It was usually played on the opening night and perhaps on the last night as well, although there were occasions when we were asked not to play it at all. I can't remember how often we played the anthems in Cardiff.

If we were in a town for more than one week we would have the advantage of free weekends rather than having to travel every Sunday. Many people, if they lived not too far away from where we were playing, would go home after the show on the Saturday night as they were not required again until the Monday evening. That applied to the chorus, the orchestra and certain principals, but other principals might have even more time off if they were not involved in either the Saturday or the following Monday's performances – a bonus that the principal tenors and principal sopranos often benefitted from. I still had no permanent home of my own and would normally use these weekends to visit places of interest, country houses, castles, museums, look round the town we were in, or, if the weather was fine, explore the surrounding countryside. It could also be an opportunity to see other friends and relatives. As this was my first visit to Wales I would normally have done something of the sort, but it so happened that on our free Sunday I had my first D'Oyly Carte in Concert at the New Theatre, Oxford; that took up most of the day. Paul Seeley and I provided the accompaniment for these concerts on two pianos and Paul eventually made a two-piano arrangement as an overture of part of Charles Mackerras's music for the comic ballet *Pineapple Poll.*

Cardiff was followed by three weeks in Brighton. We were back to that awful pit, but I had now been conducting for almost a year and was better able to cope with it. Brighton was very pleasant in June and it was here that I first conducted in a white jacket, black trousers and black bow tie. Royston had persuaded the management that our conservative dress code, particularly the black jacket and striped trousers for matinees, might be changed for the summer. The town was also very busy, resulting in another experience as part of the learning curve. Coming in from the digs for the mid-week matinee had not been a problem, but I was also due to conduct the first Saturday matinee and thought that I would drive in to town at 2pm and park in a multi-storey. I drove in as planned, but found that I hadn't taken into consideration just how busy Brighton would be on a bright Saturday afternoon in June. There were queues to get into the multi-storey and they didn't appear to be moving. I tried to park near the theatre, but I couldn't find a meter. I couldn't even find one further away, at least within walking distance. I then drove back to the theatre – still no meters. Time was going on and I was beginning to worry. I had to conduct this matinee at 2.30pm. I kept driving round and round, with a mounting sense of panic. It was now approaching 2.25pm, and just as I passed the stage door for the umpteenth time someone did drive away from a meter. I hurriedly parked the car, put in as much money as I could, rushed into the theatre, gave our stage crew some more money to be fed into the meter during the afternoon, made a very quick change, and managed to get the show started almost on time. After that, for the remaining matinees, I was careful either to find alternative transport to the theatre, or to come in early enough to park in a multi-storey. It had been an alarming experience, but another useful lesson learned.

Another of the great events of those years took place during this three-week season in Brighton: the performance of *HMS Pinafore* at Windsor Castle. It was the Silver Jubilee Year and Her Majesty the Queen had decided that some G&S would be suitable entertainment for her guests after a day at Ascot on Thursday June 16, 1977. The performance, the first by the Company at Windsor since *The Gondoliers* had been given on March 6, 1891 by command of Queen Victoria, took place in the Waterloo Chamber. It had only been made available two days before, leaving very little time to build the set and install lighting equipment. Among the distinguished audience was HRH Princess Alice, Countess of Athlone who had been at the first performance of my arrangement of 'Auld Lang Syne'. Now ninety-four, she had been a child of eight when *Gondoliers* was performed at Windsor in 1891. The Company came up from Brighton in two coaches and had a short run-through before the performance started, as the Queen had requested, at 9.45pm. A souvenir programme, with a suitably regal purple cover (doubtless now a collector's item), stated on the title page that "By command of Her Majesty the Queen... Her Majesty's servants will perform H.M.S. Pinafore".

Supper for the Company was served in an adjoining room after the performance – a small gilt-edged menu was another collectable item. The orchestra got there first and when the Company finally arrived there was not much food left. This naturally created some unpleasantness and the royal kitchens were then called upon to produce some more, a somewhat embarrassing situation, but nothing to what followed. The Company returned to Brighton by coach, although one or two elected to spend the night in a local hotel. When they arrived at the theatre for the evening performance next day, they found a notice on the board to the effect that a number of items, mainly cutlery, I think, had mysteriously disappeared from the Castle, but an amnesty had been declared and if the items were returned anonymously to a conveniently placed receptacle then nothing more would be said about it. Oh dear! In the same month, and despite this lese-majesty, John Reed was awarded the OBE. The September 1977 edition of *The Savoyard* included a Royal Command Performance Supplement, which contained reproductions of some pages from the souvenir programme and a number of photographs of the event.

On the very day of the performance at Windsor, letters were sent out about the next tour which was initially to run from August 29, 1977 to "about April 1979". Although it wasn't mentioned in the letter, this period was to include a second tour of North America in 1978 followed by what appeared to be less than a year of provincial dates in the UK. It was only later that we found out that arrangements were already under way for yet another foreign tour in 1979. My salary remained the same at £60 per week, but the subsistence had gone up to £40 per week. A second letter, dated the following day, stated among other things that the "longer period than usual" was "because of the American tour". Although I was happy to sign this contract it didn't go down too well with a number of people and the following February we received a letter to the effect that it was "the unanimous wish of the members of the Company that the present contract should end after the American tour rather than in April 1979". The management was agreeable to this so long as everyone let them know before the tour if they intended to stay on afterwards or not.

It was, I think, during that June visit to Brighton in 1977 that I first met Melvyn Tarran, a great G&S fan who has since amassed probably the world's largest private collection of G&S memorabilia after that of the Pierpont Morgan Library in New York. Melvyn ran a small restaurant with a G&S theme, which was near the entrance to the Theatre Royal, just across the road from the famous Dome. It was there that I met another D'Oyly Carte principal of former years, Marjorie Eyre, who had been in the Company from 1924 to 1946. She had been married to a fellow principal, Leslie Rands, who had died in 1972. Marjorie Eyre died in 1987. In 1979 Melvyn Tarran opened another restaurant – Sullivan's – in the nearby village of Hassocks.

We then had two weeks in Norwich, another city which, like the whole of East Anglia, was new to me. It had a very friendly atmosphere and seemed more like a large country town than a city. The Theatre Royal was run at that time by Richard 'Dick' Condon, a convivial Irishman with a definite flair for publicity. An advertisement in the British Theatre Directory, which included a photograph of Dick, referred to the Royal as "Britain's leading provincial theatre". There was a bar in the entrance foyer, which was one of the attractions that drew in the public. Dick himself would often serve behind the bar, and having acquired a taste for Guinness at the Harlequin in London I would often ask for a pint. "Ah, Chateau Liffey", he would say with a chuckle as he pulled it. He later became the first general manager of the New D'Oyly Carte Opera Company which opened in 1988; he died at a comparatively early age. The pit at Norwich was remarkably large for a provincial theatre and our orchestral players were able to spread out rather more than usual. There was a regular attender at these performances, a man who always had a stick with him. He invariably sat in the front stalls and rather than applaud items he would bang his stick on the floor – a somewhat disconcerting habit.

My accommodation here, shared with several others, was in one of those quintessentially English country cottages: black and white, timber-framed, thatched roof, low ceilings and a narrow stairway leading directly from the lounge to the bedrooms. This, of course, was *not* in the middle of Norwich, but in a little village some miles south of the city. I forget its name now. Another abiding memory of Norwich was the chocolate factory in the street behind the theatre. It was next to the stage door and every time you came in your nostrils were assailed by the smell of chocolate. (When I was a student in Birmingham I had digs in Bournville, just opposite Cadbury's chocolate factory; again, there was the same wonderful aroma, particularly on a warm summer evening.)

The Norwich factory was the home of Rowntree Macintosh, which produced that famous chocolate selection, still going strong, but under new management, whose boxes carried the representation of the soldier whose uniform reminded me of the marines in *Pinafore*. We were given a tour of the factory, with lots of samples along the way. Next door to the front of the theatre, but set back off the road, was a very nice eating house – the Assembly Rooms – which served good wholesome food. There was a serious fire there some years later, but the damage was eventually repaired, and the building continued to function as a restaurant. On the middle Sunday, June 26, I played for my old friend Sandy Oliver who was singing at a concert in Suffolk. Although Sundays were free days I had to ask permission to do this, but it was granted readily enough. We finished in Norwich on Saturday July 2, and I was back in London by the early hours of July 3; this was useful as we had a second D'Oyly Carte in Concert later that day at the Congress Theatre in Eastbourne.

We then had a further three-week season in London – a special Silver Jubilee Season – before the annual holiday. Shortly before this, on June 20, Royston had the unpleasant task of sending a letter to all members of the orchestra, saying that some members who had played in the previous London season had not always lived up to the professional standards required. There had been complaints from members of the public who had been distracted by unnecessary movement in the pit, usually by players who were not required for certain numbers – invariably the brass section, but occasionally woodwind players too – leaving the pit for long stretches, particularly during the second acts of the operas. Sometimes, if not required for certain numbers, players could be seen reading books, or even newspapers. These complaints had been discussed at managerial level and it had been left to Royston to try to sort it out. In his letter he pointed out that although players might not be aware of it they could usually be seen by the public. He said that at Sadler's Wells all but eight of the orchestra could be seen by about two-thirds of the audience all the time, and that they just had to accept this and sit quietly, even if not required for a particular number. This letter really only applied to a few players, certainly not the strings who were usually playing all the time, and most of them had now left. But it was an unpleasant reminder that not everything in the Company always worked like clockwork and situations like this had to be dealt with.

During the week beginning July 4 there were final rehearsals for the new production of *Iolanthe* and a dress parade for all those with new costumes. Reg Wilson was taking photographs for the press and although not obligatory it was requested that as many artists as possible would appear in costume. There were nominated dress rehearsals on the Thursday and Friday mornings; full costumes and wigs were to be worn, although on the Thursday only new choristers had to be in make-up. There was a third D'Oyly Carte in Concert on Sunday July 10 in the Police Sports Hall, Devizes, and understudy calls on Monday afternoon. Michael Heyland's new production of *Iolanthe* (more of a re-staging) had its first performance on July 12 and was attended by HRH the Duke of Gloucester and the Lord Chancellor, Lord Elwyn-Jones. Photographs of the opening night duly appeared in the January 1978 edition of *The Savoyard*.

While in London I took the opportunity of dealing with a more mundane, if essential, matter. Although I had a good job with a world-famous company which was now into its second century, and, as I thought, likely to see me out, I was on a yearly contract that could have been terminated at any time.

But even if that didn't happen I was a self-employed musician and I had to set up my own pension scheme. There was an opera singers' pension scheme in the Company, but that didn't apply to me. Our trumpeter, Allan Wilson, put me in touch with a broker, Charles Russell, and I saw him twice during this period.

During our long seasons in London I got to know quite a number of the regular fans who often had particular favourites in the Company. Among them were a couple from Wimbledon. At one Saturday matinee at Sadler's Wells John Reed was unwell, and was replaced by James Conroy-Ward. After the matinee I went into the Harlequin, and this couple appeared. They sat down and chatted for some time, and eventually said how much they were looking forward to the show. Not yet realising the full extent of their devotion to John and their complete aversion to James, I said that he wasn't well, and that James had done the matinee and would also be doing the evening performance. The wife immediately cried, "What!", got to her feet and said to her husband, "Come on, we're not staying". Despite having already bought their tickets, they then marched out of the pub. That was an extreme reaction, but even milder partisan attitudes from the public were not very helpful. Sometimes, when it was announced that a major principal was off, there would be audible groans from an audience – not something to inspire confidence in a nervous understudy. John Reed was understandably popular. He had honed his performances to perfection over many years and I rarely saw him put a foot wrong. I do, however, recall a matinee of *Iolanthe* when he accidentally repeated one line in 'The Nightmare Song'. My heart missed a beat, but he cleverly picked up the thread again almost immediately and we continued as if nothing had happened. I doubt if anyone in the audience except, perhaps, an over-zealous aficionado, would have been aware of the mistake.

Our last night in London was on Saturday July 23. It was not, however, a Last Night as these were reserved for the main winter seasons, but it was, for some people, their last performance with the Company. New choristers didn't always join as others left. Sometimes they joined after a season had started, sometimes before. Lorraine Daniels, for instance, had joined during the 1975–76 season, but not until January 1976, while no less than five choristers joined in May 1977 during the 1976–77 season. One of these was Susan Cochrane, a Canadian who had auditioned for us in 1976 and had been provisionally accepted despite not being able to get a work permit. Another chorister, Suzanne Sloane, who had auditioned along with Susan Cochrane, joined us in August for the 1977–78 season, and I had to be in London to take her through the music. Before this I had a short holiday in Scotland after the last performance on July 23, but I was back in time for a friend's wedding in Surrey on July 30. After that it was music calls with Suzanne. She was only with us for two seasons. She then went into the London run of *Evita*, during which she sadly took her own life.

It was also at this time that I met, through Margaret Bowden, one of the many Americans I would befriend as a result of my association with G&S. This was Frederic 'Ric' Woodbridge Wilson who latterly became the curator of the Gilbert and Sullivan Collection at the Pierpont Morgan Library in New York. Ric published, among other things, *An introduction to The Gilbert and Sullivan Operas*, based on the library's holdings, and *The Gilbert & Sullivan Birthday Book*. When I met him at a London hotel on August 8 I brought my MA thesis on Sullivan's songs, one of the few things they *didn't* have at the Pierpont Morgan Library. Paul Seeley came back on the 15th after *his* holiday, and I then had another free week – and that was the end of my second year with the Company.

Chapter 3: 1977–1978

I

My third year with the Company began in the usual way with a week of rehearsals at the end of August held at both Sadler's Wells and Finsbury Town Hall. I had now adjusted to a way of life that involved being on the road for forty-eight weeks of the year, with a good part of the time spent in London, and was perfectly happy with that. Earlier in the year it had been announced that the production director, Michael Heyland, would be leaving to concentrate on freelance work (it was on a freelance basis that he produced the Silver Jubilee *Iolanthe*), and our new production director was Leonard Osborn who had been in the Company from 1937 to 1940 and again from 1946 to 1959. After our week's rehearsal we began another provincial tour with a week in Wolverhampton from August 29. I didn't do the Saturday matinee as I had to go to Birmingham to rehearse a chorus drawn from four operatic societies in the Birmingham area. They would be joining us in a forthcoming D'Oyly Carte in Concert in September as part of the Birmingham Triennial Festival.

We followed our week in Wolverhampton with two weeks in Newcastle. While we were there we heard that Isidore Godfrey had died. We had more auditions, and I again had to go to Birmingham to rehearse the chorus for the concert. (I was getting around the country more than usual.) I was back in Newcastle for one more night before we moved up to Scotland for seven weeks. We began this section of the tour with two weeks in Glasgow, playing at the Theatre Royal, designed by the famous theatre architect C. J. Phipps, who had also designed the Savoy Theatre for Richard D'Oyly Carte. (The other great theatre architect was Frank Matcham.) On our previous visit to Glasgow in 1975 we had played at the King's Theatre because at that time the Theatre Royal was the home of Scottish Television. I had been in the STV building before I joined D'Oyly Carte, and it was obvious, even in some of the studios, that it had once been a theatre. You could see the curve of the balcony quite clearly, despite the partitions that had been put in; STV had presumably been told that they had to keep the basic structure intact in case it ever reverted to being a theatre; this had now happened.

On September 23 we gave our D'Oyly Carte in Concert in Birmingham Town Hall. The principals taking part were John Reed, Kenneth Sandford, John Ayldon, Geoffrey Shovelton, Barbara Lilley, Lyndsie Holland, who had just left the Company, and Jane Metcalfe. The line-up suggests that, with just one understudy (Michael Buchan as the Pirate King), the Company was probably performing *Pirates* in our absence – that opera had James Conroy-Ward as Major-General Stanley, Julia Goss as Mabel, Patricia Leonard as Ruth, Meston Reid as Frederic, Jon Ellison as Samuel and Michael Rayner as the Sergeant of Police. During the afternoon rehearsal in Birmingham Town Hall I had an opportunity to play the organ. I was told that it had been played by Mendelssohn and was virtually unchanged since his day, although it was soon to be renovated. I was also told not to use any thirty-two foot stops, the first to be installed in England, as the whole building would shake and the reverberations would be felt at the other end of New Street.

I was again able to stay with my parents while we were in Glasgow and they came to see me conduct an evening performance of *Iolanthe*. They had last seen it in 1961 when I was playing the Lord Chancellor in our school production in Greenock. On the Monday of the second week I had to play for an interview for Scottish Television (now in their new purpose-built studios), the first of many such events over the next few years.

From Glasgow we moved to Aberdeen for two weeks. My father had been brought up in the city and we had had family holidays there when I was younger, but I had never been in the theatre. His Majesty's Theatre, on Rosemount Viaduct, was the third of three adjacent buildings – library, church, and theatre – which the Aberdonians, with their pawky humour, referred to as education, salvation and damnation. Run by the Donald family, of whom I had often heard my father speak, it was a splendid edifice. It had a revolving stage, but of course we didn't use that facility. There was a reception at Aberdeen University's Elphinstone Hall after the performance on October 7, but the big event of our time there was the Royal Gala Night performance of *Iolanthe*, on October 11, in aid of the Queen's Silver Jubilee Appeal, and given in the presence of Her Majesty Queen Elizabeth the Queen Mother. A special souvenir programme with a silver cover was produced for this, but at £1 a copy it didn't sell out. The January 1978 edition of *The Savoyard* announced that copies were now available for 30p (post free). Perhaps that one is less of a collector's item than the *Pinafore* one from Windsor Castle.

For this restaging of *Iolanthe* Dame Bridget had insisted that the peers' costumes were not to be altered, nor was there to be any change to their famous entrance in Act I, but the fairies' costumes were now silver and black. People would often ask us why it was all a bit colourless at the beginning before the peers' entrance. They had evidently forgotten, or didn't know, that the silver was a nod to the Silver Jubilee Year. After the Gala performance the Company was invited to Haddo House, some twenty miles north of the city, the home of the Marchioness of Aberdeen, June Gordon, who was a professional musician in her own right; her performances with the Haddo Choral Society were legendary. We had been told that the Queen Mother might be present, but she didn't appear. We presumed that she had returned to Birkhall, her home on the Balmoral Estate, after the performance. This was slightly disappointing, but it didn't stop us enjoying ourselves. We gave a short concert and were well fed and watered; we didn't get back to Aberdeen until the small hours. I was to meet Lady Aberdeen again during the forthcoming tour of North America. Haddo House is now a National Trust for Scotland property.

Four of us had digs in a house that was approached from a very rough track off the Langstracht, one of the main roads leading west from the city centre. A little further along the Langstracht was Whitemyers House, the home of famous rose growers Alec and Anne Cocker who had produced a rose named Angelina, (after the Plaintiff in *Trial*), for the Company's centenary in 1975, the year in which they had also received a Royal Warrant to supply roses to the Queen. Her Majesty had given them permission to name a rose Silver Jubilee. The firm had been established in the nineteenth century and is immortalised in a tune, 'The Blooms of Bon-Accord (Cockers Roses)', by the famous Scottish violinist James Scott Skinner. (Bon-Accord is the city of Aberdeen's motto.) Alec and Anne were great fans of D'Oyly Carte and they had previously invited the Company to their lovely home. This year was no exception and it was handy for the four of us who were living within walking distance. They had just acquired a splendid grand piano. Alec was interested to hear that my father had been brought up in the city. They were both roughly the same age. Later, when most of the others had gone, we listened to a recording of Max Bruch's *Scottish Fantasia*, which now always reminds me of that visit to Aberdeen. On returning to London in December it was a great shock to hear that Alec Cocker had died of a heart attack. Anne, who continued to run the business, long survived him, dying in 2014 at the age of ninety-four. The famously moustachioed Harry Wheatcroft, another rose-grower (who, I believe, lived in the Nottingham area), was also a fan of D'Oyly Carte; he too had entertained the Company in the past, but he had died earlier this year (January 1977) and I never had a chance to meet him.

We then moved to Inverness for a week. Known as the capital of the Highlands, it has grown considerably in recent years and now has city status. The Eden Court Theatre was a modern building beside the River Ness. It had been built in the grounds of what had been the official residence of the Bishops of Moray, with part of the old house incorporated into the new building, including our dressing room, which we shared with the production department. My digs here were on the Reelig estate at Kirkhill, some six miles west of Inverness, which had chalet-type accommodation. Other members of the Company stayed there too. One was Linda D'Arcy (formerly Brindley) who, I think, had acquired a cat. Moving around the country with animals could be difficult and many theatres took a dim view of pets in their buildings. John Reed and Beti Lloyd-Jones both managed to tour successfully with dogs. I can't recall what happened to Linda's cat.

With Jimmie Marsland – combined music/production staff dressing-room, Eden Court Theatre, Inverness, October 1977.

From Inverness we moved south to Edinburgh for two weeks and Leeds for a further two weeks. As it became more difficult to get dates it was not always possible to follow such a logical route around the country, and in the last years there were some very awkward journeys from one place to another. While we were in Edinburgh Michael Rayner suffered a heart attack and was off work for some time. One afternoon Caroline Hudson and I visited Blackness Castle near Linlithgow. It was mid-week and there were not many visitors; at 4.30pm closing time we were the only two there. When we came to leave we found that the caretaker had forgotten about us and had locked the gate (just like the time on Bournemouth pier, although this caretaker had now gone). We had to get out on to the battlements to attract someone's attention. Luckily we were able to do so, or we would have been there all night – and what might have been said of our absence!

During the Leeds season which followed, I met another former D'Oyly Carte principal, the tenor John Dean, who had recently turned eighty. He had been in the Company from 1926 to 1946. It was also in Leeds that we celebrated the centenary of *The Sorcerer*. It had received a new production by Michael Heyland in 1971, and had been performed each successive year up to 1975, but it had been out of the repertoire since then. Given the Company's precarious financial position it had not been possible to stage a centenary performance, but thanks to the generosity of Pommery and Greno Champagne we had a small reception onstage on the day itself, November 17, 1977. Bert Newby proposed a toast to "an absent friend – the Sorcerer", at which point John Reed appeared in his John Wellington Wells costume to join staff and principals in a further toast to the Company. After Leeds we were in Bristol again for another two weeks. As well as the long journey between these cities we had the added problem of a D'Oyly Carte in Concert in Sheffield on the travel day. It was held in the City Hall, which had a strange acoustic. The sound we produced seemed to bounce off the front of the very low balcony, which was almost level with the stage, and come back to us. It was very disconcerting. This was the only time that I visited Sheffield during these years. I had digs in Bristol with a delightful couple, Ken and Eveline Rogers, but no sooner had I settled in than I was on my way back to London to play at a charity concert held in Inigo Jones's wonderful Banqueting Hall in Whitehall. The concert was in aid of The City of Westminster Society for Mentally Handicapped Children. During that first week in Bristol we all received a letter from the office, dated 23rd November, 1977, which began "After long and difficult negotiations it is now possible for us to undertake the Tour [sic] of the United States and Canada starting on or about 3rd April 1978". This was welcome news indeed; even better was the news that my salary would be US$600 per week (roughly £300 then), to include a subsistence allowance of $192.50. It seemed an enormous amount, given my meagre £50 per week in 1975, and no expense was spared on a meal at the Rajdoot by way of a celebration. There was an itinerary of the North American tour in the January 1978 edition of *The Savoyard*. It included Houston, St Louis and Blossom, although in the end we didn't visit these three places; perhaps they had been part of the "difficult negotiations".

From Bristol we then had another long journey, this time to Norwich for a week. Originally we were to have been in Oxford, which would have saved a fairly arduous trek across the country, there being no direct route from the west to East Anglia. But we were now into December and Norwich at that time of year was very pleasant. We could do some Christmas shopping in a fairly relaxed atmosphere. The coloured lights round the theatre entrance seemed even more of an enticement to the public to come into the foyer where Dick Condon could again be found pulling pints of 'Chateau Liffey'. I had digs here with another delightful couple, Nick and Susie McCave, who lived within walking distance of the theatre. While we were in Norwich a letter was sent to the choristers concerning a new scheme that would allow each of them to have a night off, although 'night off' was to mean exactly that: they would still be required to attend any daytime rehearsals. This would start during the forthcoming London season and would be reviewed at the end of the season before we began another provincial tour.

We opened in London on December 12 with three performances of *Mikado*. Then, as we began a half-week of *Patience*, Andrea Phillips and Richard Braebrook became the first choristers to take advantage of having a night off. *Patience* was followed by three performances of *Pirates* and on December 22 there was a meeting about *The Zoo*, the one-act opera by Sullivan (but not Gilbert) that we were to record along with *Cox and Box* in February. For those who had been in the Company during the centenary season there had been new repertoire to learn; it included the operas *Utopia Limited* and *The Grand Duke*, and one of Sullivan's anthems, 'Sing, O Heavens', for a centenary service held at St Paul's Church, Covent Garden on March 24, 1975. This had been something of a novelty, particularly for anyone who had been in the Company for a number of years and who had sung only the standard repertoire. Now, with *The Zoo*, there was more new music to learn.Another novelty at that time was receiving a Savoy Hotel Christmas card from Freddie Lloyd. It carried a reproduction of a drawing by Sir Osbert Lancaster for the programme of a Ball at the Savoy on May 31, 1977 celebrating Her Majesty the Queen's Silver Jubilee. Another card, celebrating both the Silver Jubilee and the centenary of *Sorcerer*, carried a reproduction of Sir Osbert's costume design for the *Sorcerer* bandsmen. We played *Iolanthe* over the Christmas break, Christmas Day this year being on a Sunday, and this was followed by *Princess Ida*; on December 31 we sang 'Auld Lang Syne' after the performance. We then had a two-day break, but we were working again from January 3, starting with understudy rehearsals and another three performances of *Ida*. Then there was a week of *Mikado* and, as well as the two matinees, I had to conduct an evening performance as Royston was away.

Next day I travelled north to give a talk to the Manchester branch of the Gilbert and Sullivan Society, the first of several over the coming years. I had met members of the Society during our visits to the city, and with my background of Sullivan research I soon found myself on their list of occasional speakers. I had earlier received a couple of apologetic letters from the secretary, Norman Beckett, as they had unaccountably produced some howlers in their 1977–78 syllabus: my visit was to occur on 'Thursday 10th January 1977' when it should have read 'Tuesday 10th January 1978', and all the meetings listed were scheduled for Thursdays when they should have been Tuesdays. Perhaps that little syllabus is now also a collector's item. The Society's meetings were usually held in the Manchester Post Office Sports and Social Club's premises in Quay Street, near the Opera House, and were invariably preceded by a meal at a nearby Aberdeen Angus Steak House for the evening's speaker and some office holders, who might include Norman Beckett and his wife Grace, chairman Bill Green, assistant secretary Sheila Taylor, assistant treasurer Jean Dufty, or committee member Jean Wolstenholme; she provided overnight accommodation for me on that occasion. Another mistake in the syllabus, although it was one that could not have been foreseen, was the listing of Isidore Godfrey as President. He had died on September 12, 1977 after the syllabus had been printed and just as the branch's activities were about to get under way. He was succeeded by Royston Nash. Royston died in 2016, and I was honoured when the position was then offered to me.

Back in London our season continued with performances of *Mikado, Pirates*, *Patience* and *Iolanthe*. Then came a week of *Pinafore*, a week of *Gondoliers*, and, finally, three more performances of *Mikado*, which was always the greatest crowd-puller. The only operas we didn't perform in this season were *Sorcerer*, *Ruddigore* and *Yeomen*. On January 19 I met Ray Horricks who produced the Company's recordings for Decca and on the same day I received a copy of an internal memo to John Reed to the effect that Sir Harold Wilson and David Frost would be recording an interview for ITN about D'Oyly Carte and the forthcoming tour of North America and would require him (John) to sing something in costume, possibly 'When you're lying awake' ('The Nightmare Song') from *Iolanthe*. This was to be on Monday January 23, but I don't think it actually took place: the 'ITN 2.30-5.30' in my diary for that day has been scored out.

On January 22 we gave another concert at St Michael's Church in Bray, with virtually the same line-up of principals as in 1977, minus Michael Rayner who was still recovering from his heart attack. As well as the G&S items the principals sang operatic arias ranging from Mozart to Puccini, including a performance by Julia Goss and Jane Metcalfe of the amusing *Cat Duet* by Rossini. These concerts were always followed by a splendid meal, initially in a local hotel but latterly in a marquee on the vicarage lawn. There was a return visit to the London Arts Club after the performance on February 2, but earlier in the day I also met Dr Percy Young who had been my external examiner at Birmingham in 1974. At that time his recently published (1971) biography of Sullivan was considered to be the best available, although that position was overtaken some years later by Arthur Jacobs's biography of 1984.

Percy Young was now co-general editor of an ambitious project by Broude Brothers in the United States to publish a long-overdue critical edition of the operas. He was seeking help from me with regard to band parts in the Company's possession. As well as being co-editor of the series, he was also the general editor of *HMS Pinafore* and, among other things, I was able to let him have a copy of the *Pinafore* band part that I had found in the Company office in 1976. He identified this as part of the lost duet 'Reflect my child'. This meeting was the start of a long and fruitful friendship which ended with Percy's death in 2004 at the age of ninety-one. He lived long enough to see two of the editions published: *Trial by Jury* in 1994 and in 2003, just in time, his own *Pinafore*, with more band parts for 'Reflect my child', which had surfaced in 1998. With my inside knowledge of the Company I was also invited to join the board of this series and was able to help others, particularly Gerald Hendrie, professor of music at the Open

University, and his wife Dinah Barsham, who were editing *Iolanthe*. The edition was finally published in 2018.

But back to 1978. Over four sessions in February, we recorded *Cox and Box* by Sullivan and F.C. Burnand, in which Michael Rayner, now sufficiently recovered, gave his ebullient portrayal of Sergeant Bouncer; and *The Zoo* by Sullivan and B.C. Stephenson writing under the pen name 'Bolton Rowe'. *The Zoo* is superficially similar to *Trial by Jury*, but it lacks the brilliance of the latter's libretto. Coupled with *Cox and Box* this was the only recording that the Company ever produced of operas by Sullivan, but not by Gilbert. On the following Tuesday, which happened to be St Valentine's Day, we had auditions at Sadler's Wells. Among the thirty-three aspiring performers were Simon Butteriss, Alistair Donkin and Jane Stanford. We eventually took the latter two, but never found room for Simon Butteriss. He later became a well-known exponent of the comedy roles in the New D'Oyly Carte Opera Company and also at G&S Festivals. Later that day there was a meeting about the tour of Australia and New Zealand that was to take place in 1979. Even if the Company's finances were in a parlous state, and the distant future seemed less than secure, the immediate future seemed very rosy indeed. The London season ended on February 18 with another Last Night, in three acts, the second of which was essentially a performance of *Cox and Box*. Among the by now obligatory interpolations were the appearance of John Reed and Kenneth Sandford as a couple of Chelsea Pensioners singing the Act II duet from *Patience* ('When I go out of door') and, during the 'Buttercup' duet from *Cox*, the appearance of Patricia Leonard at the set windows, which she then proceeded to clean. The fans who had secured tickets in the ballot loved it all.

We now moved to Stratford-upon-Avon for two weeks. As it was still winter, it may have been on this occasion that the heating broke down. I went up to Birmingham to see a rare production of *The Grand Duke*, which was being given by the Queen Elizabeth Hospital Operatic Society, the hospital itself being on the edge of Birmingham University's campus. The society used its own band, billed as the Asklepios Orchestra (Orchestra of the United Birmingham Hospitals). (Aesculapius, called Asklepios by the Greeks, was the god of medicine. The tenor lead, a chemist, in *The Zoo* rejoices in the name of Aesculapius Carboy.) Afterwards I met one of the performers, Bill Slinn, who was also chairman of the Birmingham branch of the Gilbert and Sullivan Society (from 1990 branches became known as Affiliated Societies). Their president was Helen 'Betty' Roberts, another former D'Oyly Carte principal, who had been in the Company from 1938 to 1948. She was now living in Australia. I knew Bill, as I had joined the Society while still a student in Birmingham. He died young, just a few years later, and the Birmingham Society itself has ceased to exist.

I was only in Stratford for the first week, February 20–25. It was during this time that we all received a letter stating that it was the unanimous wish of the Company that the extended contract (to April 1979) should end after the forthcoming tour of North America. The management was agreeable to this, but wanted to know if people were prepared to stay on for a further tour commencing in September/October 1978. I replied in the affirmative.

After a D'Oyly Carte in Concert in Malvern on Sunday February 26 I was on holiday for two weeks. I had to take holidays at odd times, as I had to train new choristers during the summer breaks. From Stratford the Company moved to Nottingham for another two weeks, and I joined them for the last week. On this occasion I didn't stay at Appleby Magna, but had digs with a delightful Irish lady, Mary Stewart-Stephen, who drank endless cups of tea, but never seemed to have a match to light the gas. As I still occasionally smoked cigars I was usually able to oblige. Before I left Nottingham I penned a few lines to Mary, which I called A Celtic Ditty, on her inability ever to have a match to hand. I then had yet another week's holiday, along with the entire Company, to prepare for our five-month tour of North America.

II

I was very lucky to join D'Oyly Carte in 1975, but I just happened to be in the right place at the right time when they needed a repetiteur. Despite the disappointment of not being part of the 1976 tour of North America, I had been retained and had even been promoted. Now, as chorus master and associate conductor, I would definitely be part of any future foreign travel – there had been no less than five North American tours in the 1960s and short visits to Denmark in 1970 and Italy in 1974. The normal round of touring in the UK, with costs rising inexorably, was incurring losses, but the 1976 tour of North America (in the USA's bi-centennial year) had been a great success and had even made a profit. It was with both of these factors in mind that a second tour was planned for 1978, the "negotiating difficulties" notwithstanding. It was to be sponsored jointly by Barclays Bank and Hanson International (Sir James Hanson was a great lover of G&S), and I was greatly looking forward to it, as I had not been to either the United States or Canada.

The tour began on Saturday April 1 with a champagne breakfast for the Company provided by Barclays Bank International in the River Room at the Savoy Hotel (where else?) after which we left for Heathrow, boarded a Pan-Am jumbo jet and took off for Washington DC, where we were to remain for a full month. It was a first visit for many of us, although some had been on the 1976 tour, others on the tours in the 1960s and a few on even earlier tours. Accommodation was always in hotels and was paid for out of our touring allowance. In some places there was a choice, but in other places we were all in one hotel. In Washington some of us had chosen to stay at a Howard Johnson, a chain famous for its ice cream. The hotel was opposite the infamous Watergate building and evidence relating to the scandal had been gathered from some of its rooms, which, like mine, looked directly on to the Watergate. We had arrived at the beginning of the Cherry

Blossom Festival (April 1–8). A local guide book, *This Week in the Nation's Capital – Cherry Blossom Souvenir Issue*, carried one of our new *Iolanthe* photographs on its cover. It showed John Reed as the Lord Chancellor and Patricia Leonard as the Fairy Queen, with Patricia Anne 'Jackie' Bennett as Fleta and Lorraine Daniels as Leila; it was excellent publicity.

The following day, in brilliant sunshine, I took a leisurely stroll downtown (I had to get used to these terms) with Leonard Osborn who had been on previous tours with the Company and knew the city well. We walked from the hotel to the US Capitol, about five miles there and back, and I was struck by the spaciousness of the city and the cleanliness of the buildings. Next day we began rehearsals with our American orchestra. We had brought two of our own players, leader Haim Lazarov, replacing Ivan Fox, and trumpeter Allan Wilson. Allan was our Musicians' Union representative at home and a useful person to have around. Unfortunately he had contracted German measles just before we left London and had to lie low for a while. The American players were very good. We were also introduced to the other Americans who would be joining us for the tour, among whom were James Kimo Gerald, company manager, and Irving Pasternak, property master.

We opened that night (April 3) with *Iolanthe*, our venue being the Opera House in the Kennedy Center, an impressive modern building with a foyer almost as big as the auditorium. Next day I walked into Georgetown where, in a second-hand bookshop, I found an early American vocal score of *Pinafore*. It contained the setting of 'Here – take her, sir' (later just spoken dialogue). On April 5 I did my first TV show, on Washington's *Panorama* programme, which went out live at around 1.40pm. As Royston didn't play the piano, and our repetiteur Paul Seeley had been left behind, I found myself playing for all of these TV spots – a wonderful, if at times daunting, experience. On this occasion I was playing for Julia Goss, John Reed and Geoffrey Shovelton. Among other people on the programme was a lady whose husband was a government official. She invited us all to dine at the Capitol, but as so often in these situations we never heard any more from her.

On April 6 we had another orchestral rehearsal, this time for *Pinafore* and *Mikado*, and in the evening we did our last *Iolanthe. Pinafore* opened the following day with two performances back to back, the first one starting at 6.30pm and the second one at 9.30pm. In between, at around 8.45pm, food was served backstage, but I didn't feel like eating anything as I was suffering from my first American hangover – too much bourbon and Coke. The back-to-backs were exhausting for the Company and had only reluctantly been agreed to. The following day was a Saturday and there were two more performances, but these were the normal matinee and evening performances with plenty of time between them. I had recovered enough to make my American debut with the matinee. Despite having conducted performances regularly for the last eighteen months I was now facing players who were less familiar with the music and who had just got used to Royston. Once again I was going into the pit without any rehearsal. It almost felt like a re-run of my first *Mikado* in Brighton. But it seemed to go reasonably well. My technique had clearly improved. I later found out that Reginald Allen, the USA representative on the board of trustees of the D'Oyly Carte Opera Trust, had been in the audience. I didn't meet him then, but did so at a later date. Known as the doyen of collectors of G&S memorabilia, he had gifted his collection to the Pierpont Morgan Library in New York and was now its curator. After the evening performance of *Mikado* I met a couple from New York, Jesse and Rochelle Shereff (friends of Royston), whom I would meet again later during the tour.

April 9, a Sunday, was a free day. The Company had been invited to a brunch, something that was new to many of us, by a local G&S group, the Montgomery Savoyards. It was held in the Devil's Fork Restaurant at the Gramercy Inn in northwest Washington. We all had to wear stick-on labels that read 'Hello, my name is… '. This was a fairly new idea to many of us and caused a certain amount of amusement. I told one of our hosts that we would normally only wear these at, say, an academic conference. He said that he had been to a conference in England where everyone had been given a label, but nobody would wear one. We sat at large round tables, a mixture of Montgomerys and Cartes, and were well looked after by our hosts. After the meal many of them offered to show us the famous cherry blossom. When it blooms people stream into Washington from far and near to see it, and this causes huge traffic jams, particularly at weekends. Caroline Hudson, Linda D'Arcy and I went with one couple, Neil and Erschel Downey (Allan Wilson would later refer to Neil Downey as Stan Duppey), who also gave us a tour of the city, including some of the less attractive parts. They then invited us to dinner at their home, some twenty miles from the city centre, as if we hadn't had enough to eat at the brunch. On the way we passed over the Francis Scott Key Bridge, named after the author of the American national anthem 'The Star-Spangled Banner'. Neil said that it was now so busy that it was known as 'the car-strangled spanner'. The Downeys entertained us generously. Erschel had had a severe stroke some years before, but one of their daughters was on hand to help with the food. If this was an example of American hospitality we had much to look forward to in the coming months. Neil's work took him around the country and he thought that we might meet up again. He will indeed feature several times in this narrative.

The following day was again devoted to sightseeing. I went to the Air and Space Museum where, as well as the many exhibits, I saw a short film on an enormous screen of a balloon trip across America. Slow-moving, but quite hypnotic, it was breathtakingly beautiful. I also went up the Washington Monument, from the top of which there are spectacular views over the city, and into the Metro (Underground), which was then very new and quite spotless. In the evening we gave our first *Mikado*, changing later in the week to four more performances of *Iolanthe*. I conducted the matinee on the 15th; the Downeys came to the evening performance. After the show Gordon

MacKenzie introduced me to a couple from Texas, Overton and Suzette Shelmire, whom he and others in the Company had known from previous visits. One of Overton's friends, Gordon Wynne, had been responsible for running three Democratic Party Conventions, and was serving a term as President Jimmy Carter's aide for energy-related matters. He and his wife Phyllis had a suite in the nearby Mayflower Hotel and, with the Shelmires, were giving a party to which the Company had been invited. We were ferried from the Kennedy Center in a fleet of taxis that included an official Democratic Party Cadillac. It was another splendid evening. I still keep in touch with the Shelmires, two of the many American friends I have made through my involvement with G&S.

A daily routine had now been established. This consisted of a leisurely breakfast, rehearsals when necessary, usually for understudies, socialising and/or sightseeing, the performance itself (sometimes two), and finally more socialising, often in someone's hotel room, until the small hours. The American breakfast was a revelation to me: eggs sunny side up, over easy or over hard (you had to know exactly what you wanted), crispy bacon, hash browns, waffles with maple syrup, as much toast as you wanted and endless refills of quite the best coffee I had ever tasted. "Oh bliss, oh rapture!" I thought of Freddie Lloyd's words to me in 1976: "like a paid holiday". Even with my conducting duties, and much accompanying at TV interviews and other functions, it still felt like a paid holiday – and "nothing like work".

The other great novelty for many of us was twenty-four hour television, including breakfast news programmes, with dozens of channels showing game shows, old films, and popular series such as *I Love Lucy*, which we had already seen in the UK. Among all of this one programme stood out for me – *The Gong Show*, a so-called talent show in which contestants were given a couple of minutes to present an act in front of a panel who, with obvious sadistic pleasure, would gong them off a la J. Arthur Rank if they felt that the act fell below a certain standard

– which it invariably did. Typical offerings were a lady who imitated an express train whistle and a man who imitated a family of flies. The show was hosted by a nervous individual called Chuck Barris who continually rubbed his hands as he exhorted the contestants to "Do it!" There were also running gags such as The Unknown Comic who told jokes with a paper bag over his head. It was quite bizarre, with more than a touch of Spike Milligan about it. A screen message at the end stated that acts were rated on "entertainment value". Anything awful, of course, is always morbidly fascinating. *The Gong Show* was on every day, and I have to confess that I found it quite compulsive viewing – if for all the wrong reasons.

On April 17 I went to the Woman's [sic] National Democratic Club at 1526 New Hampshire Avenue – the extent of the numbering in many of these addresses was something else that was novel – to play for John Reed, John Ayldon and Geoffrey Shovelton who were the main guests at a luncheon. Their short programme, which included 'If you go in' (*Iolanthe*), was very well received. Another guest at this function was Reginald Allen whom I did now meet.

In the afternoon, in an upstairs room at the Kennedy Center, we had an orchestral rehearsal for *Princess Ida*, which was opening that night. It wasn't an official Company rehearsal, but several of the principals turned up; this was particularly useful. Unfortunately Meston Reid was off, and the understudy, Richard Braebrook, had to go on as Hilarion. I recalled the occasion of my own first *Ida* when Meston was off, Richard had only just started to learn the role and Jeffrey Cresswell had to be brought back from English National Opera. There had been some talk as to why we were doing *Ida* on this tour. Despite its wonderful music it had never been a great crowd-puller at home. We did just three performances in Washington. The Downeys came to the first one and seemed to enjoy it, although Neil made some perceptive comments afterwards. On the 19th I had to contact an American lady, Pamela Leighton-Bilik, who wanted to audition for us. She didn't join the Company, but her name will be familiar to G&S enthusiasts as a production director at the International G&S Festivals, formerly at Buxton.

April 20 was another memorable day. The Company had been invited to a reception at the British Embassy at 3100 (!) Massachusetts Avenue after the evening performance of *Pirates*. It was hosted by the ambassador, Peter Jay, and his wife Margaret, now Baroness Jay, the daughter of our then prime minister James Callaghan, and was held at the ambassador's residence in Sir Edwin Lutyens' imposing original building which had opened in 1929. The principals who were not involved in *Pirates* – John Reed, Kenneth Sandford, Geoffrey Shovelton, Barbara Lilley and Jane Metcalfe – went along earlier to enjoy a buffet supper and give a short recital. As I had to play for this I was excused having to conduct the offstage choruses, leaving it to the Company, who had, after all, sung these choruses many times, to bring themselves in at the right moments. The full Company arrived at about 11pm, sang two numbers and then had *their* supper. Later, as the numerous guests were leaving, we were invited to stay on for a more informal singsong round the piano. Most of the Company declined, but Geoffrey and I were among those who did stay and we provided some impromptu entertainment for the Jays. I finally got back to the hotel at around three in the morning.

Later that day I moved from the Howard Johnson to the Intrigue Hotel, a block of self-catering apartments at 824 New Hampshire Avenue. Most of the Company were there, as many of them knew it from the 1976 tour. I conducted the *Pirates* matinee and again the Downeys came to the evening performance, this time with Neil's brother and his wife. After the show a number of us went to a Greek restaurant where we were entertained by a couple of belly dancers – a change from the usual plate smashing. We then brought the Downeys back to the Intrigue for yet another late-night party, which went on until about 4am. We were doing a lot of socialising, but, as in the UK, we were on tour, living away from home, and still doing eight shows a week. The socialising was inevitable, and it was a good way to relax.

April 23 (St George's Day) was a Sunday and about sixteen of us went to Annapolis, Maryland, east of Washington. One of our choristers, Richard Mitchell, had a cousin who lived there and she had arranged more sightseeing for us. This included tours of the Naval Academy and the State Capitol, a lovely old building *c.*1770, and was followed by yet another very nice meal. In return for this hospitality we gave a concert in the familiar-sounding St. Martin's in-the-Field Episcopal Church at Severna Park, Maryland. Many years later, in 1997, Lorraine Daniels and I were giving a concert at Tring, Hertfordshire and Richard Mitchell's cousin and her husband were in the audience. They came round to see us afterwards and later sent a tape of our concert at Severna Park. Back in Washington the routine of sightseeing, shows and parties continued. On the 24th I visited the Capitol building, and later conducted an evening performance of *Mikado*. The Downeys were again in the audience, again came back to the Intrigue, and again stayed until the small hours.

The routine changed somewhat on April 26 when John Reed and I caught a very early train to New York. John had been invited to appear on *The Dick Cavett Show* (similar to *Parkinson*), and we recorded it in the afternoon; it was due to go out sometime in May. Dick Cavett was a great lover of G&S, and as well as interviewing John he wanted to sing 'When you're lying awake' ('The Nightmare Song') from *Iolanthe* with him. After the recording John and I had a meal, but I didn't do any sightseeing, as I was quite tired. We stayed in New York that night and were up again at 6am for a live appearance on the *Today* programme for NBC. Breakfast TV is all very well if you are simply watching it, but to perform and to be interviewed at that time of the morning isn't always easy. We left New York at 10.30am and were back in Washington by 2pm. I hadn't seen much of New York, but we would be there later during the tour – plenty of time for sightseeing then.

We did two performances of *Pinafore* that night (back to back) minus the assistance of our wig mistress, Heather

Perkins, who had had to return home because of family illness. Four of us – Caroline Hudson, Lorraine Daniels, Barry Clark and myself – then had a very nice meal at the Intrigue. We had formed a little dining club and tried to have a special meal towards the end of our stay in each town that we visited, although it wasn't always possible to do this. Next day, April 29, was our last day in Washington and we finished with two more performances of *Pinafore*. In the evening, while we were in the Opera House, there was a recital in the Concert Hall given by Dame Janet Baker – a very British take-over of the Kennedy Center. Our month in Washington had been a wonderful introduction to the United States for those of us who were first-timers; now we were moving to Canada for two weeks.

We flew to Toronto on April 30, stopping at New York for half an hour. The approach to the city was spectacular. We could also see the QE2 and had heard that Lyndsie Holland, our former principal contralto (who had been replaced by Patricia Leonard), was among the entertainers on board. We had to go through customs at Toronto and discovered that our leader, Haim Lazarov (an Israeli citizen), did not have a visa for the Canadian part of the tour. No one seemed to know how this had happened. It was eventually sorted out in about an hour, but I wonder if such a situation would be so easily dealt with in today's world of heightened security. Most of us were staying in the King Edward Hotel, a vast building opposite the railway station and within walking distance of the O'Keefe Centre (English spelling in Canada) where we were playing. Canada seemed somewhat subdued after the bright lights of America, with very few shops open on the day that we arrived, but we had to remind ourselves that it was a Sunday. Some people likened it to being in Scotland on a Sunday in the days when you couldn't get a drink anywhere unless you were staying in a hotel as a bona fide traveller. (When the pubs were closed during weekdays you could also get a 'wee refreshment' on board the Clyde river steamers, as the bars were open when the ships were sailing, and many a short afternoon trip, from Gourock to Dunoon, say, was undertaken for precisely that purpose.)

I went in to the O'Keefe Centre on Monday to find a potentially disastrous situation: the band parts had been left behind in Washington. We managed to hire sets of parts for *Iolanthe* and *Pinafore* from Boosey & Hawkes (Canada), discovering not only that they were identical to our own but also that they had originally come from Savoy Hill, being stamped D'Oyly Carte Opera Trust. We were then able to rehearse *Iolanthe* in preparation for the evening performance. I was dispatched to the airport in a vast Cadillac to collect our own parts, which were due to arrive at about six that evening from Washington. But no parts arrived. They weren't on the next flight, or the one after that at 8.50pm. This was getting serious. Had the parts been lost, or even sent back to London? Reluctantly I told the driver to go back to the theatre. I had just reported that the mission had failed when the music, along with the man who had brought it from Washington, arrived at the theatre. Apparently he *had* been on the 8.50pm flight, but somehow we had missed each other, and he had simply hired a taxi. I shudder to think what it had all cost: priority freight charge; one return air fare from Washington; cost of taxi; hire of music from Boosey & Hawkes; the Cadillac and driver for four hours – to say nothing of the strain on my nerves.

Iolanthe went ahead on the Monday with the hired parts, but although otherwise identical, they didn't have our orchestral markings, such as bowing marks for the strings, and of course we had a new orchestra, most of whom were probably playing the opera for the first time. It wasn't our best performance. After the show there was a reception given by Barclays Bank International for their many guests and we were asked to provide a half-hour concert. The principals involved in this were Julia Goss, Patricia Leonard, John Reed, John Ayldon, Michael Rayner and Meston Reid. While this was going on the O'Keefe Centre management kindly threw a private party for the rest of the Company.

There had apparently been a large number of critics at the performance and the crits that appeared the following day were not very good, although I was told that they were better than the crits in 1976. I made my Canadian debut with *Pinafore* at the matinee on Wednesday May 3, and after the evening show a number of us went to see Peggy Lee in cabaret at the Royal York Hotel. At the end of her performance she drew everyone's attention to another well-known personality in the audience – Jack Lemmon who with his wife Felicia Farr was staying at the Royal York. Peter Riley, our technical and stage director, and his wife Yvonne Sommeling (herself a former Company chorister) were also staying at the Royal York. Peter had already met Jack Lemmon and the actor had invited the Rileys to join him and Felicia during the cabaret. When Peggy Lee indicated Jack Lemmon a spotlight was turned on him and his wife, but of course this also highlighted Peter and Yvonne, something they hadn't been expecting.

Next day we had a long rehearsal with the new orchestra, and in the evening began a run of *Pirates* (May 4–6). The crits for this were better, although one described the set as 'fusty'. *Pirates* was followed by five performances of *Mikado* (May 8–11), and one of *Princess Ida* on May 12. On the following day, our last in Toronto, I did the matinee of *Iolanthe*, which the orchestra hadn't seen since the opening night. Inevitably it was almost like sight-reading for them (and not the best sight-reading either), but despite some awkward moments I managed to steer them through it. This was good experience for me, if nerve-wracking at times. The evening performance under Royston was better, although the one thing that went wrong was the one thing we hadn't done at the matinee – John Reed's encore for the 'The Nightmare Song'. There was a party afterwards, again given by the O'Keefe Centre, at which I discovered that half of the staff were Scots. We also met Jill Pert, originally from London, who eventually joined the Company early in 1979.

During our two-week stay in Toronto there was the usual mixture of rehearsals, performances, sightseeing and socialising.

On the middle Sunday, May 7, a couple from the Toronto G&S Society organised a visit to the impressive Niagara Falls where, wrapped in oilskins, we entered the tunnels and were able to get right behind the water. Then there was more hospitality, this time at the home of Colonel Catto, a third-generation Scot who still contrived to sound like one. Two days later, with some other intrepid souls, I went up the still unfinished CN Tower which claimed to be the world's tallest free-standing structure – it was like being in an aeroplane. There was yet more hospitality on May 11 when we were invited to drinks and a buffet lunch at the Toronto Arts and Letters Club, similar to the Arts Clubs in Edinburgh, Liverpool and London. On this occasion I had to improvise an accompaniment to 'Take a pair of sparkling eyes' (*The Gondoliers*) which Geoffrey Shovelton had been prevailed upon to sing. Following the party at the O'Keefe Centre on May 13 (Sullivan's birthday) we prepared to move back into the United States for a week in Chicago.

We flew to the Windy City on May 14. We were all staying at the Conrad Hilton Hotel, a vast building on South Michigan Avenue overlooking Lake Michigan. At that time it claimed to be the largest hotel in the world. We checked in, and then several of us went to a recital by Anna Moffo in the Orchestra Hall just a few hundred yards from the hotel. Next morning we were in the theatre at 11am for a rehearsal with the orchestra – they were very good. The venue, the Arie Crown Theater, was part of the Chicago Exposition Center, an enormous complex at McCormick Place on the Lake, some way south of the hotel. It was yet another venue that was far too big for us – it could seat some five thousand people – and our composite set, which had been carefully designed by Peter Goffin to fit the smallest UK venue that we played, sat in the middle of the vast stage like a matchbox; black drapes had to be put up on either side to make contact with the wings. The extra distance meant that it took longer for the Company to get on and off stage, causing a number of scrappy entrances and exits. Peter Riley had already been in the theatre for about sixteen hours and he had had a lot of problems in getting everything ready. After the rehearsal Royston and I had some hot dogs in the theatre, as it was too far to go back to the hotel. I don't think they affected him, but they certainly affected me.

With all the technical problems backstage we were twenty minutes late in starting and just missed going into overtime by a couple of minutes. John Reed, as the star, had a dressing room that was more like a suite of rooms. The dressing room that Royston and I shared boasted a TV, and during the opening performance on May 15 (*Mikado*) I watched John and myself on *The Dick Cavett Show*, which we had recorded in New York in April. While I was in the dressing room a bulb exploded onstage, and this occasioned the usual hilarity when anything went wrong. It also seemed to confirm my idea that if I was out of the theatre during a performance, or at least not in the wings, something out of the ordinary would happen – as with the *Ida* bomb scare the previous year.

The hot dog that I had had at the Arie Crown Theater gave me a very sleepless night and the following morning I was violently sick after breakfast. I am very seldom ill and indisposition was something new to me. I had to spend most of the day in bed watching round-the-clock TV. This, rather surprisingly, included a showing of the famous Ealing comedy *The Ladykillers* with Alec Guinness and Peter Sellers. Later I felt a bit better and had some scrambled eggs sent up, but an hour after this I felt queasy and was sick again. This was worrying. Perhaps the hot dog had given me a dose of food poisoning. I could only hope that it would clear up fairly soon. If I couldn't conduct the matinees Royston would have to do all the shows and he wouldn't be too pleased. It reminded me of the time in Newcastle when Glyn Hale, my predecessor as chorus master, was ill with shingles. I couldn't go in to the theatre that night, and (surprise, surprise) something else happened: Julia Goss missed an entry. This was very unusual for her, but was almost certainly caused by the extra time it took to get to the actual set on this enormous stage.

I was still not well enough to get up the following day and Royston had to conduct the matinee of *Mikado*. I stayed in bed and watched more TV which included another old British comedy *The Wrong Arm of the Law* – again with Peter Sellers. This certainly helped to pass the time, but it was frustrating not being able to work, or even to get out and see something of Chicago. There were two receptions at which I should have been playing, one given by Hanson International and another at the home of the British Consul, John Heath; these were sponsored jointly by Hanson and Barclays, and I missed both of them. Although the matinee on the 17th had been *Mikado* we played *Pirates* in the evening. During the play-out at the end of Act I the curtain stuck, leaving the pirates wrestling with Major-General Stanley's daughters and 'rhubarbing' for what seemed an age until, mercifully, there was a blackout followed by an undignified scramble to get offstage – amid, needless to say, more hilarity. And again I was out of the theatre. Uncanny.

Next day I still wasn't ready to venture outside my hotel room and had to miss attending a rehearsal of the Chicago Symphony Orchestra with Sir Georg Solti who had been its principal conductor since 1969. I had to make do with more TV which included yet another British comedy, *Folly to be Wise*, with Alastair Sim as an army chaplain trying to organise entertainment in the camp; later there was *Whistle down the Wind* starring Hayley Mills. This was all very well, but I was still stuck in my room with no sign of my illness clearing up. During this enforced idleness many of the Company looked in to see how I was getting on and I was able to keep abreast of what was happening. In that week we did three performances of *Mikado*, two each of *Pinafore* and *Pirates* and one of *Iolanthe*, but I saw almost nothing of this. Virtually all I had done was watch old films and more preposterous offerings on *The Gong Show*. On Friday May 19 I woke up with chest pains; this was even more worrying, but I decided that I had to make an effort to get out and try to see something of Chicago. I managed to get to the top of the Sears Tower, which claimed to be (yes, you've guessed it) the tallest building in the world. It was certainly worth the effort as the views were incredible. Later I went to the Aquarium (more or less opposite the hotel), but by the evening I was very tired, probably having forced myself to do too much too soon.

May 20 was our last day in Chicago. I had seen very little of the city, but more to the point, I had not even been able to work. I still wasn't feeling very well and didn't have any breakfast. Royston again had to do both shows, *Pinafore* in the afternoon and *Iolanthe* in the evening. It had been a very strange week. I had never had stomach trouble before and was hoping that it wouldn't last much longer. I felt queasy again in the afternoon, but did manage to get out. It was a beautiful day and I walked along by Lake Michigan to the Arie Crown Theater. Later, while packing for our departure the following morning, I watched another old film, *The List of Adrian Messenger*. Apart from keeping me amused while I was ill, seeing these films again was another novelty. They were not then being shown endlessly on British television and were not, as now, readily available as DVDs.

At last feeling better, I was up early on Sunday to pay the hotel bill. This was always a dreary and protracted business, particularly when we were all under one roof, but this time it was enlivened by an exchange between the receptionist at the front desk and our principal tenor Meston Reid, another of the Company's great characters, and still sorely missed after his untimely death in 1993 at the age of forty-eight. There must have been something wrong with his bill, or perhaps the room itself, as I heard him say, in his broad Aberdeenshire brogue, "Ye couldnae organise a cat's arse", to which, predictably, the receptionist replied, in a deadpan voice and without even looking up, "Have a nice day". The North American tour divided neatly into three parts. We had just finished the first, and were now about to start the second: seven weeks in sunny California. The tour had been a marvellous experience so far, my illness notwithstanding, but what was to come was about to surpass even that.

We flew to San Francisco on May 21, arriving around lunchtime. Despite having been in North America for almost two months we were immediately aware of the difference in the climate and atmosphere in California. It was almost like being in another country and the city itself was like no other. We had often been asked where we were playing on the tour and as soon as we mentioned San Francisco the response was invariably "Oh, you'll love that". It seemed to be every American's favourite city. We may have thought that we knew it from countless films, such as *Bullitt* and *Dirty Harry*, and TV series such as *Ironside* and *The Streets of San Francisco*, but the reality was, as they say, something else. We performed at the Curran Theater at 445 Geary Street, close to Union Square in the centre of town and the entire Company was again in one hotel, the El Cortez, which was just across the road from the theatre at 550 Geary Street. Even the names of the hotel and the city itself seemed to suggest that we were in another country and most of the staff at the El Cortez appeared to be of Mexican origin.

We checked in, and then four of us went out to find somewhere to eat, hopefully at Fisherman's Wharf. We were lucky to find a window table in one restaurant and had a lovely meal – the first proper one I had had for a week. As we looked out over the bay we could hardly believe that we were now on the edge of the Pacific, with an eight-hour time difference between there and London. We were even so far from our last venue, Chicago, that we couldn't open on the Monday as it took an extra day for the sets and costumes to travel over to the west coast; the pattern of starting on a Tuesday was continued throughout our time in California. On that first Monday there was some sightseeing, which included a visit to the famous Chinatown near Union Square, the largest Chinese community outside China – it had to be – and the oldest in

North America. Later there was the first of several receptions, given by Barclays International and held in the Bohemian Club, an interesting building that had its own theatre where we gave the usual half-hour recital.

We were in San Francisco for three weeks and played three operas, a different one each week, although by not starting on the first Monday the schedule had to include Sundays. As in Washington there was no mid-week matinee, but we gave two performances on the Saturday and two on the Sunday – again a taxing weekend for the Company. The three operas were presented in the order of *Pinafore*, *Mikado* and *Pirates*. We had to start with *Pinafore* because in a couple of days' time it would celebrate its centenary. We opened on Tuesday May 23 to a "very good house", giving all the encores to 'Never mind the why and wherefore'. The Curran Theater was just right for G&S. After this we went to an English-style pub for a private party given by the English-Speaking Union, most of whom had been at the performance. Among the people we met were Jane Kastner, a lady of Greek extraction, and Tom and Mary Lott from San Mateo, some fifteen miles south of the city, who very kindly invited some of us to spend one of our free Mondays with them. Next day, after checking the piano at the consul-general's house for yet another reception the following day, I took a trip on a cable car – up Powell Street and down to Fisherman's Wharf, and for anyone who hasn't been to San Francisco 'up' and 'down' are not exaggerations.

And so to one of the great days of this tour – Thursday May 25, 1978 was the centenary of *HMS Pinafore*. This would have been celebrated wherever we were, but San Francisco was the perfect venue for an opera set on a ship. *Pinafore* was the first of the operas to gain widespread popularity, particularly in the United States where it became an overnight success after its first performance in Boston in 1878. This began a long association with G&S and D'Oyly Carte and it was fitting that we should be celebrating its centenary in America. The day started early for me with yet another TV appearance, on *AM San Francisco,* one of the hosts being a former Miss America, Nancy Fleming. I accompanied John Reed in 'When I was a lad' from *Pinafore* and Jane Metcalfe, who wasn't in the *Pinafore* cast, in 'When maiden loves' from *The Yeomen of the Guard.* It was the most relaxed TV show that I had yet done. Later, at about 11.15am, some twenty-five members of the Company in costume, along with staff and the Company's general manager Freddie Lloyd, who had flown over from London, boarded a sailing ship for a celebratory trip round San Francisco Bay. Refreshments were provided on board and a launch containing cameramen from various media followed us. A fire launch gave us a salute with water cannon and a helicopter from the coastguard also appeared. We sailed up to the famous Golden Gate Bridge and had wonderful views of

HMS Pinafore centenary – boarding the ship for a sail round the Bay, San Francisco CA, May 1978.

the bay, Alcatraz, which had ceased to function as a prison, and of San Francisco itself.

Later that afternoon the non-*Pinafore* principals – Julia Goss, Jane Metcalfe, James Conroy-Ward, Kenneth Sandford, Geoffrey Shovelton – and I left for the reception at the consul-general's lovely house, overlooking the bay, where we gave another half-hour recital. One of the vice-consuls was a fellow-Scot, from Port Glasgow, of about my own age. Later that evening we had the centenary performance of *Pinafore*. This was perhaps the least interesting part of the day as it was a straightforward performance with no gimmicks or any sense of a gala occasion. But just before we started Freddie Lloyd read out a telegram from Buckingham Palace with good wishes from the Queen – a thoughtful gesture as we had performed *Pinafore* at Windsor Castle the previous year during Her Majesty's Silver Jubilee celebrations (the episode of the missing cutlery had either been forgiven or forgotten). There was also a congratulatory telegram from the Admiralty.

At the matinee of *Pinafore* on the 27th I wore the white tuxedo I had first worn in Brighton the year before – it seemed appropriate in the sunny Californian climate. On our free day the following Monday four of us went to Tom and Mary Lott's lovely house in San Mateo with its heated swimming pool. Tom was something of an inventor and the house was full of gadgets of one sort or another. He had recorded our early morning appearance on *AM San Francisco* on *Pinafore* centenary day and we were able to watch it. Tom then took Caroline Hudson to the airport to pick up her father, Alec, who had flown out from England with other parents and friends of the Company and he joined us for a barbecue by the swimming pool.

The second week was given over to eight performances of *Mikado*, and sightseeing. We visited a sailing ship, the *Balclutha*, built in Glasgow in 1886, and went to a Scottish pub, the Edinburgh Castle, which did excellent fish and chips. I also went across the Golden Gate Bridge to Sausalito, which has wonderful views of San Francisco. I had acquired a second-hand cine camera and tried to shoot some film while we were there, including shots of the cable cars ascending and descending, but, for whatever reason, the film didn't come out. I did, however, take many photographs of this eminently photogenic city. Monday June 5 (5-6-7-8, something that wouldn't happen again until July 6, 1989: 6-7-8-9) was our last free day and several of us hired a car and went across the Golden Gate Bridge to Muir Woods, a National Park with famous giant redwood trees. We also visited a wine-tasting establishment at Rutherford (the Franciscan) before heading to Lake Berryessa and then back to San Francisco via the Oakland Bridge, having thus completed a circular tour.

The last week (June 6–11) was given over to *Pirates* and yet more sightseeing, including a visit to the extensive Golden Gate Park with its wonderful Japanese Tea Garden, and another sail round the bay in a further, although unsuccessful, attempt to get the cine camera working. (But it *was* second-hand – "Buy cheap, buy dear".) After the performance on Friday two of our choristers, Susan Cochrane and Elizabeth Denham, gave a party in one of the hotel's public rooms for their almost-joint birthday (Elizabeth's that day, Susan's the day before). It was a good evening, with some of our orchestra providing a jazz group, but the unexpected highlight came when two cakes were brought in. One of them was being carried by another chorister, Suzanne O'Keefe, who somehow managed to drop hers as she was walking across the room. Naturally it landed upside down – they always do. This was highly entertaining for the onlookers, but mortifying for poor Suzanne.

After the evening performance on Saturday, we went back to the Edinburgh Castle for a private party organised by the owner. The Scots among us – Gordon MacKenzie, Meston Reid, Billy Strachan and myself – found that we were not alone; several other expatriates were there too, including a man from Largs. The following day was our last in San Francisco. We were sorry to be leaving. Everyone had fallen in love with the city and had had a wonderful time there. The birthday girls' party had apparently been too much for some people, as we had no less than three understudies playing in the last two performances. Afterwards I went round to see Jane Kastner whom I had met at the English-Speaking Union function on May 23. I kept in touch with Jane for many years.

Our next port of call was Los Angeles, where we played for a week. It was very different from San Francisco and, not being a place that you could explore easily on foot, there was very little sightseeing done. Most of the Company stayed at the Hotel Figueroa and were happy to spend their free time relaxing by the outdoor swimming pool – which, rather oddly, was shaped like a coffin – and soaking up the sunshine. The Los Angeles venue was one of the most unusual that we played: the open-air Greek Theater. It was open-air for the audience, but the stage itself was covered, although that didn't stop the intrusion of flying insects – a nightmare for the singers. A raccoon had made its home in the proscenium arch and it would pop out from time to time to see what was going on. At one performance of *Pirates* – appropriately during 'With cat-like tread' – an actual cat appeared briefly on the stage. We gave just six performances (no matinees) in Los Angeles (June 13–18), two each of *Mikado*, *Pirates* and *Iolanthe*. G&S was popular not only with Americans in general, but also with 'showbiz' people, such as Dick Cavett and the late Groucho Marx. Walter Matthau was also twice seen at performances here.

On the first evening, following an afternoon rehearsal, we had the understudy, Richard Braebrook, playing Nanki-Poo (*Mikado*). No matter how well the understudies played any part it was always an added strain on the performances when we had orchestral players who were not familiar with the music, and there were a few awkward moments. After the performance I met a man called Manny Weltman who claimed to have an early set of *Pinafore* band parts that I was keen to see. Next day, after another rehearsal, I met him again, and he took me to the Los Angeles Variety Arts Center where he kindly bought me a meal. We then had a look at the parts, which turned out to be someone else's arrangement, and didn't appear to be particularly old. I was hoping that I might have stumbled on a rare nineteenth-century set – no such luck!

Manny and I then went to the Magic Castle, clubhouse of the Academy of Magical Arts, membership of which was open to both amateur and professional magicians. Originally a private house, it was a fascinating place full of little tricks and surprises for the uninitiated. One of these was Invisible Irma, a piano that not only played itself, but played anything you asked it to – all done with mirrors of course, but still quite spooky. There was another reception on June 15, this time at the consul-general's house in Hollywood, where those principals not involved in the performance (*Pirates*) gave another half-hour concert. Once again excellent food was provided; the rest of the Company came along after the performance.

Next day some of us went to Disneyland at Anaheim, where we sampled the delights of, among many other things, the Space Age Roller Coaster, Matterhorn Mountain Railway, Haunted Mansion, and Pirates of the Caribbean. It was great fun and, like so much that we had seen in America, very well organised; one could spend days there and not see everything. Caroline Hudson's father was still in California and he joined us when we had another brunch, this time with Michael and Mary Anne Scheff, friends of Jane Kastner in San Francisco. Michael was a writer, one of his credits being the film script of the recently released *Airport 77*. Mary Anne was an actress turned author who had written a play with a title something like *Waiting for the number 23 bus, having just missed one.* One lady at this brunch (her name escapes me now) claimed to have been in D'Oyly Carte, and another said that she had been a leading lady to toothy ukulele player George Formby. After the brunch we went to Venice City beach at Santa Monica, an area frequented by street entertainers and local hippies.

On June 19 we moved on to Long Beach for a week, a city about twenty-five miles south of downtown Los Angeles. We had been given a choice of two hotels, a Downtown Travel Lodge and a Hyatt. But this was no ordinary Hyatt: the Queen Mary Hyatt Hotel was part of the Cunard liner RMS *Queen*

Mary, which had been permanently moored at Long Beach since 1967. It was more expensive than the other option, and not everyone stayed on board, but a number of us felt that it was an opportunity not to be missed. After our performances at the Terrace Theater – we were back to eight per week, two *Mikados*, two *Pirates* and four *Pinafores* on the Saturday and Sunday – we would come back to the *Queen Mary* and have drinks in the semicircular observation lounge situated just under the bridge. You could almost imagine you were actually at sea. We also explored the ship, including the bridge and wheelhouse. The engines had been removed and part of the huge space had become an exhibit called Cousteau's Living Sea. The cabins (not much changed) were fun to be in and although we had got used to American plumbing it was still an unexpected pleasure to see a familiar trademark on the porcelain – Shanks of Barrhead. There was also a very nice restaurant, the Lady Hamilton, where our little dining club had a meal, something we hadn't done since Washington.

While we were in Long Beach I met a delightful couple, Joe and Ducelia Contreras, through a family connection. My cousin June had met Ducelia in the late 1940s when they were both travelling on *Queen Mary*'s sister ship RMS *Queen Elizabeth*, and they had kept in touch. Joe was a Mexican-American. They met me at the ship on the day that we arrived and took me back to their home where they were having a meal to celebrate the birthday of a friend; it was here that I first tasted guacamole. A few days later they took me to Marineland where we had more delicious Mexican food, something that was still fairly new to me. Later that afternoon, while browsing in a second-hand bookshop, I found an early American edition of the *Iolanthe* libretto, which contained extra dialogue, Strephon's song 'Fold your flapping wings' and Mount Ararat[sic]'s 'De Belville was regarded as the Crichton of his age', all of which was deleted in subsequent editions. Needless to say I snapped this up – for just 50 cents. Even back in 1978 this was a bargain.

June 24 was, for me, the most memorable day of our time in Long Beach. In the morning I took a short helicopter ride over the harbour area, seeing the *Queen Mary* herself and the hangar that contained Howard Hughes's famous Spruce Goose aeroplane. In the afternoon I conducted the matinee of *Pinafore*, and in the evening, after I had conducted the ladies' offstage chorus 'Over the bright blue sea', I was collected by an official car and driven back to Los Angeles to attend the Queen Elizabeth Birthday Ball, an annual event held in the prestigious Beverly Wilshire Hotel. This year it coincided with the twenty-fifth anniversary of Her Majesty's Coronation. As a visiting British group the Company had been asked if it would provide some cabaret. Again, this fell to those who were not in the evening performance – in this instance Jane Metcalfe and Geoffrey Shovelton – and again it was my "privilege and pleasure" to be the accompanist; there was also a display of Scottish country dancing. Among the guests were the British consul Tom Aston, actress Jenny Agutter of *The Railway Children* fame, former superstar Virginia Mayo and Ben Lyon, also a former film star but better known in Britain for his radio show *Life with the Lyons*, with his wife Bebe Daniels and children Barbara and Richard. During the meal I was seated at Ben Lyon's table. He was charming and unassuming, and it had been a privilege to meet him. He died the following year. Joe and Ducelia came to the *Pinafore* matinee the next day, after which we had a very English-style afternoon tea on *Queen Mary* – a pleasant way to end our stay in Long Beach.

We were now at the final stage of our seven-week period in California and on June 26 we travelled, again by coach, to San Diego, a longer journey, which enabled us to enjoy the spectacular coastal scenery. We played in San Diego for two weeks and stayed at the El Cortes Hotel. It was a tall building on a hill and had a bar on the top floor. We were sitting there shortly after checking in, when to our alarm a very large plane flew past the window. Having come from Long Beach by road we hadn't realised that the airport was very close to the city centre. Later that year, on September 25, just a month after we got back to the UK, there was a major disaster in San Diego when two planes collided over the city, killing everyone on board and several people on the ground.

Our performances were at the Fox Theater, and, as usual, we had to cope with yet another orchestra. They were not the best players we had had, but they were very pleasant. Their contractor, originally from Czechoslovakia, and known as Papa, was quite a character. He was not afraid to tell them to "Look at your music" and "Be on time to get your car parked". Despite all this the opening performance of *Mikado* was one of the worst we had yet done, not helped by having perhaps the least responsive audience we had ever had. I conducted the matinee the following day and this was better, both as regards the orchestra and the audience reaction. I decided not to come in for the evening performance, and what happened? The curtain almost failed to go up on Act II. I rest my case. Our schedule here was slightly different as it was the last time we would start each week on a Tuesday. We gave our usual eight performances in the first week (four each of *Mikado* and *Pinafore*), although now with our traditional Wednesday and Saturday matinees, and just one performance on the Sunday, but there were only seven performances in the second week (five of *Pirates* and two more of *Pinafore*). We were to have ended our season here with *Iolanthe*, but it was eventually decided that it would be better to play our centenary (and perhaps more popular) opera *Pinafore* again in the hope of attracting bigger audiences - and the orchestra had already played it.

San Diego was home to the USA's Pacific fleet, with probably some forty capital ships, and the harbour area was much more interesting than the city itself. On June 29 I took a two-hour trip round the bay. Another attraction was the *Star of India* – not another Indian restaurant, but a sailing ship listed (are you surprised?) as 'the oldest merchantman afloat'. We went on board and when it was discovered that we were from the UK we were allowed to look around without being charged an entrance fee. The next day I was up early again to do a TV show with John Reed. In the afternoon Julia Goss had a birthday party. Alcohol-fuelled, like most of these events, it turned into quite a boisterous affair, with some of us ending up in the hotel's indoor pool – properly attired in our swimming costumes I hasten to add.

We were now into July, and had been away from the UK for exactly three months. July 1 happened to be Ken Sandford's twenty-first anniversary with the Company and a surprise party was laid on for him by Jane Metcalfe. Most of those present, who had been told to come early, managed to hide in the kitchen of Jane's apartment and in true theatrical fashion leaped out when Ken arrived later. He claimed to have had no inkling that anything was afoot, but must surely have suspected that something might happen. The following day was a Sunday, and there was just one performance, a matinee of *Pinafore*. After this some of us set off for Mexico. There were no delays as we crossed the border, ushered in by smiling Mexican officials keen for us to spend our dollars, but we were aware that there were long queues waiting to get back into California, with vehicles being scrutinised by less friendly-looking officials, and we duly encountered delays on the way back. Illegal immigration was as much of a problem then as it is now. The little that we saw of Mexico between Tijuana, Ensenada and Tecate seemed more like a third world country than the supposed delights of Acapulco. It was an interesting experience (I even bought some Mexican jumping beans), but it was a relief finally to be back in the United States.

July 4 was Independence Day. We still had a hired car, and we drove east across the Anza-Borrego Desert State Park. Again, this was interesting, but it wasn't a place in which to break down or run out of petrol. We performed *Pirates* in the evening. The audience, which numbered less than five hundred, really seemed to enjoy it, particularly the Act II chorus 'Come, friends, who plough the sea'. Americans sing their own words to this – "Hail! Hail! The gang's all here". This was obviously the right opera for Independence Day. After the performance there was another treat in store when we were invited to the home of a G&S fan whose name was Howard Stein. He had his own private cinema and we were shown the 1939 film of *The Mikado*, one of the first full-length colour features, and one that I had not yet seen. There were several old D'Oyly Carte performers in the cast, Sydney Granville (as Pooh-Bah) and Martyn Green (as Ko-Ko), but there was also another star, although he was not then a principal: Leonard Osborn. Leonard, who of course was with us on this tour, had joined D'Oyly Carte in 1937 as a chorister and he appears in the film as a guard. I was sitting beside him that night and at the appropriate moment he pointed up to the screen. "That's me there", he whispered. It was another fascinating evening.

I conducted the *Pirates* matinee on July 5. The orchestra had played it once under Royston, but now they had to get used to me. It wasn't too bad, but compared with our orchestra at home, which knew all of the operas backwards, I found that I had to work really hard to get results. But it was all good experience. Next day there was a Barclays reception at the Westgate American Hotel. Tom Aston, the consul from Los Angeles, was there. Afterwards we went to a second event, hosted by the English-Speaking Union, where the principals again gave a short concert. Tom Aston came with us and introduced the artists. He got John Reed's and Geoffrey Shovelton's names right, but Jane's became Janet Metcalfe, mine became David MacNee and Ken Sandford was introduced as Kenneth Kendall (the well-known BBC announcer). Directly behind me, as I sat at the piano, was, of all things, a four-foot long model of a ship that had been built by the Greenock Dockyard Company in 1925: two of us, so far from home! On our last free day, July 7, I went to the world-famous San Diego Zoo. I was there from 11am until 5pm, but still didn't manage to see everything. After the evening performance Royston and I had drinks with the orchestra to thank them for their hard work. They had been a friendly and approachable group.

Aside from sticking curtains, errant tannoy systems and other mishaps, awkward situations would arise from time to time, and there was one on our last day, July 8. I did the matinee performance of *Pinafore* and that went quite well considering that the orchestra hadn't seen it for a week. During the evening performance I was in the wings waiting to conduct the offstage chorus prior to the ladies' entrance in Act I. There seemed to be an unusual amount of suppressed chattering and as the chorus was nearly on us and no one seemed to be ready for it, I felt that I had to make some gesture to attract their attention. I chose to clap my hands, which came out louder than I had intended. It did have the desired effect, but unfortunately it also distracted the principals on stage. It turned out later that the ladies had just heard of cheap accommodation at our next port of call, Denver, which was a mere $20 a night (admittedly sharing a room) and this had naturally been a great talking point and was the root cause of the problem. From a distance of forty years this little incident may seem rather trivial, but, for one reason or another, similar things would happen every so often. It was all part of being on the road continuously for forty-eight weeks of the year.

Having now completed the second part of the tour we reluctantly left sunny California and flew to Denver, Colorado where we played for a week. It was raining when we arrived. We hadn't seen rain for literally months and it almost seemed as if the tour was over and we were back in the UK. We had only been given one hotel for accommodation (the Executive Tower Inn), but as soon as we arrived those who had decided to try the cheaper alternative went to have a look at it. Not surprisingly it turned out to be very down at heel and in a very seedy area, so none of them stayed there after all. This made the *Pinafore* incident the previous day seem all the more ridiculous and unnecessary. Denver is a mile above sea level and our venue, the Auditorium Theater, had oxygen in the wings for anyone who needed it. Some of the Company certainly found the altitude difficult and this led to a number of problems, usually with vocal entries. We were back to eight shows a week, opening with *Mikado* on Monday July 10 to one of the best audiences we had had since Washington. We played *Mikado* again on the Tuesday, and also at the Wednesday matinee, but in the evening we changed to *Pinafore*, which we also played on Thursday and Friday, with two performances of *Pirates* on the Saturday.

Neil Downey, who had entertained Caroline Hudson, Linda D'Arcy and me in Washington, was in Denver on a business trip, and we took him for a meal to return his earlier hospitality. He came to *Pinafore* in the evening, and afterwards we all went to a place called Basin Street Blues where a jazz group was performing. On July 13 we had a full chorus rehearsal to tidy up a number of things, which resulted in a very lively performance in the evening. The rehearsal had been prompted by the fact that the next stop was New York, perhaps the most prestigious of the tour, and we had to be at our best for the critics there. After the show we went to a bar at the top of the Security Life Building – there seemed to be no end of these top-floor bars in America. This one (Stouffer's Top of the Rockies) apparently afforded wonderful views of the Rockies – if one could have seen them at midnight.

Our week in Denver was almost over, but not without another memorable day on July 14 – a visit to Central City in the heart of what was once known as 'the richest square mile on earth', gold having been discovered in the area in 1858. The appellation 'city' (as so often in America) is misleading, and belies its size: the population in 1978 (according to the Rand McNally atlas I had purchased in Washington) was a mere two hundred and twenty-eight, but it was doubtless much larger in its heyday. Central City lies about thirty-five miles west of Denver and is approached through an impressive gorge. Rebuilt in the 1870s following a disastrous fire, its attractions included Diamond Lil's Mine, the Teller House, with its famous painting 'Face on the Barroom Floor', and an Opera House. Opened in 1878 it too, like *Pinafore*, was celebrating its centenary. Among the season's offerings was a production of Balfe's popular

The Bohemian Girl, the first opera staged in Central City (by amateurs in 1877). The weather was warm and sunny. We arrived in the late morning, and were shown round the Opera House. We then had lunch in a hotel and were entertained by some of the cast of *The Bohemian Girl*. After this we gave an impromptu concert. This was followed by an afternoon of sightseeing before returning to Denver.

D'Oyly Carte was no stranger to Central City, having played there in 1955 and 1968. A number of the present Company, including business manager Bert Newby and his wife Ceinwen Jones, who had been in the Company from 1946 to 1963, had been on both of these tours. Bert and Ceinwen had become engaged in Central City on the 1955 tour and had married later that year in New York. Although out of the Company by 1968, Ceinwen had accompanied Bert on that tour, the year in which he had been given a Wheel of the West certificate in recognition of his 'Sterling Character' and his 'Golden Deeds for the Central City Opera House Association'. Now, following his stroke in 1977, she was with him again on this tour. Many years later she kindly gave me a book on Central City (*Gulch of Gold*) which was given to them by the author, and has an inscription which reads "for Cienwen [sic] and Herbert Newby whom it was delightful to meet in Central City, Cordially [,] Caroline Bancroft [,] July 14, 1968". "This hallowed volume" is now a treasured memento of Bert and Ceinwen, of my own time in the Company, and particularly of that day in Central City in 1978.

Before the Saturday matinee on our last day in Denver (a very hot one) I bought some books, adding to the not inconsiderable amount of material I had acquired in North America: books, programmes, postcards, publicity material and memorabilia of one sort or another. I would never have been able to take all of this on to a plane as hand luggage, but I did have a somewhat unorthodox way of getting it back home. We had a music department skip, which contained our vocal scores (Royston and I each had a complete set from *Cox and Box* to *The Grand Duke*), dress wear and various other things, but there was still a certain amount of space, which I soon managed to fill up. We also had specially designed wooden boxes for the orchestral music that were rather like Boy Scouts' patrol boxes – painted green, with a rope handle at each end, and subdivided by a partition. This enabled a set of band parts to sit comfortably in each section, but there was still plenty of room round the sides to add things, which I did. To say that this was "Temptation, oh, temptation" to an inveterate collector ('hoarder' would be more accurate) such as myself to continue to buy things and to hang on to just about everything that came my way, would be something of an understatement.

The skip and the boxes travelled with the sets and costumes and I eventually picked up all the extra material when we returned to the UK. I don't think that I could have been accused of smuggling (a la *Brandy for the Parson*), but I often wondered if the sheer volume of stuff that I acquired might have broken some obscure bye-law. If anyone in the UK had ever seen all of the material that I collected during the tour they might have been forgiven for thinking, "How did he manage to get it all home?" Now you know. Royston, on the other hand, rarely bought or kept anything. He had a briefcase which seemed to contain only a few relevant Company letters, and I think he finished the tour with no more than he had started with, possibly even less. I could never understand how he managed to do this, but he would sometimes say, "When I was in the grey funnel line [the Royal Navy] space in the cabins was at a premium, and anything that wasn't essential was filed". (He meant, of course, thrown out of the porthole!) We gave two performances of *Pirates* on that last day, July 15. The usually dependable Julia Goss was indisposed, possibly due to the high altitude, and Mabel was sung by the understudy, Vivian Tierney; it was her first *Pirates*. Next day we flew to New York.

Having left Denver in sweltering conditions we arrived in the Big Apple to fog and rain. Our venue was the New York State Theater (part of the Lincoln Center) near Central Park and our hotel, the Empire, was nearby at the junction of Broadway and 63rd Street. In a departure from our normal routine we played a full week (July 17–22) and then just the first two days of the second week. We opened with *Iolanthe* on the 17th and played it again on the 20th. We also gave three performances of *Mikado*, three of *Pinafore*, and two of *Pirates* the following week. As we were now in New York, and *Pinafore* was our centenary opera, Royston decided to conduct both performances on the 22nd, but I conducted the *Mikado* matinee on the 19th, enabling me to state, in subsequent CVs, that I had conducted at the Lincoln Center (if only once, but I didn't have to add that). I was glad that I had now had almost two years' experience of conducting the operas. This gave me more confidence to go into the pit and face these new players, who were excellent, without having had any rehearsal with them.

After the evening performance on the 19th we went to the home of Jesse and Rochelle Shereff whom we had met earlier in Washington. They both loved G&S, and had once owned a dog, which they had named Basingstoke after the reference in *Ruddigore*. Jesse also had a sizeable collection of G&S memorabilia. I have kept in touch with them too. The following day Royston and I met Ronald Broude of the publishing firm Broude Brothers, which was preparing a critical edition of the operas. Over a pleasant working lunch on the thirty-sixth floor of a skyscraper off Fifth Avenue, we discussed mutual problems relating to the operas and to the publishing project itself. I then went to the Pierpont Morgan Library whose collection of G&S-related material is undoubtedly the greatest in the world. They had mounted an exhibition for the *Pinafore* centenary which even included Sullivan's autograph full score. The library's curator, Reginald Allen, was out of town, but I had met him briefly in Washington. Next day I had to play for Michael Rayner and Julia Goss, who were taking part in a prestigious two-hour radio programme, *The Don Sherman Show*. The Company had been asked if it could supply four or five artists, but only Michael and Julia turned up – so I was also invited to take part in the chat. Michael and Julia did most of the talking, but I contributed from time to time; it was another interesting experience.

In a city like New York it was perhaps not surprising that every minute of our spare time seemed to be taken up with one thing or another. But unlike our leisurely month in Washington, we were only here for ten days. My sightseeing included a three-hour Circle Line trip round Manhattan Island and saw much of the city's skyline as well as other landmarks such as the Statue of Liberty. The skyline included the iconic Twin Towers, which I photographed from the boat but didn't ever manage to visit. In 1978, of course, no one would have believed that in the not-too-distant future they would be toppled in the dreadful events of 9/11. After the opening *Pinafore* on July 21 several of us went to the top of the Empire State Building, which stayed open until midnight. The spectacle of the city at night, with its myriad lights, was mesmerising.

On our free day, Sunday July 23, a number of the principals and I provided entertainment at another reception, this one given jointly by Barclays International and the Hanson Trust. It was at the invitation of the British consul, but was held at the home of Mr and Mrs John MacCulloch at East Hampton on Long Island. John MacCulloch was chairman of the English-Speaking Union in America; their lovely home was on the coast and had its own private beach. Several members of the Company were also with us as we had been told that we could all bring a partner. Long Island is aptly named, and East Hampton itself is about one hundred miles north-east of New York. It took over two and a half hours to get there. We travelled in a rickety minibus whose driver was a real New York character. He drove like a madman, tooting his horn at any car that dared to overtake him. Among the guests at the reception were two from the UK, Lady Aberdeen whom we had met the previous year at her home, Haddo House, after the Gala performance of *Iolanthe* in Aberdeen, and

Colonel Kenneth Osborne whom some of us had met at a sponsorship function at his home in 1976. We had dinner in a marquee and after this we gave our usual short recital. Eventually the time came for us to leave, but just as we were boarding our minibus we were presented with a case of wine – with all the bottles opened! As we had already partaken of seemingly endless drinks throughout the evening I will draw a veil over the return journey.

Another guest at the East Hampton reception was Gale d'Luhy, who was Reginald Allen's assistant at the Pierpont Morgan Library, and she invited me to come in next day to see some more of their extensive collection. It had been started by Reginald Allen when he was a student in the 1920s; he had then given it to the Pierpont Morgan in 1949 and they had continued to add to it. We did our first *Pirates* that evening and after the show we went to the University Glee Club where we were treated to yet more hospitality. There was also some entertainment by the club's members. July 25 was our last official day in New York and it was another memorable one. In the morning I fulfilled a long-held ambition, namely, to visit Radio City Music Hall to see a programme of what we call variety and the Americans call vaudeville. Early in the tour I had heard a report that Radio City might have to close, and I thought that I might never have an opportunity to see a show there, but there had been such an outcry about the possibility of closure that by the time we got to New York, the "threatened cloud" had "passed away". The programme included a full-length film about a boxing kangaroo (*Matilda*, starring Elliott Gould and Robert Mitchum), an illusionist, a line of chorus girls, a ballet and the Radio City Symphony Orchestra. The latter made a spectacular entrance coming up out of the pit on a hydraulic ramp, playing as it did so – 'showbiz' at its best.

After this I headed off to a very special event, the wedding of two of our choristers, Vivian Tierney and Gareth Jones. This took place at the Community Church, just off Park Avenue, and was very much a Company affair. Our wig mistress Heather

Perkins attended to Vivian's hair, choristers Suzanne O'Keefe and Barry Clark were maid of honour and best man, the bride was given away by Gordon MacKenzie, and Geoffrey Shovelton and Roberta Morrell were designated official photographers. There was a small reception for the wedding party and immediate family at Sardi's restaurant, where people used to wait for reviews after a show opened on Broadway, but there was also a reception for the rest of the Company at the Empire Hotel. The performance of *Pirates* that evening, our last in New York, certainly had an extra edge to it.

There now followed a rather unusual interlude, with two free days before our next date at Saratoga Springs in upper New York State where we were to give just four performances. We were given a choice: we could either travel to Saratoga Springs on the following day, Wednesday July 26, or stay in New York for another day and travel on the 27th. A number of people, including the newlyweds, decided to stay in New York; the rest of us travelled by coach on the Wednesday. We were staying at the Holiday Inn, Latham, some twenty miles south of Saratoga Springs, near the city of Troy. There wasn't much to do there, but the hotel had an outdoor swimming pool with plenty of open space round it and it was decided to organise some games for our free day; this developed into the never to be forgotten D'Oyly Carte Olympics.

The great event began with a drinks party held in Meston Reid's room. Afterwards we paraded round the grounds waving plastic fly swatters (there was one in every room). I don't know what the other residents thought of it all. Then the action began. We had a wheelbarrow race, an egg-and-spoon race, five-a side-football and a tug-of-war – across the swimming pool! It was all great fun. Even Bert Newby, still recovering from his stroke, took part in the football match, although virtually all he did was stand in the middle of the field, turning every so often in the direction of play. He later gave a speech and presented prizes. There were numerous minor bumps and bruises, but there were also some more serious incidents. Ken Robertson suffered an arm injury and I sustained a blow in the side during the football match. Enjoying ourselves on a day off was one thing, but a series of minor injuries was quite another – we were there to perform, not to indulge in wild shenanigans. The rest of the Company arrived later and the following day, Friday July 28, we opened with a single performance of *Pirates*. The Performing Arts Theater was an unusual building in that the sides and back wall were open – very useful in the hot summer weather.

We gave two performances of *Pinafore* on the Saturday, but Royston conducted both, as I didn't feel like doing the matinee after the incident at the Olympics. I did, however, manage to conduct the offstage choruses, but with some difficulty. Between the shows some of us had a picnic by the side of Saratoga Lake and after this I went to the local hospital where an X-ray revealed that I had a hairline fracture of one rib. I was given a surgical belt to wear, which helped to ease the pain. I managed to get some painkillers, which also helped. This treatment had to be paid for (no National Health Service here), but the Company took it on board. I was grateful, but it was an embarrassing situation to be in. On our last day in Saratoga Springs, Sunday July 30, we went to an area called the Green Mountains, near Bennington, the site of an American War of Independence battlefield, in the neighbouring State of Vermont. In the evening we gave a performance of *Iolanthe*.

It was now time to return to Canada; we drove to Ottawa by coach. The day after our arrival, August 1, we celebrated the *Pinafore* centenary on a boat called the *Black Jack*. This was similar to the event in San Francisco, although it was a quieter occasion. But we did have CBS News to record it all. Some Sea Scouts appeared later in three small boats and gave us a ceremonial salute. We were then provided with a meal. We opened our week at the National Arts Centre that evening with *Iolanthe*. Next day we had a rehearsal for *Princess Ida*, which we hadn't performed since our season in Toronto in May. I then met a lady, Ferne Stonham, who had been in the Canadian

Wrens during World War Two and had been stationed in Greenock where, with other Canadian service personnel, she had met my parents. They had kept in touch over the years, but had not met again. I managed to phone home from my room in the Beacon Arms Hotel and they were able to talk to each other for the first time in thirty-three years. With modern communications, including Skype, the concepts of distance and separation have almost been eliminated, but in 1978 it was quite a

Second *Pinafore* centenary celebration – on board *Black Jack*, Ottawa, Ontario, August 1978. L-r: Richard Mitchell, Patricia Rea, Patricia Leonard, Alan Spencer, Vivian Tierney, Geoffrey Shovelton.

thrill for them to talk to each other again. Ferne came to our second performance of *Iolanthe* in the evening.

It was raining heavily on August 3, which was unfortunate as Ferne was still in Ottawa. She had come from New Brunswick and we wanted to do some sightseeing. We managed to avoid the rain by having a tour of the Parliament Building where we also climbed the Peace Tower. In the evening Ferne came again to the theatre where we gave the first of two performances of *Princess Ida* which she much enjoyed. We then had drinks in the bar and said our goodbyes. On August 4 we had a four-hour orchestral rehearsal for both *Pinafore* and *Mikado* and in the evening we gave our second performance of *Ida*. We knew that it would be the last for some time, although we thought that we might do it again during the next London season, but it turned out to be the last performance of the opera that D'Oyly Carte gave. It was certainly going to be the last for those who knew that they would be leaving at the end of the tour and the performance was marred by a certain amount of hamming by some individuals. There were two more performances of *Pinafore* and of *Mikado*. The tour was almost over.

We went back into the United States for the final two weeks, playing at the Colonial Theater, Boston. So far, on this momentous trip across North America, we had been singularly lucky with travel. Now, almost at the end of the tour, our luck ran out. We left Ottawa at 10.30am on August 7 for a ninety-minute bus ride to Montreal, but then had to wait two and a half hours before our flight to Boston. It was supposed to be a short one, just fifty minutes. It was sunny when we eventually took off, but as we approached Boston it was obvious that the weather was getting worse and the captain announced that we couldn't land. We circled for a while, then abandoned Boston and headed for Portland, Maine where we refuelled. After some time we took off again, but had to return to Portland when the captain was informed that we still couldn't land at Boston. Once again we took off, and finally arrived at Boston sometime after 8pm. What should have been a fifty-minute flight had taken almost six hours. We then had to find our own way to the hotel, with groups of two or three people sharing taxicabs. The Copley Plaza turned out to be a lovely old building *c.*1912. It was completely dwarfed by its neighbour, the sixty-storey John Hancock Tower, named after the first signatory of the American Declaration of Independence. We checked in and then went down to get some food in the hotel dining room, which had been decorated to look like the library of an English club or stately home. It was warm and extremely comfortable, and the food was excellent – almost too good for the price. It was a welcome end to a somewhat fraught journey from Ottawa.

We opened next day with *Iolanthe* to a wildly enthusiastic audience. We also discovered that the houses were virtually sold out for the two-week season – a good end to the tour. The following day, August 9, we gave two performances of *Pinafore*, both of which Royston conducted. The opera had had its first American performance in Boston almost one hundred years previously on November 25 (my birthday), 1878. In the evening I had to play at a reception hosted by the British consul-general but held at the home of Mr and Mrs Peter Lombardi. The house was in an older part of the city and it had wonderful wood panelling and plaster work. I hadn't seen anything like this since we left home, although we had been in some fairly spectacular, although modern, houses during the tour. I remarked on this to Mrs Lombardi, who said, "Well, they were going to pull it down so we bought it to save the place". How nice to be able to do that! When I got back I found that in my absence something else had happened. Barbara Lilley had started off the evening as Josephine, but suddenly felt unwell and had to be replaced by the understudy, Vivian Tierney; once again it was her first time in the role. I was beginning to think that I should refuse to play at any function that took place during one of our performances. We did *Pinafore* twice the following day and I conducted the matinee, my first since the Olympics incident. I was still wearing my surgical belt and there were not a few twinges, but at least I was able to conduct again.

Two days later, I played for John Reed and Kenneth Sandford on an *Elliot Norton Review*. Elliot Norton was one of the Boston critics and he had been very kind to us. The TV station was having a major fund drive and had asked John and Ken to do a promotional plug after the interview. They sang a short parody of 'I am the very model of a modern

Major-General', which began "I am the very model of a public TV President". We did *Mikado* that evening to another wildly enthusiastic audience and attended a reception given by the New England G&S Society. Andrea Phillips, my travelling companion in the UK, would soon be leaving the Company to marry the BBC producer Richard Cawston, and she had chosen her wedding dress in Boston. On the morning after the G&S reception I went along with her to see it. I'm no expert in these matters, but it did look rather wonderful. In the afternoon, now pretty well recovered from my accident, although still wearing my surgical belt, I conducted the matinee of *Mikado*. John Reed's voice showed signs of strain and it almost went completely during the evening performance.

John was not staying at the Copley Plaza, but had digs with friends who gave a party for the Company one night after the show. I eventually found that I was the last to leave. I had forgotten that John was staying there, and I now had to find my own way back to the hotel. It wasn't too far away and I decided to walk. Halfway there I suddenly realised that I was going through an area known as 'the combat zone' – one to be avoided if at all possible. It was now about three in the morning and there wasn't much traffic around, so from then on I walked very quickly – actually, more of a run – down the middle of the road, casting nervous glances from side to side as I went along. But I got back safely with no unpleasant incidents.

Sunday August 13 was another memorable day, perhaps the last such of the tour – and there had certainly been plenty of them. The entire Company had been invited to spend the day with Mr and Mrs Gerald Mayer who lived in a lovely house at Cotuit, on Cape Cod, which had its own private beach and a jetty. (There had been a similar day's outing during the 1976 tour.) We left Boston in a coach at 10.30am and arrived at Cotuit at noon. With us on this trip was Anne Egglestone, a former chorister who had been to the Mayers' house in 1976. She had left the Company in 1977, but she happened to be in the States on holiday, and joined us for a second visit. Drinks and sandwiches were laid on and after this most people headed for the beach. The Mayers owned a sizeable motor launch and we went out in groups of about fifteen at a time for a cruise round a small island. After this I went back to the house, along with several others, as it was too hot to stay out for long. Drinks were served again at 5.30pm, and we all set off for a clam bake. This took place on another beach in a large wooden hut furnished with long tables and benches. We were served with clams and little bowls of butter and water in which to wash the clams. For those of us who were new to this we were told clearly which bits *not* to eat. We were each then given a lobster and a large corn cob, all washed down with a liberal supply of beer. We offered our grateful thanks to the Mayers, said goodbye, and left Cape Cod at around 9pm. It had been another wonderful day of American hospitality at its best.

We were now into the last week of the tour, but there were still things of interest to see and do. We had occasional rehearsals for understudies, but as it was very hot and humid

A visit to Cotuit, Cape Cod MA. The Company being welcomed by Mrs Mayer. August 1978.

at that time of year it wasn't very pleasant working in clothes that were always damp. But signs of strain were beginning to show. In one *Mikado* during the first week Richard Braebrook (the Nanki-Poo understudy) had to go on for Geoffrey Shovelton. After the Act I quartet, with chorus, 'So please you, sir, we much regret' there is a general exeunt, leaving Yum-Yum alone on the stage. Nanki-Poo then enters with the line "Yum-Yum, at last we are alone!", but at this point Richard failed to appear, leaving Julia Goss to wander around the set humming to herself and trying to look as if nothing untoward had happened. She eventually had to go offstage to tell the stage manager to find him – pronto! – before going back onstage to await his arrival. He eventually made his entrance and the scene got underway – but he got a good telling-off from Julia afterwards. For the last performance of *Mikado*, on August 14, we fielded more understudies, this time for John Reed and John Ayldon, and during the first performance of *Pirates*, on August 15, Meston Reid had to go off after the opening scene. We had all had a wonderful time on the tour, with sightseeing, hospitality and general socialising, but the Company was still giving eight performances each week. We had been away for five months, and everyone was in need of a holiday.

On August 16 Geoffrey Shovelton and I appeared on another TV show, *Woman '78*, which was hosted by a charming lady whose name was Sharon King. The programme went out live at 12.30pm and we went on air half an hour into the programme, Geoffrey being interviewed before singing. As soon as it was over we were taken back to the Colonial Theater, where I had to conduct a matinee of *Pirates*, and when *that* was over we went to the City Hall for yet another reception, this one given by the Mayor of Boston for the casts of three shows that were running in the city – ourselves, *The Wig* and *Man of La Mancha*. I met some people who had been at the Lombardis' lovely house the previous week and was able to spend more time talking to them. After the evening performance we went to the Tennis and Racquet Club in Boylston Street for a meal laid on for us by James Nederlander who had brought the Company over to North America (and also in 1976). This was to thank the Company as a whole for making the tour such a success. It was a splendid evening, finishing off with speeches from Gordon MacKenzie, Bert Newby and Peter Riley. But this was not the end. We were then ushered into another room and the best-kept secret of the tour was finally revealed. This was a cabaret that was put on by several members of the Company who had been in a dance class run by one of the choristers, Alan Spencer. It consisted of routines in varying styles, often guying members of the staff, with one or two serious numbers as well. Richard Braebrook redeemed himself by accompanying for most of the evening, but I had to play for him when he sang 'The Flower Song' from *Carmen*.

The cabaret had started with a performance of the first movement of a Bach concerto for oboe and violin given by our own two orchestral players – Haim Lazarov (violin) and Allan Wilson playing the oboe part on the trumpet – accompanied by another chorister, Edwin 'Eddie' Rolles. Allan Wilson introduced the performance, saying it was dedicated to "the one person who has not been mentioned so far, namely Royston Nash". The previous speeches had tended to concentrate on Bert Newby, mention being made of both his recent stroke and his forthcoming retirement after so many years with the Company – he had also spoken himself – but it was still unnecessary, and was embarrassing for Royston; it also annoyed Gordon MacKenzie (Bert's assistant) who took Allan aside afterwards and gave him a dressing down in no uncertain terms. It was an unfortunate blemish on what was otherwise a splendid evening. The entertainment also included a barbershop quartet with Eddie Rolles, Michael Westbury (Kevin West), Patrick Wilkes and Allan Wilson, and some singing from the other Company members. At risk of omitting someone I think the following were also involved: Jackie Bennett, Susan Cochrane, Lorraine Daniels, Elizabeth Denham, Roberta Morrell, Suzanne O'Keefe, Patricia Rea (Elliott), Hélène Witcombe, Malcolm Coy, Richard Mitchell and Alan Spencer himself. With no axe to grind concerning our eight performances a week, rehearsals, general working conditions or any other issues, they had all put a tremendous amount of work into the cabaret; it was a very good show.

The following morning I was woken up by a phone call from a man called Robert Walters who asked me if I would do a tape for him for a radio broadcast. He had heard that I supposedly knew something about Sullivan. Then there was an understudy call with Richard Mitchell and after that I met up with Neil Downey who was on yet another business trip. He had a colleague with him this time and we all went to a bar called Top of the Hub, at the top of the Prudential Building. It was run by Stouffers who also ran Top of the Rockies, which we had visited in Denver. It was now time to say goodbye to Neil who, having seen us several times during the tour, felt that he knew us quite well and was genuinely sorry to see us leave.

Next morning, our last free day, I went to Filene's department store to see if I could pick up any bargains. They had a policy of selling off unsold stock each week at reduced prices, in the basement of the building. Gordon MacKenzie had been there on previous visits to Boston and had told me about it. There were plenty of suits at throwaway prices, but unfortunately there were only a few in my size and they were in styles that I didn't much like. But I did get some shirts and ties, which was a change from second-hand books, although later that day I acquired even more of those. After visiting Filene's basement I was supposed to meet Steven Ledbetter who was editing *Trial by Jury* for Broude Brothers, but somehow I missed him. I then decided to go to the top of the John Hancock Tower ('Tallest building in New England' – what else!) from where there were wonderful views of the city; it was also strange looking down on our hotel from such a height. We played *Iolanthe* again that evening, the first performance since the opening night. After the show our little dining club went out for a farewell meal, this time to Chinatown.

August 19 was our last full day in Boston. At 11am Robert Walters appeared with a tape recorder and we recorded a half-hour programme for his radio show. I didn't hear the broadcast as it went out after we had gone home. Royston had decided to do both shows (again, *Iolanthe*) and I did the offstage choruses. After the matinee I finally caught up with Steven Ledbetter and, as Royston and I had done with Ronald Broude in New York, we talked at length about the operas over another very pleasant meal. The last performance of the tour was notable for the depositing on the stage, during Act I, of some imitation dog mess. This caused a great deal of hilarity among Company members, but given the outstanding reception we had received from the Bostonians it really wasn't at all funny – quite the opposite. Royston was justifiably furious. Mercifully the second act passed without any further nonsense, ending appropriately with 'Soon as we may/Off and away! Up in the sky/Ever so high'. After the performance most people went straight back to their rooms to pack or just flop, the tour having taken a lot out of everyone. I said goodbye to the Americans, including property master Irving Pasternak, who had been with us on the tour. The company manager Kimo Gerald was not there, but I saw him the following morning.

It was now Sunday August 20 and the tour was effectively over. I made sure that I had one last (and large) American breakfast – two eggs, bacon, sausages and hash browns, with plenty of toast and coffee. It was just as well that I did, as we were again hit by a plague of delays. We left Boston in the mid-afternoon, and arrived in New York at about 5pm. We were due to leave again at 8.30pm, but by that time we were still in the departure lounge. We were then told that there was a delay and we wouldn't be taking off until 11pm; at this point everyone wandered off to find something to eat. Shortly afterwards there was an announcement to the effect that meal tickets up to the value of $2.50 (this, remember, was 1978) could be acquired at the gate. Half the Company had joined a queue for these tickets when there was yet another announcement, this time to say that the plane was ready to leave, and would everyone please get on board; but the other half of the Company had gone off to look for alternative food and drink, and not many of them heard this. It was now beginning to look like a scene from a Jacques Tati film. It was almost eleven before everyone eventually turned up. Then there was a further delay, because the passenger list didn't tally with the numbers on board, and the plane was also carrying luggage for people who were not there, a situation that was suspicious even in those days.

We finally took off just before midnight much to everyone's relief, but our troubles were not over yet. Something had gone wrong with the air-conditioning unit and at one point the plane was like an oven. Then they served dinner – at 1am. I was glad that I had had that large breakfast, which had helped to sustain me throughout the numerous delays. They were particularly frustrating as we had had virtually trouble-free travel throughout the five-month tour. The meal helped to calm everyone down and a good Disney film, *Candleshoe*, was then shown. Much of it had been shot at Compton Wynyates, a lovely old Warwickshire house, and it almost seemed as if it was being shown to welcome us back to the UK after five months in North America.

We landed at Heathrow shortly after 11am on Monday August 21 and then had to go through customs. I managed to get away with £3, but Gordon MacKenzie had to pay about £20 – he *had* bought a gold watch and a set of golf clubs. As well as all the material I had stored away in our orchestral boxes, I also had a carrier bag full of guide books, postcards and other things, and on the way to the shuttle service to Glasgow this bag burst, spilling all the contents on to the floor. At that point I almost gave up, but there was a shop nearby where I bought another bag and soon had everything packed away again. Gordon and I, along with Billy Strachan who was going home to Ayrshire, then caught the 2.05pm flight to Glasgow. It had been quite sunny when we left Heathrow, but it was raining when we arrived. I got my luggage through quite quickly, but Gordon had to wait for about twenty-five minutes – almost half as long again as the flight. By 3.30pm Gordon and I were in a taxi and we arrived in Greenock at 4.15pm. It was not merely raining there but pouring, but Greenockians are used to rain and this in no way dampened our enthusiasm for what had been a wonderful five-month tour. It had been quite literally the highlight of my life so far.

And that was the end of my third year with D'Oyly Carte. I had three weeks at home catching up with family and old friends and then headed back to London. Andrea Phillips married Richard Cawston at the Savoy Chapel on August 25, and another two of our choristers, Jackie Bennett and Patrick Wilkes, almost certainly the only Old Etonian ever to be in the Company, were married on September 16. For this second wedding Geoffrey Shovelton prepared the invitation card. There was a cartoon on the front, with the text inside in his inimitable calligraphic hand. Several of us, including members of our orchestra, attended the wedding and provided some entertainment at the reception, including items from the barbershop quartet that had been part of the cabaret entertainment in Boston. A week later I began my fourth year with the Company.

Chapter 4: 1978–1979

I

My fourth year began in September 1978 with the usual Company rehearsals of the operas we would now be performing – *Pinafore*, *Pirates*, *Iolanthe*, *Mikado* and *Gondoliers*. From the public's point of view there was a definite batting order of popularity and this meant that we always had to have certain operas with us on our provincial tours: *Mikado*, *Pirates*, and usually *Pinafore*, although it wasn't on the first tour that I did in 1975. Then we might have *Iolanthe*, *Ruddigore* or *Yeomen* – sometimes all three, as in 1975, or sometimes none of those, as in 1976 when we took out *Pinafore*, *Pirates*, *Patience*, *Mikado* and *Gondoliers*. (*Gondoliers* had once occupied the number two position, except in the United States where it was known as 'The Gone Dollars'.) Of the ones that we performed least, my particular favourites were *Patience* and *Ruddigore*, and the former provided me with two of the biggest laughs I ever had during my time with the Company.

The men's first chorus in *Patience* is a brilliant piece of theatricality, the Dragoon Guards' scarlet uniforms and martial music contrasting vividly with the green and yellow costumes of the ladies and their languid music in the opening scene. But the effect was certainly sabotaged one night. The men had cavalry boots with proper spurs and new choristers were told that they must be very careful not to bring their heels together in case the spurs locked. The long introduction before the men sing allows them to make an impressive entrance. In our production they marched on from stage right and finished up in a semicircle, before launching into 'The soldiers of our Queen'. On this particular night one new chorister was doing his first *Patience*. As luck would have it he was fairly near the head of the marching line. He got about halfway across the stage and then either forgot about keeping his heels apart or simply misjudged his steps, with the result that the inevitable happened, his spurs locked and he went crashing down. The queue behind him sidestepped, or stepped over him, and, although they kept going, by the time that they got into position (shoulders heaving) no one could sing for laughing, gales of laughter also coming from the audience. I was standing in the wings and witnessed this addition to the long list of things that went wrong on the stage. The gentleman in question took a long time to live that one down.

The second incident, really more amusing and less immediately obvious, concerned Barbara Lilley (as Patience), and probably happened during one of the London seasons. Halfway through Act I, Bunthorne sings his song 'If you're anxious for to shine', after which Patience enters. Bunthorne sees her, and says, "Ah! Patience, come hither". In our production she came on at the back, stage right, dancing, and singing in a disarmingly naïve way, "Fal la la la la" to the tune of "For I am blithe and I am gay" from her earlier aria 'I cannot tell what this love may be'. She then stopped at Bunthorne's "Ah! Patience" to continue with the dialogue. Bunthorne's 'If you're anxious for to shine' never received an encore ("What, never?"), but there must have been a particularly good audience that night (rare for *Patience*) as Royston decided on the spur of the moment to give one and held his baton upright – the signal to the orchestra for an encore. Barbara, standing in the wings, couldn't see this, and having thought that she had heard the last of 'If you're anxious for to shine', started to dance on, singing "Fal la la la la". She was already in full view of the audience as the music started again and the only thing she could do was to continue right across the stage and exit stage left, still singing "Fal la la la la". You had to know what was supposed to happen here for the absurdity of this to register. I could imagine people who didn't know the opera, or at least our production of it, turning to their neighbours with puzzled expressions and saying, "What was that all about?" I saw this episode from the front of house. Being so unexpected it really was extremely funny, although Barbara was justifiably annoyed at being made to look rather silly, if unintentionally.

The recent North American tour had been such a wonderful experience that I wondered if touring again around the UK might be something of an anticlimax, a feeling that was perhaps only natural. Many of the older artists such as Leonard Osborn, Bert Newby and Jimmie Marsland had been on a number of North American tours and in earlier days had gone by sea. Leonard had even been on the 1939 tour, just before World War Two, sailing on the stately four-funnelled RMS *Aquitania*. Leonard, Bert, Jimmie, Jon Ellison and Gordon MacKenzie (still as Michael Lynch) were all on the 1955 tour. Gordon told me that they were due to sail from Southampton on RMS *Queen Mary* and had actually embarked, but the following morning, still at the quayside, they were told that there was a strike, and the ship would not be sailing. They had to disembark and head back to London. Shortly afterwards it was arranged that the Company would, for the first time, fly to the United States, on a Boeing Stratocruiser. For some, then, the recent tour was not such a novelty, but it certainly was for me – the first time for anything is always particularly memorable.

Despite any misgivings that I might have had I was still very happy to be with the Company and to continue touring – wherever we went. But if much of my working week was 'the mixture as before' there was also something else to look forward to. By this time we already knew that a tour of Australia and New Zealand, which had been in the planning stage even before the start of the North American tour in April, was now definite and would take place the following year.

Even by September 1978 dates had been fixed for the shipment of sets and costumes early in 1979, with our performing schedule adjusted accordingly. I couldn't quite believe my luck. I had joined the Company in 1975, had been promoted in 1976 and had started to conduct the operas. I had just had five wonderful months in the United States and Canada and was now looking forward to another foreign tour on the other side of the world. It all seemed to be an endless upward progression, although I did wonder how long this could continue. I would just have to wait and see.

There was a return visit to Devizes in September for another D'Oyly Carte in Concert and we opened our season the next day with three weeks at the Wimbledon Theatre (September 25–October 14). The dressing rooms there were rather shabby with, unusually, armchairs and sofas instead of ordinary chairs. I also remember that there was a refreshment bar backstage. I was looking forward to conducting our regular orchestra again, my technique having definitely improved with the experience of having had to conduct so many players in North America who were less (or not at all) familiar with the music. In situations like that the conductor really does have to know what he is doing. I did my usual matinees, but I had to do some evening shows as well: an *Iolanthe*, a *Pinafore* and a *Mikado* – ominously on Friday October 13, although it seemed to go off without a hitch. I also had to go up to the Savoy Theatre on two occasions to play for more auditions. Among those we heard on October 6 were Felicity Forrest, Alexandra Hann, Jill Pert, John Roper (later Coe-Roper) and Ray Simmons, all of whom eventually joined the Company. On October 12 we heard Robert Crowe, Suzanne Cullen (later Houlden) from Australia, and Peter Lyon (Barbara Lilley's husband) who also joined us later.

The next dates after Wimbledon were Birmingham, Oxford, Bournemouth, Bristol and Norwich. We were then back in London for our annual Christmas season. I had already been to all of these places, some of them, like Oxford, more than once, but even in towns and cities that I now knew quite well there was always something different. I was, for instance, able to indulge my passion for browsing in second-hand bookshops. I could go into a WHSmith or Waterstone's anywhere and find exactly the same goods on offer, but the beauty of touring was that in every second-hand bookshop I would find different things. Now that my interests were focussed on G&S, I was on the lookout for as many books on the subject as I could find. As well as books about the operas, and individual biographies of Gilbert and Sullivan, there were books of reminiscences by former Company members such as Rutland Barrington and Jessie Bond. Many of these were quite rare items, and long out of print, and it was only in second-hand bookshops that I was going to find them. Travelling all around the country at the Company's expense, I soon acquired a number of these. I also acquired many rare vocal scores.

There was a second-hand bookshop in Arlington Way, near the old stage door at Sadler's Wells, and the owner knew that when we had a long season in London he would do very well with his G&S items, but his prices were high, and it was sometimes better to wait until we were out of London in the hope that such and such an item on one's list of 'wants' might turn up at a more reasonable price. Ironically one of the best bargains I ever found *was* in London, but in Charing Cross Road. This was a piece of music that had belonged to Nancy McIntosh, long-time companion of Gilbert and his wife Lucy. It is the alto part of a set of five songs by her singing teacher Sir Georg (later George) Henschel and her unmistakable signature is on the front cover. As it is just one vocal line the music is not worth very much in itself, but the bookshop owner presumably didn't know who Nancy McIntosh was and had obviously assumed that the signature was simply that of some obscure music student. The asking price for this item was 20p. I proffered it with a trembling hand, feeling that I was cheating him. I'm quite sure that our man in Arlington Way would have known who Nancy was and he would almost certainly have charged me £20 rather than 20p.

We were in Birmingham for two weeks from October 16–28. I stayed with the Oakleys again in that lovely Georgian rectory in Appleby Magna, but spent most of my time in the city. There were morning rehearsals on the non-matinee days and I would then have to find something to occupy my afternoons. Having been a student at Birmingham University I would sometimes go back to the campus at Edgbaston to renew old acquaintances. I didn't neglect my second-hand bookshop browsing either and was somewhat taken aback on a visit to one shop (Birmingham Bookshops) to find items that had been in the Barber Institute's music library – items that I had often consulted, and wished that I could own myself. It turned out that the library had disposed of them as it was acquiring new stock, needed some space, and presumably thought that few students, like me, would be consulting old nineteenth-century books, scores and periodicals; and so I did finally acquire some of them. One, a vocal score of Sullivan's last completed opera, *The Rose of Persia* (1899), had belonged to a famous director closely associated with the Birmingham Repertory Theatre, Sir Barry Jackson. It had been very nicely bound and his name – B.V. Jackson – was printed on the front. I bought this along with other rare Sullivan items, which were similarly bound, but with the initials C.G.B. on the spine. I thought that these might have belonged to the composer Sir Granville Bantock who had been the second professor of music at Birmingham (Elgar was the first), but found out later that his full name was Granville Ransome Bantock – G.R.B. I'm still trying to identify C.G.B.

After the performance of *Gondoliers* on Wednesday 18th there was a reception at the Albany Hotel given by Barclays Bank, which had had about one hundred guests at the theatre. As usual we had to provide a short concert, the artists on this occasion being Barbara Lilley, Patricia Leonard, John Reed, John Ayldon and Meston Reid. Two days later I had to play for Geoffrey Shovelton who was giving an illustrated talk at King Edward's Grammar School for Girls in Handsworth in the north of the city. Geoffrey, as a former teacher, was particularly good at giving talks of this nature – informative and amusing. There were yet more auditions on October 24, but these were for principal roles and the majority of the auditionees were our own choristers. We didn't take any of the others who auditioned. While we were in Birmingham I received a very nice letter from Muriel 'Poppy' Dickson recalling her days in D'Oyly Carte (1928–35) and particularly her friendship with Marjorie Eyre. She also wished us good luck for the Australasian tour. I was to be in touch with her again.

Soon it was time to move on, this time to Oxford. It was always a pleasure to be in "that sweet city with her dreaming spires" and I found digs here with a lovely couple, Paul and Tina Briand, in Cowley (Oxford's 'town' to the university's 'gown'). I stayed with them again and also several times after the Company had closed. Our little dining club usually had an outing here, as we had found a particularly good restaurant on the Cowley Road just outside the city centre. I had once been a regular smoker and although I had given up cigarettes before joining the Company I still enjoyed a cigar after a nice meal. I had come back from the USA with a box of King Edward cigars and on these nights out Barry Clark and I would indulge ourselves at the end of the meal along with coffee and a liqueur. Now you can't smoke anywhere in public places and these bursts of dissolute behaviour and wanton extravagance are sadly but a fond memory.

Oxford was followed by two weeks at the Pavilion Theatre in Bournemouth, the first week being a particularly busy one for me. On Tuesday November 7 I had a morning session with Geoffrey Shovelton on *Trial by Jury*, as he would soon be singing the role of the Defendant in a special performance in London. After this I had to travel up to London to give a talk to the Friends of Sadler's Wells about the Company, and particularly about the recent tour of the USA and Canada. Royston was then away for two days, and I had to conduct both performances on the Wednesday and also the Thursday evening performance. In preparation for the London season we even had two chorus calls on the Thursday – morning and afternoon, which was unusual – on the music of *Yeomen* and *Ruddigore*, and as if all of that wasn't enough for one week I was back in London on the Friday playing for more auditions. On this occasion we heard Jillian Mascall, Jane Stanford and Paul Weakley, all of whom joined us for the Australasian tour. Thankfully this was an exceptional workload, and the second week reverted to a more normal routine. Barclays were again in evidence while we were in Bournemouth. They had sixty guests at the performance of *Gondoliers* on Wednesday 8th, and another sixty at *Pinafore* on the following Wednesday, and after each of these they held receptions to which the principals and some choristers were invited. On neither of those occasions was a performance expected from the Company. For me, however, the big event of the second week was my first meeting with Frances Yorke Batley.

Mrs Yorke Batley, by then a widow, had been married to the theatre chaplain, and they had always invited whomever was performing at the Pavilion to afternoon tea at their home, Kit's Close. Frances continued with this tradition after her husband died, and was assisted by a couple of young clergymen. If the weather was fine there would be croquet on the lawn, then sherry indoors and a game of cards. During the game Frances and the clergymen would come round taking orders for tea: "One egg, or two?" (boiled, of course). Frances would invariably add, "Most people usually have two". Although it was an open invitation not everyone would come, and depending on what was on at the theatre there might only be a handful of people. On the two occasions that I was there only about a dozen to fifteen Company members turned up, although others may well have been there on previous visits to Bournemouth. (I remember once seeing the magician Paul Daniels at the Pavilion stage door. He was presumably coming in after us and he may well have sampled the delights of Kit's

Close.) At some point in the afternoon a group photograph was taken and eventually added to albums containing photographs of previous occasions. These albums were laid out for perusal and they were a veritable treasure trove: snapshots of artists from all branches of the profession who had played at the theatre over the years. Bournemouth Borough Council now owns the albums, and a plaque at the Pavilion commemorates the Yorke Batleys.

Among the many performers who had been to Kit's Close were Hinge and Bracket and when they produced their TV series set in the village of Stackton Tressel they managed to get Mrs Batley's name into one episode. The pair of them were having breakfast, with Dame Hilda reading the local newspaper and commenting on the goings-on in the village. I forget the exact details now, but it started with the Dame saying, "I see Frances Yorke Batley has… [done something or other]". Most viewers would have assumed that this was just a made-up name, but anyone in the business who had played at the Pavilion would have recognised it immediately: this was the ultimate 'in joke'. I kept in touch with Mrs Batley, usually at Christmas, and in response to my 1981 card (by which time the Company's demise was almost certain), she sent a card on which she had written, "We are so terribly sorry the D'Oyly Carte C[ompany] is closing. It really is a shame after over 100 years isn't it? We miss you all coming here so much". Mrs Batley's quaint old-fashioned hospitality was certainly as much of an institution as D'Oyly Carte itself.

From Bournemouth we moved to Bristol for another two weeks. During this visit I managed to catch up with John and Con Moore, a couple I had stayed with when I was a student in Glasgow. John was now a history lecturer at Bristol University. There were more auditions on November 30, and we heard Robert Eshelby who also joined us later. It was on one of our visits to Bristol that the Company, with its historic links to G&S, was invited to the opening of the Pinafore wine bar in Park Street. A certain amount of cynicism was in evidence

Afternoon tea at Kit's Close, Bournemouth, November 1978.
Standing (l-r) Leonard Osborn, David Mackie, Gordon MacKenzie, Heather Perkins, Patricia Rea, Elizabeth Denham, Shaun Britten (Stage Assistant), Gillian Swankie, Peter Riley; seated (l-r) Mrs Eileen Osborn, Caroline Hudson, Suzanne O'Keefe, Beti Lloyd-Jones, Suzanne Sloane.

before the event, with comments such as, "We'll get one glass of something and then be expected to sing", but most of the Company turned up. We were indeed given a glass of champagne when we arrived, but it wasn't long before there were waiters at our elbows with refills that just kept on coming; this certainly silenced the cynics, and it all became quite lively. Then there was an announcement – "The food is now ready". We hadn't expected food (perhaps just 'nibbles'), and with it came wine – and many refills of that too. And so it turned into a really good afternoon – and no one was asked to sing. But by now most people had forgotten that there was a show that evening and the after-effects of the alcohol were obvious during the performance, with not a few hangovers the following day.

After Bristol we were in Norwich for two weeks. This was the second year in which we played Norwich in the run-up to the London season and again it was very pleasant to do some Christmas shopping there. I had to conduct both shows on Wednesday December 6 (*Pirates*), as Royston was in London conducting the special performance of *Trial* for the Bar Musical Society for which I had rehearsed Geoffrey Shovelton in Bournemouth. This event, which had been organised by Albert Truelove, was given in the presence of Her Majesty Queen Elizabeth the Queen Mother. On the Friday of the first week, after the performance of *Gondoliers*, the Company was invited to supper at Broad House, a substantial property some five miles north-east of the city at Wroxham that was the home of Major Edward Trafford and his wife June. The following week there was yet another Barclays reception, less formal this time, held in the theatre bar after the performance; again no singing was required. We finished this two-week season on Saturday December 16 and on the following Monday began a ten-week London season at Sadler's Wells, ending on February 24, 1979. We performed all of the operas except *Sorcerer* and *Ida*. (*Cox* and *Trial* had now been permanently withdrawn.) Once again, although it was just another part of the tour, coming in to Sadler's Wells felt like coming home; the extended length of the London season meant that even people who didn't actually live there (like myself) usually felt more settled.

Despite the valiant efforts of our little touring orchestra, particularly the small, hard-worked string section, it was always good to have a larger orchestra while we were at Sadler's Wells. I gradually got to know some of the extra string players who were provided by the Philomusica of London. Two of them, husband and wife Charles Beldom and Donna Chapman, played for me many years later when I became the musical director for the G&S performances at Grim's Dyke (Gilbert's last home) in Harrow Weald near Stanmore, and they became good friends as well as colleagues. Our regular touring orchestra consisted mainly of younger players who were just recently out of college. The orchestral playing and the touring itself were useful experiences for them, but of course we were always losing them as they found other employment. It has to be said that playing the same material over and over again can become a bit monotonous, particularly so with inner parts that, while essential to the harmony, are not always very interesting for the players.

Apart from the younger members we did also have some older players who had had wide musical experience elsewhere, but were now happy to be in a relatively stress-free job. Three of these were Joe Brady (cello), John Taylor (viola), whose wife Philippa was one of the Company's keenest fans, and David Catchpole (bassoon) who also acted as librarian. Of these three Joe was the senior; he was probably in his seventies at that time. Seldom seen outside the pit without a cigarette dangling from his lips, he was jokingly referred to in the orchestra as 'I was Lord Kitchener's batman'. One of the worst incidents that I can recall during those years happened to Joe during a London season. After a matinee performance everyone went off to have something to eat. Instead of putting his cello in its case, which might have been a soft one anyway, Joe left it, as cellists often do, sitting on its side by his chair, right in by the wall separating the pit, which was deep, from the auditorium. When the house opened at 7pm a member of the public came in early, wandered down to the foot of the stalls, peered over into the pit, and then fell in – right on top of Joe's cello, smashing it completely. When Joe came back from his meal he was confronted with the remains of his instrument. It was particularly unfortunate that this had happened at Sadler's Wells as he was using a better instrument that he always kept at home in London (he used another one for touring). I don't think he ever fully recovered from the shock; he left the Company soon afterwards.

I also recall another incident that happened during a London season, this time to viola player Jack Fleetcroft, one of the regular extras. The pit at Sadler's Wells was quite commodious, which allowed Royston to arrange the players as he wished. The strings formed an arc in front of him, with, from left to right, the first violins, the second violins and the violas; the cellos were immediately to his right, with the double basses behind. The violas were therefore in front of the conductor, but slightly to his right; Jack Fleetcroft, facing Royston, was sitting just forward of the stage.

One feature of D'Oyly Carte's performances, and one much criticised, was the encores for specific numbers, some of which were given in the evenings whether they were really called for or not. Sir Joseph Porter's six-verse song 'When I was a lad' (*Pinafore*) was adjusted to make it appear that it ended after verse five, so that the sixth verse gave the impression of being an encore. On this particular occasion we were doing *Mikado* and James Conroy-Ward (John Reed's understudy) was playing Ko-Ko. The Act I trio 'Here's a how-de-do!' had several encores, one of which involved Ko-Ko sitting cross-legged on a little trolley (reading, fishing, or perhaps knitting) which appeared from stage right and travelled across to exit stage left into the prompt corner: the rope for pulling it had earlier been laid across the stage, although this wasn't obvious to the audience.

The encore was certainly very funny, particularly for anyone who hadn't seen it before, but it was quite tricky for the performer to remain seated while being pulled across the stage. John Reed had done it countless times and never had any difficulty with it, but James Conroy-Ward wasn't on very often as Ko-Ko, and this encore was one that could not really be practised, but could only be done during an actual performance. James was also a somewhat nervous performer, which didn't help matters. On this particular evening the trolley started its journey across the stage, but it could be seen immediately that James was having difficulty in maintaining his balance. (I witnessed this from the prompt corner.) He was about halfway across when the inevitable happened and he fell off. The stagehands immediately tried to haul the trolley across the remaining stretch as quickly as they could, but shorn of its human ballast, it suddenly developed a life of its own, exacerbated by the fact that the stage at Sadler's Wells had quite a steep rake. Despite their frantic efforts to get it safely into the wings the trolley veered downstage and toppled over into the pit, striking Jack Fleetcroft a glancing blow on the back of the neck. I don't think he was seriously injured, but the incident seemed to have endless repercussions, with Jack complaining that it had permanently affected his playing.

Starting a show at Sadler's Wells involved being sent down from the prompt corner (as in most theatres), but with the added hurdle of a set of traffic lights – red and green – at the entrance to the pit. Having arrived there you invariably found that the lights were still red and so you had to wait until they turned green before going in. You then worked your way through between the players and climbed up on to the high podium. At one performance, having negotiated all of this, I lifted my baton to start the overture and was startled to see a well-known face smiling up at me from virtually under my nose: a girl who had been at college with me in Glasgow. I had no idea that she was in London doing freelance work and seeing her so unexpectedly nearly threw me off my balance. By that time, however, I had had enough experience *not* to be thrown by such an unexpected encounter. The North American tour had certainly boosted my confidence and I felt more at ease with the larger orchestra for this 1978–79 season, but even with increased confidence I found that it wasn't easy to attempt to interpret the operas in my own way, such as by changing the tempi for individual artists' numbers, or even for those of the chorus, and I often found that it was simpler just to carry on as before – "It's expected of you". (But I did once get a crit that said my slightly slower tempi in some numbers gave the singers a little more time to breathe.)

Rehearsals continued in the usual way, normally either in the opera rehearsal room or the ballet rehearsal room, or occasionally in the church hall in Exmouth Market, but on

December 29 a nominated dress rehearsal of *Mikado* took place on the stage. It was to assist Joe Davis and Bruno Santini in lighting the new set; costumes were to be worn, but no make-up was required. Just a few days later we were into the New Year, and beginning to look forward to the tour of Australasia – the January 1979 edition of *The Savoyard* referred to the forthcoming "tour of Australia and possibly New Zealand", suggesting that plans had not quite been finalised – but any excitement in anticipation of this event was almost immediately dampened by the sad news of the death of Bert Newby, the business manager, on January 2. I remember coming in to the theatre and being met by a solemn-faced Leonard Osborn who told me what had happened. Bert would have been sixty-five later that year and he had intended to retire in April. Like Jimmie Marsland and Gordon MacKenzie he had given most of his working life to the Company; now he had died in harness. His widow, fellow-chorister Ceinwen Jones, long survived him, dying in January 2010 at the age of ninety-seven.

A few days later, on January 4, there was another nominated dress rehearsal, this time of *Patience*, in the presence of the Friends of Sadler's Wells and Friends of the Vic-Wells Association. Costumes were not required on this occasion. On Sunday January 7 several of us gave a concert at St Mary's Church, Lambeth. Situated at the entrance to Lambeth Palace it is the burial place of the Tradescants (father and son) who were gardeners to the House of Stuart in the seventeenth century. The concert was sponsored by the Tradescant Trust, which was hoping to turn the redundant and deconsecrated building into a museum of gardening. It was in this church, on July 31, 1842, that Arthur Sullivan was baptised, and one of the trustees, Rosemary Nicholson, kindly arranged for me to have a copy of the relevant entry in the church's baptismal register. Those who took part in the concert were Julia Goss, Jane Metcalfe, John Ayldon, Michael Rayner, Geoffrey Shovelton and myself. We also had four members of the orchestra – our then leader Geoff Short, Pam White (second violin), Malcolm Murray (viola) and Barry Newland (cello). They called their group the Sullivan String Quartet. I wrote a piece for them – *A Sullivan Overture*, based on themes from the operas – and they opened the programme with it. Malcolm had also made arrangements of all the G&S numbers and the quartet accompanied these while I played for the other items, which were mainly from the operatic repertoire. A recording, which I still possess, was made of the concert. On the following Tuesday, January 9, Bert Newby's funeral took pace at Golders Green Crematorium. Members of the Company sang the part-song 'The Long Day Closes', and the organist played the overture *In Memoriam* – both by Sullivan.

There was another Sunday concert a few days later when we were once again at Bray and on the following Thursday there was a third nominated dress rehearsal, this time of *Yeomen*. Once again costumes and make-up were not required, but lighting took place during the rehearsal. That evening we auditioned Victoria Klasciki (Scottish mother, Polish father) who joined the chorus for a year, singing under the name Victoria Duncan. January 25 is Burns Night and I had an evening off to play at a Burns Supper at the London Hospital in Whitechapel. This had been arranged by an old Greenock friend, Peter McCrorie (brother of Ian, and husband of the singer Linda Esther Gray), who worked there. I had to play for Laureen Livingstone, another fellow student from my college days at the RSAMD, who would later sing with the Company. This was also the evening that we had again been invited to the Arts Club in Dover Street, but as this didn't happen until after the performance I was able to get to that too. I had played for a *Ruddigore* rehearsal in the morning, and so all in all it had been quite a busy day.

The following week was taken up with our annual recording; this year it was *Yeomen*. Although we didn't know it at the time it turned out to be the Company's last recording. Some months earlier I had received a note from Freddie Lloyd asking me if I could inform Ray Horricks (Decca's manager for our recordings) of the exact timing of the opera minus the dialogue; I duly did this. It was recorded in six sessions over three days at Decca's number three studio at Broadhurst Gardens, West Hampstead. On the Thursday afternoon, after a nominated dress rehearsal of *Ruddigore*, I saw the manuscript full score of *Yeomen*, which Sullivan had bequeathed to the Royal College of Music (later, I also saw the full scores of *Iolanthe* and *Ruddigore*). There were many interesting differences, but as the Company did not have the time to effect any changes we simply recorded it more or less as we performed it. We did, however, include Sergeant Meryll's Act I song 'A laughing boy but yesterday', which had been cut after the opening night, and the Act I duet 'Rapture, rapture!', which was not then in our production (it was reinstated in 1981). As with some of our recent recordings there was room for a filler: we included the Suite No. 1 from the ballet *Victoria and Merrie England* that Sullivan had written for Queen Victoria's Diamond Jubilee in 1897. I was allowed to write the sleeve note for this, but as usual Freddie Lloyd provided the sleeve note for the opera. The cast list on the record sleeve contains a delicious howler: Wilfred Shadbolt (Head Jailer) is listed as Wilfred Shadbolt (Head Sailor).

After the recording we had another three weeks in London. There were more auditions, among the hopefuls being future choristers Clive Birch and Peter Robinson (later James-Robinson) and Michael Freeman (later Lessiter). During the week's run of *Yeomen* I had to deputise for Paul Seeley and play the dreaded offstage bell, but it behaved itself this time and didn't fall off its stand. On February 23, the penultimate day of the London season, I had to travel north to give a talk to the Birmingham branch of the Gilbert and Sullivan Society. While I was away there was a full Company rehearsal for the Last Night on the 24th. We had finished the season with a short run of *Patience* and the Last Night was played on that set. It was nominally another performance of the opera, but with the usual interpolations and substitutions for certain numbers. The Dragoon Guards' brilliant entrance was preceded by the town band from *Sorcerer* and there were also numbers from *Pinafore*, *Ida*, *Yeomen* and *The Grand Duke*, including from the latter 'Take my advice – when deep in debt' ('The Roulette Song'), with which John Ayldon had scored such a success in the centenary concert performance in 1975. For one scene I put together a set of fanfares from four of the operas: *Mikado*, *Ida*, *Gondoliers* and *Patience*.

The first date on our short provincial tour was Eastbourne where we played for a week. Known as 'God's waiting room', its high proportion of elderly inhabitants meant that you often had more people at the matinees than the evening performances as they didn't like to be out too late. At one matinee there the show had just ended, and I was about to leave. In the Congress Theatre the conductor was just inside the barrier separating the pit from the auditorium, and you were easily accessible to the audience filing out. Someone tapped me on the shoulder and said, "That was the best performance… (I turned, smilingly, ready to offer profuse thanks) …of the national anthem I have ever heard". At least I was doing something right! (We clearly played it at every performance here, if not at every venue.)

I had taken a liking to Eastbourne, partly because it was on the coast. Having been brought up in Greenock I missed the sea when we were inland. Now that I had what seemed like a settled job that should last for many years, if they still wanted me and if I chose to stay, my thoughts were beginning to focus on buying property somewhere. As we toured permanently I was never going to be at home, wherever that might be, for any length of time, and that was one reason why I didn't want to buy in London. I wouldn't have wanted a property there to be empty for months on end. But there was also the fact that, whatever you could afford, you would get more for your money outside London. I did feel, however, that I ought to be reasonably close to the capital, and the south coast seemed an attractive proposition. I had already considered Brighton, but that was quite expensive. Bournemouth was also very nice, but it was just a bit too far away from London. Eastbourne seemed the ideal place. On the day that we opened there, February 26, Freddie Lloyd sent out a letter to members of the Company, which read, "As you will appreciate, I have to make plans for the tour which will begin after your return from Australia. I hope it will be possible for you to remain with this Company. Will you please let me know your decision on this matter not later than 24th March, 1979". It was good to know that one was still wanted, but it was also very comforting to know that the Company would be continuing for the foreseeable future, despite ominous rumours of financial difficulties, and this was definitely a deciding factor – before the end of week I had made up my mind to purchase a property in Eastbourne.

The next five weeks were spent in Manchester; once again we were at the Opera House. Having so often been accused of not moving with the times the Company now had some new publicity material, which noted further sponsorship from Barclays Bank. The flyer for the season was in dark blue with gold lettering and featured an airborne Lord Chancellor on the front cover ('Up in the air, sky-high, sky-high'). The Company's previous publicity material had included little cards with the season's offerings for each town or city. They were printed in red and black and had rather unkindly been likened to programmes for boxing matches. For the moment, however, they continued to be produced. With a five-week season we needed a bigger repertoire and we had no less than eight operas with us: *Pinafore*, *Pirates*, *Patience*, *Iolanthe*, *Mikado*, *Ruddigore*, *Yeomen* and *Gondoliers*; we opened on March 5 with *Iolanthe*. The theatres that we played could only take one opera at a time, and so the articulated pantechnicons that we used to transport the sets and costumes were a permanent feature of the Company as they were retained in each town to store the material for the other operas. Even with just five operas on tour this was a major expense. With eight operas we needed even more vans, adding to the ever-rising costs of touring.

On Tuesday 12th I had to give another talk to the Manchester branch of the Gilbert and Sullivan Society, preceded as usual by a very nice meal (this time at the Café Royal) with the secretary Norman Beckett, his wife Grace, and other members of the committee. On the 29th I had lunch with one of the younger members of the committee, David Walton, who later became chairman of the Manchester Society.

On one of my free Sundays in Manchester I saw my cousin Norma and had a meal at her home; I was able to get her a ticket for *Pirates*. There were more auditions and, out of some twenty that we heard, Alistair Donkin, Pamela Searle (later Baxter) and Michelle Shipley all came into the Company. On Sunday 25th our little dining club went out for a meal and on the last Sunday, April 1, several of us went to the home of one of our choristers, Hélène Witcombe, at Bramhall in Cheshire. Hélène was one of those people who seem to light up a stage when they are performing. She had joined the Company in 1977 and was with us when we closed. Sadly she died in 1998, aged just forty-two, from a rare form of liver cancer.

During our last week in Manchester we were given a tour of Granada TV, the studios being not too far from the Opera House; later that day I wrote a letter to Spike Milligan. I had long been a fan of *The Goon Show* (see the alternative title of this book), but this wasn't just a fan letter. I had heard that he had saved the door of a house (about to be demolished) that Sullivan had lived in, and had presented it to a museum. I didn't receive an immediate reply, but did eventually get one, which was dated 30th May. By that time we were in Sydney. He explained that he liked to try to preserve old buildings, had managed to acquire the door and had presented it to the museum, as he thought it should be preserved after all that Sullivan had given us. He also said that he was delighted to learn of my interest in this matter and that it was good of me to have written to him. It was signed in the usual way: "Love, light and peace, Spike". Another one for the collection.

We finished our extended season in Manchester with two performances of *Gondoliers* (which so appropriately ends with the line "We leave you with feelings of pleasure!") and then moved to the Grand Theatre, Leeds for two weeks. This was the last venue on the tour, and the last for several members of the Company, including principal tenor Geoffrey Shovelton and musical director Royston Nash. Geoffrey had decided to leave because his mother was very ill and there was a distinct possibility that she might die while we were away (in fact she died not long after our return). Royston had actually decided to leave before the North American tour began on April 1, 1978. In a letter to me from the Royal Shakespeare Theatre, Stratford-upon-Avon, dated March 4, 1978, he set out his reasons for wishing to leave. He had become increasingly frustrated with the Company's management, particularly over an episode with our leader Haim Lazarov who was with us on the North American tour in 1978. As yet he had no other job lined up, and he had often said to me that with his unusual background for someone in the operatic world (he had been in the Royal Marines), he doubted if he would get very much further in this country. But he also wanted to pursue a more purely orchestral career, although he felt that even that might be difficult in the UK. The North American tour in 1976 had convinced him that there might be more opportunities there – he followed up this idea in 1978 – and it was partly with this in mind that he had tendered his resignation. Although it took some time, his gamble did pay off, and he latterly became music director of the Cape Cod Symphony Orchestra in Massachusetts. He and Geoffrey Shovelton, who also later moved to the United States, died within months of each other in 2016.

Auditions on April 10 produced two more choristers, Bruce Graham and Janet Henderson. There was a staff meeting on April 12, and among the items discussed was the possibility of an extra night off for John Reed. He no longer played Major-General Stanley (*Pirates*), but it was also suggested that he might drop all the matinees; this would give James Conroy-Ward the opportunity to play all, or most, of the roles more frequently (a similar situation to my own as associate conductor). Unfortunately this never happened. We also learned that the London season would begin on a Tuesday (December 18), as there would be lighting on the Monday. On April 14 I caught up with Frank and Ruth Bowler, my old friends from Birmingham with whom I had stayed in Newcastle on my first tour in 1975 (when Frank's home-brewed beer didn't agree with me). Four days later several people, including some of our own choristers, auditioned for the principal tenor vacancy occasioned by Geoffrey Shovelton's departure; among them were Colin Wright, formerly with D'Oyly Carte (principal from 1970–75), and Harold Sharples who eventually held the position for the 1979–80 season. On April 19 there was a party in the theatre's Grand Hall to say goodbye to those who were leaving. I was sorry that Geoffrey and Royston were going as I got on well with both of them. Geoffrey eventually returned to the Company in 1980 and we remained close friends. I kept in touch with Royston, but after he went to America I rarely saw him. As president of the Manchester G&S Society he attended two G&S Conventions in Stockport and I met up with him at each of those. He conducted his last performance with D'Oyly Carte on Saturday April 21, 1979.

We then had a two-week holiday, but I wasn't entirely free of G&S. First of all there was a letter inviting me to become a vice-president of the Birmingham branch of the G&S Society, an honour I was more than pleased to accept. Then, on the night before our departure, there was a further concert at St Mary's Church, Lambeth for the Tradescant Trust. I had earlier received a letter from Jane Metcalfe asking if I would be willing to be the accompanist for this, despite the fact that the Company was leaving for Australia the following day. This wasn't going to affect the soloists as every one of them – Julia Goss, Jane Metcalfe, Geoffrey Shovelton, Michael Rayner and Jon Ellison – had left the Company and wouldn't be going 'down under'. I was quite happy to play for them again knowing that I would have a very long flight in which to recover. Geoffrey produced a splendid cartoon of the soloists who performed under the name Gilbert and Sullivan Unlimited. The following day we set off on our Australasian tour.

II

The letter that I had received the previous year, which suggested that the next contract would not terminate until the end of the Australasian tour, set out my salary for touring both at home and abroad. Having started as the repetiteur in 1975 with a salary of £32 per week I was now being offered £66 as the chorus master/associate conductor (the letter actually said assistant conductor), double what I was getting just four years previously, but the salary for the Australasian tour was to be £116 per week which was almost double again. This was less than my salary for the North American tour, but it was still very welcome. Strangely, despite the annual increases in wages and subsistence, my dress allowance remained the same each year at £65, but my costliest outlay had been in the early days, and I now had everything that I needed. The money was usually spent on extra white shirts. Each contract also stipulated that I wear a morning suit for matinee performances and a tail coat, white tie and waistcoat for evening performances. Thanks to Royston it was tacitly understood that we might also wear our white jackets on appropriate occasions.

Our tour of Australia and New Zealand began on May 7, 1979 with an afternoon reception at the Savoy Hotel, courtesy of Barclays Bank. One of our sponsors was the tobacco giant Benson and Hedges. They paid for the famous gold programme produced for the tour, in return for which they got a full-page advertisement in the programme and some free seats in each venue. While it may seem surprising now that singers were being sponsored by a tobacco company there were still many smokers in D'Oyly Carte at that time (although this wasn't always appreciated by their fellow performers). We left the Savoy at about 6.45pm, being seen off by many well wishers, including some of our stalwart fans, and flew out of Heathrow on a British Airways jumbo jet at around 10pm.

This was the Company's first visit to the southern hemisphere, and the tour was being presented by Derek Glynne and the Australian impresario Michael Edgley. Derek Glynne had contributed an article entitled The Australasian Tour to the May 1979 edition of *The Savoyard* which had appeared just prior to our departure; in it he told of the initial planning for the tour (it took almost three years), and mentioned the problem of getting costumes and scenery sent out. He had been in Washington DC when we were performing there in 1978 and had seen many of our performances during the 1978–79 London season. He had also spent some time in Australia and New Zealand visiting all of the cities we would be playing in and had even met former members of the Company who were now living there. The article also included useful information on various things such as tipping in restaurants (not usually done), adaptors for electrical appliances, and so on.

The following day, May 8 (VE Day), was spent in transit. It was difficult to estimate exactly where we were, and also 'when'. As we were travelling east we kept putting our watches forward every so often, which was a little confusing. The journey to Sydney took almost twenty-four hours. We stopped first at Bombay and were sent out of the plane while it refuelled. I wasn't particularly impressed by the 'International' lounge with its four-bladed fans going round and its apparently single telephone. Even at 6am the temperature was something like 88 degrees Fahrenheit, and it was very humid. I was glad to be back on the plane. We then stopped at Brunei, although we were not allowed off – possibly for security reasons. Throughout our time on board we were wined and dined endlessly, and this certainly helped to pass the time. It was also useful to get to know the new members who had joined the Company. We had of course seen them prior to the tour, although this was on a more formal basis, but the biggest change for the Company was having a new musical director. Fraser Goulding was a graduate of Bristol University and a former assistant conductor of the Arts Council-sponsored Opera for All. He had also been assistant director of opera at the Guildhall School of Music and Drama where he had known our principal soprano, Barbara Lilley. I had met him before the tour began, but got to know him better on this very long journey.

The tour, like the North American tour, divided neatly into three parts – Australia, New Zealand, Australia – but, mirroring the great trinity of Gilbert, Sullivan and D'Oyly Carte, almost everything about it was in threes. There were three dates in each part: Canberra, Sydney, Brisbane; Auckland, Wellington, Christchurch; Melbourne, Adelaide, Perth and we took just three operas: *Pinafore*, *Iolanthe* and *Mikado*. It was felt that these would best show the Company's versatility. There had been quite an exodus after the recent UK tour of principals as well as chorus and this had necessitated a number of cast changes. Meston Reid, who played Ralph Rackstraw (*Pinafore*), also took Geoffrey Shovelton's role as Earl Tolloller (*Iolanthe*), but we had a new Nanki-Poo (*Mikado*) in Philip Potter, a former principal tenor with the Company (from 1961 to 1971) who had been brought back just for this tour, and specifically for this role. (During the 1960s he was partnered in *Mikado* by Valerie Masterson as Yum-Yum; their performances in these roles had been highly acclaimed, and were still fondly remembered.) Barbara Lilley (Phyllis in *Iolanthe*) took over the role of Yum-Yum from Julia Goss. Barbara had also played Josephine (*Pinafore*), but to have continued with this would have meant that she was in all three operas, and Josephine was given to Vivian Tierney. Peter Lyon, Barbara's husband, had joined the Company in January and had taken over Michael Rayner's former roles: Strephon (*Iolanthe*), Pish-Tush (*Mikado*) and Captain Corcoran (*Pinafore*), with, in the latter, occasional performances by Gareth Jones. Long-standing Company member Jon Ellison had also left and his Boatswain role (*Pinafore*) was taken over by Gareth Jones, with occasional performances by Alan Rice. Lorraine Daniels now took over Jane Metcalfe's roles, which included Pitti-Sing (*Mikado*) and the eponymous Iolanthe.

During the London season everyone had been photographed and had been asked to provide short biographies for the large programme (some sixteen inches by almost a foot) with its gold cover – again probably a sought-after collector's item. Most of the photographs were taken at Sadler's Wells – the two of me were taken in our small dressing room – and they were in the main fairly casual. For her biography one of our new choristers, Jillian Mascall, had been asked, "What are your favourite roles?", and she had impishly replied, "Ham and cheese", thinking no more about it. To everyone's astonishment, this duly appeared in the programme. "When asked to name her favourite G&S roles, she included 'ham and cheese'". There were other odd things too. It was claimed that chorister Robert 'Bob' Crowe had played the part of Robert in *Yeomen*, but there is no such character in the opera. The compiler had obviously got muddled and had substituted Bob's own name.

We arrived at Sydney on May 9. Although we had been travelling for some twenty-four hours it seemed, on paper, to have been almost *thirty*-four. There was some apprehension among one or two of the Company as we approached the runway, but when it was obvious that we had landed safely there was a spontaneous burst of applause. After an interminable time going through customs and immigration procedures, we were met by Derek Glynne and his wife Kate and were treated to coffee in a private lounge while we waited for yet another flight (mercifully a short one) to Canberra.

We touched down there at about 9.30am, but to our bodies this was the previous midnight. Anyone who had complained about jet lag on the North American tour must have suffered badly here. Our accommodation was at the Kythera Motel, named, according to its own publicity, after a Greek island popularly known as the Island of Love, where Venus had apparently emerged from the sea. I shared a twin-bedded room with Gordon MacKenzie. Some people went to bed immediately and woke up again at about six that evening. I tried to stay awake, and went out to get some groceries, but I felt so tired that I came back and went to bed around four, waking up again at eight. It takes time for the body to adjust to such a major change and we had the luxury of several free days before the first performance on May 14. We played just one week in Canberra.

Over the next few days we did a lot of sightseeing. Our AUS$6 tour of the city included a visit to Parliament House and the impressive War Memorial Museum. I watched Derek Glynne interviewed on a TV programme called *The Mike Walsh Show*, which included a performance of 'Three little maids from school' (*Mikado*) by Barbara Lilley, Lorraine Daniels and Roberta Morrell. Fraser played for this. As there were now two of us who could play I didn't do as much as I did on the 1978 North American tour. Fraser and I then went to see Warwick Ross, a double bass player who was organising the orchestras for us (a different group in each city). He called his agency Strings 'n Things, and we immediately christened him Warwick the Fixer. He told us that while we were in Australia we would have to become temporary members of the Australian Musicians' Union. I can't remember if Fraser was a member of our own Musicians' Union, but I wasn't. Royston, with his Service background, was not a member and he had advised me not to join. Fraser and I didn't have much choice in the matter and we had to comply with the requirement. Warwick then took us out for a very nice lunch. Afterwards Fraser and I went down to the theatre where we unpacked the music and prepared some band parts for our first orchestral rehearsal that evening. The leader, Bob Ingram, would be with us for parts of the two Australian legs of the tour; Warwick himself played in a number of the performances. The players were good, but as in the United States and Canada few of them were familiar with the music and despite having a full three hours we only got to the middle of the Act I finale of *Iolanthe*.

We had more rehearsals the following day, the first one being in the theatre in the afternoon. The pit was large, with plenty of room for the orchestra; it also had a floor that could be raised or lowered. We were shown how this operated, but I don't think we used the facility. After the rehearsal Fraser and I were treated to another meal, this time by Derek Glynne, in his hotel, which was a bit more upmarket than ours. We then had an evening rehearsal during which we finished *Iolanthe* and started on *Mikado*. Anyone in possession of the large gold programme will see that we were only supposed to be doing *Iolanthe* in Canberra, but there were several changes to the itinerary during the tour and we did some performances of *Mikado* here. During the rehearsal I found that I couldn't stop yawning; this was very embarrassing.

The following day, May 13, was Sullivan's birthday. The weather was beautiful and several of us went on a cruise up and down the seven-mile-long Lake Burley Griffin, named after Walter Burley Griffin, the American architect who had produced the prizewinning design for the city of Canberra. In the evening we went to a restaurant called the Esquire. Next day we had the first full Company rehearsal – of *Iolanthe*, which had been considered the obvious choice for the seat of government. It started at 10.30, and the Act I finale ended more or less on the dot at 1.30pm, at which point Fraser said, "Now I just want to do one thing". This might have lasted only a few minutes, but we were then informed by the Equity representative that we were in overtime. Leonard Osborn asked if there might be a little give and take, but this was not to be, despite the fact that many in the Company would have been prepared to spend a few minutes longer for the sake of whatever it was that Fraser wanted to do; some were clearly upset by the incident as there had also been some unpleasant exchanges. We were about to open the season and we had a new conductor who was obviously anxious to make a good impression. We also had several new choristers and even some of the principals were new to their roles. With all of this the opera was not yet fully run in, but artistic integrity certainly took a back seat that morning – yet another of the seemingly endless confrontations between unions and management.

We opened that evening, and there were, inevitably, a few mishaps, but despite these it seemed to go down well. Afterwards there was a reception hosted by Benson and Hedges. Among the guests were the British high commissioner and one of our former chief constables, Sir Robert Mark. I found myself having a long conversation, through an interpreter, with the Chinese ambassador. When I later told an Australian that I had been speaking to His Excellency his reply was, "Oh yeah? A pain in the arse". An interesting start to the tour! The crit of *Iolanthe*, which appeared two days later in *The Canberra Times*, was very positive, saying that the production had "strength" and "beauty". It also spoke of the "excellent diction from every member of the cast".

The day following our opening performance nearly ended in disaster, again due to jet lag. Four of us hired a car and set off early, driving south to a town called Cooma where we had a late breakfast – mine was the largest toasted sandwich I had ever seen. We then moved on to the Kosciusko National Park, which contains the Snowy Mountain range. The range includes Mount Kosciusko, the highest mountain in Australia. It was a lovely day, but it was the equivalent of our mid-November and there was enough snow on the ground to build a snowman – a strange experience for mid-May. This was all fine, but by the time we got back to Canberra at about 7pm I was again beginning to feel the effects of jet lag, and

I lay down for half an hour. I didn't feel like getting up again, but managed to get to the theatre by about 8.10pm (the performance started at 8.15pm), only to find that Fraser wasn't yet there. He too was still 'adjusting', had been asleep, and had only been wakened by a phone call to his room. Thinking that I had to stand in I changed into my evening clothes – and then Fraser arrived a few minutes later. Seeing me dressed for action he suggested that I conduct the performance, but as I didn't feel like conducting a bus, never mind an opera, I persuaded him to change quickly, and the show got under way at 8.20pm. I think that if I had had to go on I would almost certainly have had to come off again halfway through.

Next morning we had a rehearsal for *Pinafore* in preparation for our visit to Sydney, and in the afternoon, as there was no matinee, we had another orchestral rehearsal to finish off *Mikado*; in the evening we did our final *Iolanthe*. Several members of the Company were still having problems with jet lag and there also seemed to be other health problems. Barry Clark, who had been with us to the Kosciusko National Park, was off that evening. This was turning out to be worse than anything that people had experienced on the North American tour. I don't know when everyone finally conquered the jet lag, but I think it took some time.

On May 17, with Barry Clark now recovered, our little group hired another car, but we didn't go so far this time. We finished up at the Tidbinbilla Nature Reserve where there were a number of kangaroos. High above us in a tree there was also a lone koala – it was fast asleep. The highlight of this visit was the feeding of the birds, most of which were crimson rosellas – parakeets that are native to eastern and south-eastern Australia. There was no show that evening, but we had a final orchestral rehearsal for *Mikado*. Although not a scheduled rehearsal for the Company, some of the principals came to it, and this was very helpful.

There was yet another rehearsal on the 18th, this time for chorus only, and with piano. Fraser played for this and I conducted. I also conducted the evening performance of *Mikado*, our first there and my Australian debut. The British high commissioner, who had been at the Benson and Hedges reception after our opening performance, was in the audience. The chorus sang well and the orchestra, despite the lack of rehearsal time, pulled out all the stops, but some of the principals were not so good that night. I thought it was brave of John Ayldon to go on as he had heard only the previous day that his mother had died; he had decided not to go back for the funeral. (Fearing just such a situation with his own mother was what had prompted Geoffrey Shovelton to leave the Company.) May 19 was our last day in Canberra, and once again we did *Mikado* – two performances, both of which I conducted as Fraser was going ahead early to our next stop, Sydney. I had now conducted all three performances of *Mikado* in Canberra. The orchestra played well on Saturday after their baptism of fire the previous evening. The matinee had the better audience. Between the shows some of us went again to the Esquire restaurant for a final visit. The first date on the tour was now over.

We flew to Sydney on May 20 for a three-week season – not at the iconic Opera House but at a somewhat inferior venue, the Regent Theatre. It had originally been a cinema, and lacked adequate dressing rooms and a proper pit. Our accommodation here was rather different to the Kythera Motel. We were in the Hyde Park Plaza complex, a series of very large well-appointed apartments with either one or two bedrooms. There was also a roof-top swimming pool. I shared a two-bedroom apartment with Caroline Hudson and Hélène Witcombe. Just across the passage was a similar apartment, where two of the new choristers, Jillian Mascall (of the 'ham and cheese' roles) and Jane Stanford, were sharing with our guest tenor Philip Potter. Once we had settled in, the six of us went out for a meal. I was awakened the next morning by a phone call from Peter Riley's wife Yvonne to say that I was required in the theatre to help with publicity. John Reed, Philip Potter, Meston Reid and some of the chorus were also involved, but, as so often during these sessions, we all sat around for a long time before being used – and then only for five minutes. In the afternoon I went down to have a look at the Opera House. It is certainly very eye-catching, whatever one thinks of the actual design. We then had a rehearsal onstage at the Regent, but only with an old piano that was in the pit; this wasn't very satisfactory. We didn't see the orchestra, which had a slightly larger string section, until the evening. We opened with *Pinafore*, but there were problems with balance and, with some justification, Fraser wasn't too pleased with the performance. There was an after-show function laid on by Derek Glynne, and a surprise guest at this was Britain's Ronnie Barker. The two Ronnies, Barker and Corbett, were among several Michael Edgley presentations in the 1979–80 season, including ourselves, the Red Army Choir and Liberace.

Next day we had another rehearsal onstage, again with the old piano in the pit. *Pinafore* was better in the evening for having had a 'dress rehearsal' the night before; it was followed by the first Barclays reception of the tour. Some of the principals had to sing at this and Fraser suggested that we improvise piano duet versions of the accompaniments. This wasn't really very successful and I said that we simply ought to take it in turn to play at any future functions. Finally, in the afternoon of May 23, we had an orchestral rehearsal for *Mikado*, which we would be presenting during the second week. It was while we were setting up the pit that we became aware of two people standing at the front of the stalls – Ronnie Barker and Ronnie Corbett. They were performing shortly after us and had come in to have a look at the theatre. Although we had now done *Pinafore* twice the orchestra still found the pit difficult. But *Pinafore* went quite well in the evening; everyone seemed to be getting used to the theatre at last.

There was a further rehearsal next morning which I didn't attend as I had to play for Meston Reid and Vivian Tierney who were being interviewed live on radio. They sang 'Refrain, audacious tar' (*Pinafore*). In the afternoon I went on a Coffee

Cruise, which headed out to the edge of the Tasman Sea and also hugged the many inlets to let us see yacht clubs and much desirable real estate. I then had an Indian meal (still something of a rarity in Australia at that time), and in the evening I conducted my first *Pinafore*. This performance also went well and I was particularly pleased, as it was May 25, the opera's 101st anniversary. The previous year we had celebrated its centenary in style in San Francisco. Sydney rather reminded me of San Francisco, being similarly situated on a bay at the edge of an ocean. There was another Benson and Hedges reception after the show and again we met many interesting people; among them were Brian and Dulcie Chaseling who invited a number of us to their house for a Sunday barbecue.

We finished the week with two performances of *Pinafore* on the Saturday. Afterwards Fraser and I were invited to a party at the home of one of our violinists, Eva Kelly, who was married to a publisher, Alan Ziegler. On Sunday there was more hospitality when several of us were collected by Ian and Marylou Arnold, a couple we had met earlier in the week. Strangely, they had also met Caroline Hudson's father in San Francisco in1978. They took us first to Waratah Park, a small nature reserve which was one of the filming locations of *Skippy the Bush Kangaroo*, a programme that had been popular in the UK. We then had a pleasant drive, finishing up at Manly, north of Sydney, and also on the coast, where we called in on some friends of the Arnolds. (The husband was quite a character and looked like a thinner version of Gomez in *The Addams Family*.) They kindly provided us with a barbecue lunch in their garden, which gave on to the beach. The lunch included a splendid pavlova dessert, something of a novelty for most of us, and I took a photograph of it. We walked along the beach after lunch, and left at about 4pm. The Arnolds then took us back to their house where we had even more food; we finally got back to the Hyde Park Plaza at 9pm.

In common with many of the Company I took a number of photographs during the tour and got them developed as we went along (this was a pre-digital period). In photographing the pavlova at the Arnolds' friends' house I had concentrated on the dessert itself, but you could also see the upper bodies, although not always the faces, of those around the table. When I eventually got this batch of photographs developed the print of the pavlova had a sticker on the back – "A tip from Kodak", which said, "Problem? – Some of the subject matter is missing from the print... Solution! – Keep important subject matter [i.e. the people] well centred in the viewfinder". It clearly hadn't occurred to whoever was developing the negatives that anyone would want to photograph such an everyday item (to an Australian) as a pavlova.

Our second week in Sydney was devoted to *Mikado*; it opened on May 28. The orchestral rehearsals had certainly helped and the shows all went reasonably well. During each week there were occasional rehearsals in the mornings, with the afternoons usually devoted to sightseeing. I was also able to indulge my fondness for browsing in second-hand bookshops, but didn't find anything of interest. The morning rehearsal on May 30 was on the stage and instead of having to use the piano in the pit we were allowed to use the one that was kept in the wings – a AUS$35,000 Steinway, certainly one of the most expensive pianos I have ever played. After this rehearsal Fraser and I were given a tour of the Conservatory of Music. The conductor and composer Sir Eugene Goossens had been principal there from 1947 to 1956, and the man who showed us round (Ronal [sic] Jackson, now the head of the Opera School) had been one of his pupils. It was all very casual and in typical forthright Australian fashion he even told us how much he earned: "Twenty-six thousand dollars for just eight hours teaching a week". (Sometime after we returned to the UK I found a recording of some pieces by Percy Grainger, which featured Ronal Jackson as soloist.) In the evening I did my first *Mikado* in Sydney and the next day I went on a Captain Cook's Luncheon Cruise, which went under the famous Sydney Harbour Bridge to let us see something of the inner part of Port Jackson, one of the finest natural harbours in the world.

By the end of that week we were into June, and we had already been away for almost a month. I was given a night off on June 1, and went to the cinema to see *Death on the Nile*, with Peter Ustinov as Hercule Poirot. I then came back to the theatre, and when *Mikado* had finished our little dining club went out to find somewhere to eat. We had heard about the notorious King's Cross area, where there had recently been a clean-up campaign, and wanted to have a look at it, but we also hoped to find a restaurant there that would be open – so many in Sydney seemed to close at 11pm. We found an excellent French restaurant – I had escargots, rack of lamb and profiteroles – and didn't leave until 2.30pm. Fraser did the matinee on Saturday; I went to a museum, and then took a ferry to Mossman on the north side of the harbour. This was becoming another paid holiday – and "nothing like work".

Sunday June 3 was our second free day and was one of the highlights of our time in Sydney. At 11am Caroline Hudson, Hélène Witcombe, Victoria 'Vicki' Duncan and I were picked up by Ellis Glover, who was involved in some aspect of the sponsorship of the tour, and his wife Helen, and taken to Brian and Dulcie Chaseling's house for the barbecue to which we had been invited on May 25. The food, washed down by a great amount of alcohol, was wonderful, and throughout the afternoon Ellis Glover kept up an endless supply of Australian banter and instant Polaroid photographs. The alcohol soon did its work and before long we were all screaming with laughter at every one of Ellis's jokes. Finally, at about 4.30pm, we thanked the Chaselings and said our goodbyes. We then went to another party, which lasted from 6.30pm until 8pm.

Later that evening there was a third party, this time at the home of Sybil Ghilchik and her husband Terence O'Donoghue who had both been in D'Oyly Carte – in the years 1945–47 and 1946–47 respectively. (Sybil was the daughter of the cartoonist David Ghilchik.) Food and drink were again in plentiful supply

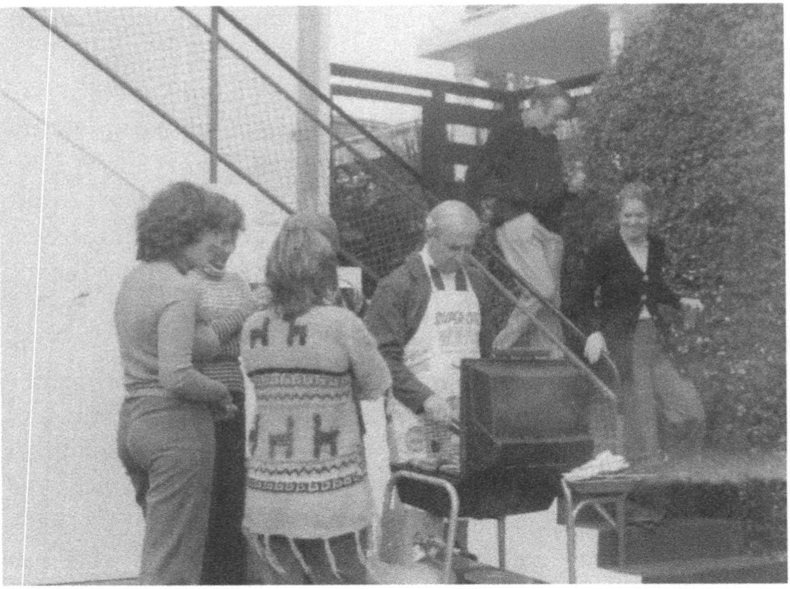

Australian hospitality – a barbecue at the home of Brian and Dulcie Chaseling, Sydney, New South Wales, June 1979. L-r: Hélène Witcombe, Helen Glover, Vicki Duncan (back to camera), Dulcie Chaseling (hidden), Brian Chaseling, Ellis Glover, Caroline Hudson.

and afterwards we had an impromptu singsong. As well as our hosts there were two other ex-members of the Company at the party – no less than former principals Helen 'Betty' Roberts and her husband Richard Walker. Richard, then eighty-one, had joined the Company as far back as 1924; Helen, some fifteen years younger, in 1938. They both contributed to the entertainment. Helen sang, 'Were I thy bride' (*Yeomen*), but at such a pace that I could hardly keep up with her. Did they really take things so quickly thirty years previously? Richard's contribution was 'I'm getting married in the morning' from Lerner and Loewe's *My Fair Lady* (complete with actions) as he had sung the role of Doolittle in Australia. Helen was president of the Birmingham branch of the Gilbert and Sullivan Society of which I had recently been elected a vice-president, and before we left the UK I had been told to pass on the Society's best wishes to her if we managed to meet up. All in all it had been a memorable, if exhausting, day. We eventually got back to the Hyde Park Plaza at around 1am, and, not surprisingly, I went out like a light and slept for about ten hours.

We were now into the last week in Sydney. Originally we were to have given eight performances of *Iolanthe*, but we continued with *Mikado* for the first half of the week, beginning a short run of *Iolanthe* on the Thursday. There were regular staff meetings throughout the tour; the one on June 4 included Freddie Lloyd who had flown out from London. Next day we had a rehearsal for *Iolanthe*. After the evening performance (*Mikado*) Warwick Ross, who wasn't coming to Brisbane, invited us to supper to say goodbye to Fraser and me; unfortunately Fraser couldn't come, as he wasn't feeling very well.

June 7 was another memorable day. We took a ferry across the harbour to visit Taronga Park Zoo, an outing arranged by Patrick Wilkes and Jackie Bennett (now Mrs Patrick Wilkes) who were staying there with Jackie's uncle, one of the zookeepers. It was a beautiful day and the view of Sydney from the zoo, and particularly from Jackie's uncle's garden, must be one of the best views in Australia. That evening we opened our short run of *Iolanthe*. The following morning we were given a tour of the Opera House followed by a reception. I had to conduct the evening performance (and the two on Saturday) as Fraser was again moving on early to our next stop, Brisbane. After the Friday performance our two choristers, Elizabeth Denham and Susan Cochrane, who had given a joint birthday party in San Francisco the previous year now gave another one, taking advantage of the Hyde Park Plaza's large apartments. This time it was a fancy dress party and many unusual and inventive costumes were in evidence, acquired from various sources. Our hostesses appeared as Minnie Mouse (Elizabeth) and Dracula (Susan). Patrick Wilkes came as a koala, and his wife Jackie, with her Taronga Park connection, was a zookeeper, Gareth Jones was Batman and Peter Riley was in a gorilla skin. I went as Groucho Marx. I simply wore my formal matinee outfit of black jacket and striped trousers, my grey tie was not quite straight, to give that slightly seedy touch, and I also painted on a moustache and sported a large cigar. The star turn of the evening, however, was undoubtedly Ken Sandford who appeared as Barry Humphries' exotic creation Dame Edna Everage. It was a splendid outfit and won him the prize for the best female costume. I won the prize for the 'most corny effort'. Next day was our last in Sydney. Between the shows Caroline Hudson and I went to a Mandalay restaurant with Patrick and Jackie Wilkes and Jackie's uncle and aunt from Taronga Park. An enthusiastic audience at the last performance threw streamers at the end – a splendid send-off.

Batman (Gareth Jones) and Groucho (David Mackie) at the fancy–dress party, Sydney, June 1979. Behind D.M. is Warwick Ross, orchestra fixer, of Strings 'n Things.

We flew to Brisbane for two weeks on June 10, and played at Her Majesty's Theatre. I was in the Heath Court Hotel in East Brisbane. It was some distance from the theatre, but the best way of getting into town was by ferry on the Brisbane River. On June 11 we had a rehearsal in the morning with yet another orchestra. The string section was back to smaller numbers, but we still had Bob Ingram as leader. The rehearsal went quite well, which is more than can be said for the opening performance that evening (*Pinafore*) when we had another of those (mercifully rare) situations when a principal failed to appear on stage. Peter Lyon, as Captain Corcoran, had finished his opening aria, 'I am the Captain of the *Pinafore*!', and was left onstage, after the chorus had exited, waiting for Little Buttercup – but she didn't appear. This is another of those instances where there is no underlying music to cover any such non-appearance. Buttercup enters, and sings, unaccompanied, the long opening part of a recitative, 'Sir, you are sad! The silent eloquence/Of yonder tear that trembles on your eyelash', before a chord is sounded; with no singer there is little that one can do. After what seemed an eternity the orchestra, or at least some of them, started an encore for the previous number, but just at that moment Little Buttercup (Patricia Leonard) finally appeared on stage and the encore rather died a death. The opera took some time to settle after this, but by the time we got to 'Never mind the why and wherefore' in Act II we seemed to have won over the audience. There was another Benson and Hedges reception after the show; among those present was Ellis Glover from Sydney.

I conducted the matinee on June 13, my first time with the new orchestra. But owing to Fraser's indisposition I also had to do the evening performance and this gave rise to another of those curious coincidences in my life that are connected with G&S. The first opera that we did when I was at school, under the redoubtable Donald 'Minty' Miller, was *HMS Pinafore* in 1958. Donald Miller had since retired, but the operas had continued and 1979 was now the twenty-first anniversary of these productions. It had been decided, therefore, to have a Gala Night for the opening of its latest presentation (Johann Strauss ll's *Die Fledermaus*), followed by a dinner in Greenock Town Hall to which all who had taken part in the operas over the years had been invited. I couldn't attend as I was in Australia, but both my parents were present, as was Donald Miller. This was to take place on June 13, the very day on which I was conducting *Pinafore*, although I had worked out that the evening performance in Brisbane had finished before the Greenock one had started. Even more incredible was the fact that my old school had been demolished and a new one built on a different site – at the end of Brisbane Street! And as if that wasn't enough of a coincidence, Donald Miller's daughter and her husband were living in Brisbane. ("Spooky, Possum!" as Dame Edna might have said.) They couldn't come to the performance on the 13th, you can't have too many coincidences, but they did come to a later one.

We continued with *Pinafore* for the rest of that week. On June 15 I played for Barbara Lilley, Lorraine Daniels and Roberta Morrell who were singing 'Three little maids from school' (*Mikado*) for a TV show, not live this time but recorded at the studio. The accompaniment to 'Three little maids' is quite tricky on the piano, although it isn't too bad if you only have to play it once, as at a live performance. But there were numerous takes for the recording, and I found that I was getting more nervous with each one. Eventually, however, we managed to get it in the can. The Company, more used to a different opera each night (apart from during the London seasons), was perhaps beginning to tire of eight performances of one opera on the trot and that evening's show was not one of our best, but there were just two more to go. After the last *Pinafore* Fraser and I took some of the orchestra for a drink to say goodbye to Bob Ingram who had been with us since Canberra.

Next day, Sunday, Caroline Hudson and I saw Donald Miller's daughter Betty and her husband Alistair Urquhart, another Scot. They took us to Toowoomba, a two-hour drive south of Brisbane, where we had lunch. We then went to a famous vantage point, at some 2,000 feet, before going back to the Urquharts' house for drinks. I discovered that Alistair had been a prisoner of war in Italy during World War Two, but he had escaped and had lived in a cave for five months. He also knew a famous wartime character (Lieutenant-General Vladimir Peniakoff, known as 'Popski'), who had written a book about his experiences – *Popski's Private Army*. It had been an interesting day, although a little less frenetic than some we had experienced.

The second week was devoted to *Mikado*. Again I had to do the last three performances, as Fraser was flying early to New Zealand to prepare for the second leg of the tour. The weather was not so good this week, but on the Monday we managed to get to the Gold Coast, south of Brisbane, stopping first at Surfers Paradise. Although it was the middle of winter it seemed like fairly average British summer weather to us, but we saw someone on the beach wearing a fur coat. The first *Mikado* that evening was attended by Sir James Ramsay, the governor-general of Queensland, but there was no reception afterwards. We also had a new orchestra, with only three of the players who had been in *Pinafore*. Next morning, although it was now raining, we had a barbecue at the hotel. After the evening performance there was a small reception given by the Australia-Britain Society; among those present were the president Sir Charles Barton and a lady from Pittenweem in Fife. Next day the rain really started in earnest. In Australia, certainly in those days, many of the buildings had corrugated iron roofs. The theatre was one of them and as it rained incessantly throughout both shows, you could hardly hear the dialogue. It rained again the following day, but I managed to see something of the city. In the evening, with fellow Scots Meston Reid and Gordon MacKenzie, I went to the local Caledonian Club where we performed to a small band of enthusiastic expatriates. Like so many events in Australia, this came to an end at 11pm, which was really quite early for us.

The weather changed again the following day and a number of us went upriver to the Lone Pine Koala Sanctuary where most people had a photograph taken with one of those lovable little creatures. They are gentle, but their claws are very sharp. Betty and Alistair Urquhart came to the evening performance, and we had another meal together, this time being joined by our new leader Valentina Abaza, a lady of Russian/Romanian extraction. June 23 was our last working day in Brisbane, the evening performance being enlivened by a man in the front row of the stalls who screamed and cackled at every joke, much to the amusement of the orchestra who were now more accustomed to the music and were playing very well. Between the shows I had tea at the home of one of our cellists Colin Fox, a brother of Ivan Fox who had been one of our leaders in the UK. (Another brother, Eldon, also a cellist, played in the Royal Philharmonic Orchestra and was usually present at our London recording sessions, and there was at least one other sibling whom I was to meet later in Adelaide.)

We should have travelled to Auckland on the Sunday, but there was a grounding of DC-10s and we found ourselves with another day in Brisbane. Our dining club took advantage of the lovely weather, hired a car and headed north to the Sunshine Coast. It was so pleasant that we were able to swim in the sea. We then treated ourselves to another meal, one of the best we had yet had in Australia. The first part of the tour was now over.

We flew to Auckland, some twelve hundred miles away, on June 25, 1979 leaving Brisbane at 3.30pm. The flight took about two and three-quarter hours. As it was winter, and with a time difference of two hours, it was nearer 8.30pm, and dark, by the time we arrived. We had to go through customs again, although one advantage was that you could stock up on duty-free goods. We also had to discard any food that we were carrying; many people had forgotten about this. I seem to recall sandwiches, fruit, chocolate bars and even half a jar of marmalade among the items deposited in the strategically placed bins.

We were in Auckland for two weeks. I stayed at the Barrycourt Motor Inn whose rooms were characterised by a distinct lack of furniture: no tables, not even a dressing table – just beds. We were playing at the St James Theatre and after our rehearsal on June 26 there was some filming in the theatre. The footage was shown on the six o'clock news. In the afternoon I found the best second-hand bookshop so far and spent about NZ$20 on various items. That evening we opened our season with *Pinafore*. It went quite well, although the new orchestra was a bit rough. The next day there was more filming, this time for *The Ray Woolf Show*, with John Reed and the 'three little maids'. It was due to be screened a week or so later at 9pm, but we would still be in the theatre and unable to see it. Later that day there was another TV slot, now with Meston Reid and some of the men's chorus. The second performance of *Pinafore* was, if anything, even more ragged than the first, but the orchestra was at last beginning to get the measure of it.

Next day there was a rehearsal for *Mikado* followed by a meeting with Derek Glynne. We discussed several things including a proposed televising of *Mikado*. The proposal had to be put before the Company who voted on it during the evening performance, the consensus of opinion being a majority in favour. But for some reason the televising never happened. We rehearsed *Mikado* again on the 29th, this time with the understudies, which was very constructive. Afterwards I did some coaching for the Field Day on July 3. The main purpose of these Field Days was to hear all of the choristers; they had to sing one song from the operas and prepare some dialogue. But in this instance there was the added attraction that understudies were still required for a number of roles, including several major ones in operas that we were not performing on this tour: *Pirates*, *Yeomen* and *Gondoliers*. On that same day information reached us from London about the forthcoming UK tour and the operas we would be playing. Initially these were to be *Pirates*, *Mikado* and *Yeomen*. We could not immediately play either *Pinafore* or *Iolanthe* as these would still be in transit after the Australasian tour, but we could still play *Mikado* (the number one box-office draw) as we could use the old Disley Jones set for it.

June 30 was matinee day and Fraser did both shows. During the break between them we went to the home of our clarinettists David and Shirley Smith. It was David's birthday and they laid on an alfresco meal with some very nice New Zealand wine. After the evening performance four of us took part in a telethon at the studios of TV2. This somewhat unusual event was a twenty-four hour charity stint that had raised some NZ$3 million the previous year – not bad for a country of just three million people. The charity benefitting from the 1979 telethon was the International Year of the Child. Artists who were appearing in Auckland were asked to give a short performance and then read out 'pledges' – money donated to the cause without any strings attached, e.g. NZ$10 from Anonymous of Auckland, and NZ$103.83 from a ladies' bowling club from somewhere or other, which had organised a 'table-tennis-a-thon'. The event had started at 8pm. We arrived after 9.30pm, were given something to eat, and then performed. Meston Reid and Vivian Tierney had been asked to do this, and again they sang, 'Refrain, audacious tar' (*Pinafore*). I was ostensibly only there to play for them, but Gareth Jones (Vivian's husband) had also come along and he and I were invited to do some pledge-reading, although Gareth didn't sing. For some reason we were given more airtime than the other two. It was another interesting experience, but an added bonus was the presence on the panel of no less a person than Lauren Bacall. She was appearing in a play in Auckland and had agreed to take part. That was definitely the icing on the cake for me.

On the following day, July 1, about forty of us had planned to visit the famous hot springs at Rotorua. Unfortunately, the rain was coming down in torrents and the coach was late in arriving at our hotel. The rain was showing no sign of stopping and several people, already rather wet, had decided not to come. The driver then informed us that it was pointless going to Rotorua in these conditions, but said that he would take us to the end of the motorway (some twenty-five miles away) and assess the situation there. We stopped at a tourist shop and the driver phoned ahead to see what it was like at Rotorua. It was apparently just as bad there and it was already worse at the tourist shop than when we had left Auckland. Reluctantly, on a majority vote, we then decided to abandon the outing. But the tourist shop did well.

We played *Mikado* in the second week (July 2–7), and Fraser asked me to conduct the first performance. Despite a few unsteady moments I thought it had gone reasonably well, but the following morning there was a less than euphoric crit. Fraser thought it was rather unjustified, and bought me a very nice bottle of claret by way of compensation. The show was better in the evening, but our oboist seemed to be having problems. He eventually found that there was a feather stuck in one of the instrument's keys. Next day was matinee day, and James Conroy-Ward was playing Ko-Ko at both performances. There had just been a strike of refuse collectors, and in the afternoon performance James inserted the line "the waste disposalist" in the 'little list' number. It didn't make much impression as the audience was composed mainly of schoolchildren, but his evening line "the Maori tattooist" got a better reception. John Reed also made regional variations where these were allowed in the text: in Sydney, for example, "King's Cross" was an obvious variant in the reply to the Mikado's "His address" in Act II (the reply in the original is "Knightsbridge"). But while we were in Australia John added a line to his Act I speech on receiving the letter from the Mikado, which states that unless someone is beheaded within one month the post of Lord High Executioner will be abolished and the city (Titipu) reduced to the rank of a village. He read the letter from bottom to top which invariably got a laugh, and then, with a rueful expression, turned to the audience and said, "Life wasn't meant to be easy". This always got an even bigger laugh as it was a catchphrase used by the Australian prime minister.

Having just got used to Australia we were now beginning to appreciate how different it was in New Zealand. It seemed so much more British in many ways, with place names like Hamilton, Warkworth, Christchurch – and the Firth of Thames! Even the atlas that I bought in Auckland had been prepared by the AA. The sacred ritual of afternoon tea was much in evidence, as were many old British cars such as the Standard Vanguard of *c.*1950. Caroline Hudson had friends in Auckland who owned a 1960 Ford Anglia and we went out in that on July 6. We managed to find an almost deserted beach, and later went to a vineyard. After that we went to a thermal pool where I nearly lost my glasses going down a water chute. They came off as I hit the water and I was lucky to catch them before they went under. Fraser did the show that night, but went off next day to Wellington. I then had to conduct the last two shows. The matinee audience was possibly the quietest yet, but the evening was a bit livelier. Afterwards there was a small party at the home of Ray and Janice Hope, a New Zealand couple who had played in our orchestra at home. Despite his British-sounding name Ray was, at least partly, of Maori descent. Janice, with ginger hair and freckles, was very obviously of Scottish descent. It was good to see them again. And that was the end of our time in Auckland.

Next day, July 8, we flew to Wellington, New Zealand's capital city. We were there for just one week, playing at the State Opera House. We were supposed to be staying at the Royal Oak Hotel, but something had gone wrong with this booking and various other hotels were used instead. Several of us ended up at a block of self-catering flats called Melksham Towers (again sounding very British). Having settled in we went out for a meal at 7pm. We were just in time as restaurants closed at 8pm on a Sunday. This was even worse than Australia. Wellington is built round a bay, then called Port Nicholson, and has an attractive inner harbour. It is also hilly and, although smaller, like Sydney it reminded me of San Francisco. Once again I found some good second-hand bookshops. We were originally due to play a week of *Iolanthe* there, but, perhaps wisely, this had been changed to the perennially popular *Mikado*. It went well on the opening night, although the encore number 'Here's a how-de-do!' seemed to take the orchestra by surprise. A more pleasant surprise was seeing Helen Moulder, a former chorister who had been with us in my first year. Helen, Andrea Phillips and I had stayed with Mrs Walford in Norton during our two-week season in Billingham in 1975. A New Zealander, Helen was now at home again pursuing a career as an actress and singer, and she turned up after the opening performance. Patrick and Jackie Wilkes were staying with her.

Fraser Goulding was staying in a flat owned by Harry and Phyllis Brusey, the only New Zealand husband and wife each to have been awarded the OBE. Harry worked in shipping and Phyllis dealt in antiques, but both were keen musicians. Phyllis played the violin and Harry had been the chorus master of the enterprising New Zealand Opera Company which, sadly, had closed in 1971. One of its musical directors had been James Robertson CBE who latterly became director of the London Opera Centre. Fraser had worked there and it was through this connection that he was now staying in the flat. It was high above the city and there were splendid views of the bay and harbour. The Bruseys' main home was a large house full of wonderful antiques on the other side of the city, and they kindly invited some of us for afternoon tea on July 10. The show that evening went well, but just before the curtain went up half of the set collapsed and had to be removed. It was a new set, replacing the old Disley Jones one (often referred to as Disleyland), and had already given us some trouble. The general opinion in the Company was that it had been money needlessly wasted.

Phyllis Brusey had written a book about her life, *Ring Down the Curtain*, covering her interests in antiques and the New Zealand Opera. A signed copy of it is another of my treasured possessions. Among the many photographs of the Opera Company's performances is one of Grahame Clifford, who had played the comedy roles for D'Oyly Carte during World War Two, as Frosch in *Die Fledermaus* in 1966. He was still living in New Zealand and attended a performance of *Mikado* while we were in Wellington. Afterwards, he met James Conroy-Ward and a short article about this, with a photograph of them, appeared in the January 1980 edition of *The Savoyard*.

At the end of our week in Wellington Fraser flew back to Australia to prepare for the last leg of the tour (Melbourne, Adelaide and Perth), and this meant that as I had to conduct all of the performances in Christchurch, our last stop in New Zealand, I would have to leave Wellington a day early to organise this – on Friday 13! Dr John Drummond, my tutor in Birmingham for my research into Sullivan's songs, was now professor of music at the University of Otago in Dunedin. We were not visiting that city, but I managed to phone him, only to find that on the day I was flying to Christchurch, he would be in Wellington. This could only happen on Friday 13. Fraser did the matinee on July 11, and I did the evening performance. Afterwards we had another visit from Helen Moulder. She was giving a party on the Friday night, but unfortunately I would miss that. On my last day, Fraser took a chorus rehearsal, which was being televised, and after this John Reed and I were whisked off to the local TV station for a live performance at 1pm. John wasn't interviewed, but he was announced as being "New Zealand-born", as they had mistakenly believed that Auckland had been his birthplace. He was in fact born near Bishop Auckland in County Durham. He sang 'When I was a lad' (*Pinafore*), but there was only about twenty seconds of it, which seemed a bit pointless. Next day I flew to Christchurch and checked in to the United Service Hotel in Cathedral Square. Despite the ominous date, the flight had been pleasant and uneventful – the calm before the storm.

Our week in Christchurch (July 16–21) was devoted entirely to *Pinafore*, although originally it was to have been *Mikado*. The orchestra here was the least experienced I have ever had to deal with (we didn't have Warwick Ross in New Zealand to fix the players). The first rehearsal on the Friday evening was a real Friday 13 experience. The first trumpet didn't turn up and he had the only copy of the music (both parts were in one book, written together on the same stave). The timpanist was young and his father was with him to see that he was all right! He had no bass drum and cymbal and couldn't play the side drum – and his timing was abysmal. Despite all of this we got through the overture and Act I, which is the bulk of the work. Afterwards I unwound over a few drinks with our local contact Tony Goodliffe who, I discovered, had met my old school friend Peter Morrison when he too had toured here recently. After some sightseeing the following morning, we had a second rehearsal, which wasn't too bad despite the obvious weak spots. The Company arrived on Sunday July 15. There was a French restaurant in the United Service Hotel. It had just opened the previous day, and six of us had a very nice meal there.

Next morning I went in to the theatre to set up the pit and then tried to relax in the afternoon. I found another good second-hand bookshop, which had some G&S items, and this helped to take my mind off what was to come. At the opening performance the orchestra, who had only just met the Company, seemed to be suffering from stage fright, and the audience was quite the deadest I had yet encountered. Sir Joseph's entrance, minus the side drum, was something of a damp squib and I was more than a little damp myself, not having sweated so much for a long time. When I went back in to the pit after the interval there was a smattering of applause, and I motioned the orchestra to get up. At first they looked at me in blank amazement. Then, just as a few of them started to get to their feet, I turned round to acknowledge the applause – at which point it ceased altogether. My morale had now reached rock bottom. In an effort to whip up the audience we did all the encores for 'Never mind the why and wherefore', and that brightened up the atmosphere. It also helped the orchestra and by the time we got to 'He is an Englishman!' they were playing with a little more gusto. But it was perhaps the longest two hours of my life. Next day, to my astonishment, there was a very praiseworthy crit headed "The best 'Pinafore' to visit New Zealand". Unfortunately it also referred to "Musical Director Fraser Goulding". A later crit, which was a little less euphoric, managed to get my name right. Typical!

Our venue here was the James Hay Theatre, part of the Christchurch Town Hall complex which was greatly damaged in the earthquake of 2011. On the day that the crit appeared, the complex had another visitor from the UK, Her Royal Highness Princess Anne. As she came out of the building the Princess stopped to chat in the time-honoured way, doubtless assuming that she had picked on a New Zealander. She had in fact picked on our wardrobe mistress, Vera Carnegie. I don't know who was the more surprised. (A photograph of the Princess, which appeared in the local paper, showed Vera standing in the background.) The show was a little better that evening, but the audience still seemed incapable of laughter and rarely clapped after numbers. It continued like this throughout the week. The mid-week Thursday matinee was quite lively, but the evening was again very quiet. Conversely the Saturday matinee was dull, while the evening performance had the best audience of the week, laughing and applauding numbers.

The orchestra gradually improved as they became more familiar with the music, but there was nearly a disaster on the last night during the long section in Act II beginning with 'Carefully on tiptoe stealing'. It all seemed to be going quite well until we came to Captain Corcoran's, 'My lord – one word', at which point it almost fell to pieces. This is one of those danger points where there is a break in the music, with the soloist giving the upbeat before the accompaniment begins. It hadn't been a problem so far, but on this occasion Peter Lyon (as Captain Corcoran) took longer to come in. Not expecting a pause, I had already started the orchestra, and now had to stop them – at which point Peter started to sing. This was confusing for the players, as they were not familiar enough with the opera to realise what had happened. I got them going again, although there were only spasmodic sounds coming from the pit for the next few bars. But I gritted my teeth and kept on conducting, somehow managing to indicate the start of the next section – Sir Joseph Porter's 'I will hear of no defence'. At that point, things started to improve and by the time we got to the last section it was, mercifully, more or less back on track.

As usual there was much sightseeing, including a coach trip to Lyttelton, the main port of the area, where we sailed round the harbour on a sixty-five-year-old launch. On the way back we stopped at a restaurant, which was listed as being in Tudor style but was more like Victorian Gothic. This had all been pleasant enough, but two days later we had a really wonderful day in the Southern Alps in well-nigh perfect weather. We travelled about three-quarters of the way across the South Island, stopping for lunch at Arthur's Pass. On the way back we came to a lake whose waters were so still that you could see the sky and mountains perfectly reflected. It was all quite breathtaking and cameras were much in evidence. I remember thinking that only the big screen could really do justice to such scenery and it is not surprising that Tolkien's *The Lord of the Rings* was filmed entirely in New Zealand. This certainly made up for the day we didn't manage to get to Rotorua, but all too soon we were back in Christchurch for another *Pinafore* and the "uncongenial gloom" of a colonial audience. On our last day, between the shows, I had a drink with some members of the orchestra. It had been a hard week for me and I was glad we were moving back to Australia.

We flew to Melbourne on July 22. After just a week each in Wellington and Christchurch it was good to be settled again for a three-week season. We played at an old Victorian theatre – the Princess. It was planned that we should give a week each of *Pinafore*, *Iolanthe* and *Mikado*. Now that we were back in Australia we again had Warwick Ross to look after the orchestras, a great relief after the problems I had had in Christchurch. There was an orchestral rehearsal in the late afternoon of July 23, followed by our first *Mikado*, one of the best opening nights so far. This in turn was followed by yet another champagne reception. Next morning I had to play for John Reed who was doing a radio interview. It was all very casual and this suited John who didn't like a lot of fuss. In the evening we had another very good house for our second *Mikado*. The shows went well for the rest of the week, although occasionally there were some strange sounds coming from the orchestra. Sometimes there was less than full sound, as when the brass and timpani failed to come in at one point during the Wednesday evening performance. Throughout the tour we had rehearsals for the next UK tour. At one of these, Jimmie Marsland could be heard muttering about the ineptitude of the latest intake: "They're doin' it all wrong, you know". Nothing new there.

My leisure time in this first week was partly taken up with an exploration of the city. It had a central grid layout that reminded me of Glasgow and it had retained its trams, which also reminded me of earlier days in Glasgow. One day I found a second-hand bookshop, which had a vast amount of old music. I bought quite a lot of it, ever thankful again of our skip and the music boxes for our band parts without which I would never have been able to get all my purchases back to the UK. Along with Patrick and Jackie Wilkes and Caroline Hudson I also met Victor Brown who had been an assistant master at Radley when Patrick's father had been headmaster there. He was an Australian by birth, and was now retired. He kindly took all of us out for the day in his 1962 Humber Super Snipe automatic and later he showed us round Ivanhoe Grammar School where he had latterly been headmaster.

On our first free Sunday, July 29, members of the Melbourne G&S Society took about twenty of us to Sovereign Hill, Ballarat, some sixty miles west of Melbourne. Ballarat had been a gold-mining town, and at Sovereign Hill, on a thirty-six-acre plot, there is a reconstruction of the town as it was in the 1850s. We went down a mining shaft and then had lunch in a hotel. In the afternoon we tried our luck at panning for gold. I didn't find anything, but one or two of the group did find some tiny specks. On the way there and back, I had long conversations with Violet Jackson, a charming lady who had been a principal in the famous J.C. Williamson Company which had first presented G&S in Australia, and had closed just three years earlier in 1976.

Next day Patrick and Jackie Wilkes, Caroline Hudson and I set out to visit Hanging Rock, the setting of Joan Lindsay's novel *Picnic at Hanging Rock* in which a group of girls from a school party inexplicably vanish during a Valentine Day's picnic. Peter Weir's film version had been made in 1975 and was fresh in our minds. The place itself is a vast outcrop of rock, several hundred feet high. It looks as if a giant has just thrown a large number of huge boulders together. It was deserted when we arrived, and was strangely atmospheric. When we got to the top we found a koala fast asleep in a gum tree. Back at ground level we encountered four coachloads of screaming children who were just beginning the ascent. We wondered if their teachers were hoping that some of the noisier ones might also vanish. We then found a table, and had our own very pleasant picnic.

We opened our second week in Melbourne with our first *Pinafore*. It went quite well, but Fraser complained of some inattention to his beat and had to go round the dressing rooms afterwards to tell everyone to watch more carefully. During the interval I met Lady Tait who had been one of the directors of the J.C. Williamson Company. As Viola Wilson she had been a principal with D'Oyly Carte from 1938 to 1939. Helen Roberts, Richard Walker and Leonard Osborn had been

Caroline Hudson, Jackie and Patrick Wilkes enjoy a picnic at Hanging Rock near Melbourne, Victoria, July 1979. No-one vanished!

among her fellow artists in those days. She had married Frank Tait, one of five brothers who eventually took control of the Williamson organisation; he had later been knighted for his services to the theatre. I also discovered that she was from Paisley (although not born there), had been a student at my old college (known as the Scottish National Academy of Music in her day), and had known many of the staff who were still there in *my* day, including former D'Oyly Carte principal Muriel Dickson.

On the morning of the 31st Fraser and I went to the Grainger Museum, repository of manuscripts and other effects relating to Percy Grainger (born in Melbourne), one of the great musical eccentrics. The exhibits included models dressed in clothes that had belonged to his composer friends Balfour Gardiner, Roger Quilter and Cyril Scott. This was certainly rather unusual, but Grainger had also wanted his skeleton to be put on display after his death; wisely, this was not done. During our time in Melbourne Grainger's widow Ella died aged ninety.

We were almost three-quarters of the way through the tour. Fraser decided to do the matinee on August 1, and during this I met Gordon MacKenzie's cousin and some other people from Greenock; we all went out for coffee. The audience that afternoon consisted of some pensioners and a horde of screaming children who chattered very loudly through the overture and most of the first act. When Fraser came out after the interval the noise was even worse and he had to shout at them to be quiet or they wouldn't hear anything (the second act starts quietly). I don't know if this had any effect. Once again it had happened while I was out of the theatre and I missed it all.

I did the evening show, and it was then my turn to experience something. After the performance an eccentric fan came to the stage door with a letter written in a school jotter that he was going to send to Dame Bridget – he spelled it Bridet [sic] – asking her to use her influence to have all of Sullivan's extant works recorded. I told him that it was an admirable idea, but it was highly unlikely that this would happen. (Thankfully most of his considerable output has now been recorded). He then said that he loved G&S and would like to be in the Company ("heaven ha'mercy"). He informed me that he had "a very good voice, not trained, of course, but a damned good voice". I was finally rescued by Caroline Hudson and we literally had to run out of the theatre to get away from him. I made some very good friends among the Company's fans, but that fellow wasn't one of them.

The following morning we had a rehearsal for *Pirates* (for the UK), and the day after that we had one for *Iolanthe*, due to open in Melbourne on Monday August 6. On the Saturday, we had the last two performances of *Pinafore* which went very well. After the evening performance the Company was invited to the theatre bar to celebrate the official centenary of the D'Oyly Carte Opera Company (originally Mr D'Oyly Carte's

Opera Company), which had fallen that week. The centenary had been celebrated in 1975 because that was the year of *Trial by Jury*, the first of the series (after *Thespis*) to involve Richard D'Oyly Carte, but there was no opera company in 1875. Gordon MacKenzie and I missed this celebration as Gordon had already invited me to meet another distant relative. At his home we listened to a number of recordings that Gordon had made, some of which he had forgotten about. One LP had been made in Dublin when D'Oyly Carte was on tour there. Gordon told me that visits to Dublin in those days were very well received; even a number like 'When Britain really ruled the waves' (*Iolanthe*) would get a rapturous ovation. But with the later advent of 'the Troubles' we visited neither Dublin nor Belfast during my time with the Company.

On our second free Sunday, August 5, there was an evening event with the Melbourne G&S Society which took place on a farm belonging to the man who had organised our trip to Ballarat. Some members of the Company had formed a group and they sang arrangements of popular numbers such as 'Stormy Weather' and 'Money, Money, Money'. Afterwards the 1939 film of *The Mikado*, which we had seen the previous year in San Diego, was shown again. The following day we opened the third week with *Iolanthe*. We hadn't done it since Sydney, and the orchestra had only had one rehearsal for it, but despite this it went remarkably well. Before the show Patrick and Jackie Wilkes, Caroline Hudson and I treated Victor Brown to a meal to thank him for his hospitality during the first week. After the show the Company recorded 'Hail, Poetry' (*Pirates*) and 'Three cheers' for *This is your Life, Sir Charles Mackerras* which was to be shown the following week. The eccentric fan appeared again, but we avoided him and instead met Harry and Phyllis Brusey from Wellington.

On August 7 Jimmie Marsland and I went to see Dame Joan Sutherland as Donna Anna in Mozart's *Don Giovanni*, conducted by her husband Richard Bonynge. Now in her fifties her voice was still excellent. We heard later that our second *Iolanthe* hadn't been so good that night. August 8 was matinee day and it had been decided that the evening performance would be the last *Iolanthe*. Between the shows we had some drinks in the band room to thank the orchestra for their work. John Reed had already intimated that he would be leaving the Company at the end of the tour and this was his last appearance as the Lord Chancellor, although this went unheralded by just about everyone. We returned to *Mikado* for the last three days. Fraser did the first performance on the Thursday, but, as usual, he was flying on ahead to our penultimate stop, Adelaide, and I had to do the last performances. On the Saturday both Barbara Lilley and Philip Potter were off due to illness and it had also been decided that John Reed could have a day off. Days off had become quite common, but not on the last Saturday of a season – and particularly in one of the best dates of the tour. In the circumstances it was an unfortunate decision to allow this one.

We flew to Adelaide for two weeks on Sunday August 12. For some reason the staff left much earlier and as there were only about a dozen of us we were ferried to the airport in several taxis. When we arrived we found that something had gone wrong with our wig mistress Heather Perkins' cab, and the boot had become red hot. This had caused damage to her case and to several items in it, including some cine film she had taken – something one can never replace. Adelaide time was half an hour behind Melbourne, an arrangement I had not come across before. The Festival Theatre, right in the centre of the city, was very modern and to my mind very ugly. It looked like nothing more than a gigantic geometric shape, but it was well appointed inside. We stayed at the Arkaba Court Motel at Fullerton, some way out of the city centre, and I had an entertaining time sharing with James Conroy-Ward who was a clever mimic (often imitating Freddie Lloyd). We opened with *Pinafore*, but only gave four performances of it before changing to *Mikado*, which we also did throughout the second week – twelve performances in all.

There was another live TV spot on the Monday morning, but this one almost didn't happen. Once again the artists were Meston Reid and Vivian Tierney. We met first at the theatre where they were to change into their *Pinafore* costumes, but the skips had only just arrived and it took some time to locate everything. At 11am when the show was due to begin, we were still in the theatre, but after a mad dash across town we arrived at the studio and managed to go on at 11.25am. Just as the interview preceding their duet ('Refrain, audacious tar') was about to start, the soprano June Bronhill walked in to the studio. She and Meston knew each other very well, but neither knew that the other was due to be there, and the shock on their faces was very obvious. As the show was now under way they couldn't shout out and to see them mouthing ecstatic greetings in complete silence was extremely funny. It quite put Meston off his stride and he didn't sing very well. Afterwards, in the studio, they did get together, embrace and arrange to meet later – all still in complete silence!

In the afternoon, this time in the theatre, there was another TV spot (filmed as a rehearsal), which Fraser played for; this was followed by an orchestral rehearsal before we opened in the evening. The players here were very good. After the performance, which went well, there was another Benson and Hedges reception. It had been an interesting first day. I discovered later that there had been a lady at the reception whose mother, still alive at ninety-nine, had supposedly been the youngest Yum-Yum (*Mikado*) ever – presumably as a teenager, which would have been in the late 1890s when Gilbert, Sullivan and D'Oyly Carte were all still alive. Another link with history.

We had various morning rehearsals for our forthcoming autumn tour in the UK, with the usual free afternoons to explore. One place we visited was the German-speaking community and township of Hahndorf. We went there on a minibus with several other people, including a couple from Tasmania who had come to see *Mikado* that very evening; there was also a professional musician from San Diego who had played for the Company on its 1968–69 tour – a small world. Our opening *Mikado* went well, but there was a very odd crit the following morning. After the show Meston Reid appeared in the motel bar with a man from his hometown of Banchory. They had known each other as children, but hadn't met for some twenty years; Meston was soon singing bothy ballads with gusto. There was another TV spot on August 17; this time I had to record something with Barbara Lilley. It was shown at six that evening, and we managed to watch it in the theatre. After the performance there was a party given by Elizabeth Silsbury, a local musician of some standing who, it turned out, had written the strange crit of *Mikado*.

On the Saturday I did the matinee and Fraser did the evening performance. During the interval he seemed rather depressed and I gathered that there had been developments at home. Apparently the Musicians' Union was demanding higher rates for the orchestra and if the money wasn't forthcoming then the orchestra would be reduced – to ten players if necessary, with all the scores rewritten. This was certainly rather depressing news. A rare event after the evening performance was a Company party. Not everyone turned up, but it was good fun, and went on until the small hours. Luckily next day was Sunday and I spent most of it recharging the batteries. In the evening we watched *This is Your Life, Sir Charles Mackerras* to which we had earlier contributed two items – but they only used the 'Three cheers'.

On Monday August 20 five of us set out early to explore the Barossa Valley, a famous wine-producing area, in a car that Barry Clark had hired for the week. I had noticed that there was a place there called Greenock and I wanted to see what it was like. It turned out to be a small community, but it did have a post office and a few shops. I bought a number of souvenirs and took some photographs. We then moved on to Chateau Tanunda, the home of Seppelt, one of the largest companies in the area. We toured the vineyard and sampled their wares. I bought a bottle of Greenock Sauterne [sic], 1977 vintage. I still have the empty bottle with its label. In the evening we had a very small audience for our first *Mikado* of the week. Apparently this was due to incompetence on the part of the publicity department. Afterwards we took Warwick Ross out for a meal to thank him for his work fixing the various orchestras during our time in Australia.

Wednesday 22nd was matinee day, and during the interval I met some distant relatives of Dame Bridget. They were members of the Black family, descendants of John, the brother of Helen Couper Black, Richard D'Oyly Carte's second wife and Dame Bridget's step-grandmother whom she had met when she was a small child. The matriarch of this group was John's daughter, now eighty-two. There were apparently many family members in the Adelaide area, but few of them had ever been in touch with Dame Bridget. It was another interesting connection with the early days of the Company. As I had conducted the matinee I had a night off and I went to see Joan Fox, sister of Ivan (our former leader in the UK) and Colin who had played for us in Brisbane. Unlike her brothers Joan wasn't a professional musician, but she had an enormous Bechstein grand piano, which I played for about an hour after a very nice meal. Joan also had two beautiful Burmese cats, which seemed to enjoy the vibrations from the piano. On the Friday I took a tram to Glenelg on the coast and then met Joan for a meal in town. She came to *Mikado* in the evening. After the performance Beti Lloyd-Jones had a birthday party (although her birthday was the following day). Everyone made an effort to dress a bit more formally for this. Many of the men were in dinner jackets and the ladies were resplendent in various attires. It was a good evening, and there was even some old-time dancing.

Saturday was our last day in Adelaide and again I had to conduct both shows as Fraser had flown ahead to Perth. There were quite a few hangovers from Beti's party and the matinee was a bit subdued – like the audience. The evening performance was our last *Mikado* in Australia and the last for a number of the cast. Inevitably it occasioned some silliness on stage, such as people changing costumes, and this didn't go down very well. Although a production should be presented in the same way at every performance it is accepted that deviations do sometimes occur for one reason or another – "but the line must be drawn somewhere". John Reed was leaving at the end of the tour and this was to be his last performance as Ko-Ko, at least for D'Oyly Carte. It should also have been Philip Potter's last appearance as Nanki-Poo, but he was suffering from laryngitis and hadn't appeared at either performance. John didn't seem in any way concerned that this was his last Ko-Ko, but I was particularly pleased to be conducting on this occasion. We said goodbye to the orchestra, and I discovered that one of the players came from Wishaw, near Glasgow, and had also studied at the RSAMD – a small world indeed.

We had now arrived at the last date on the tour, and on August 26 flew to Perth, Western Australia – the State was celebrating its sesquicentennial. We were there for just under two weeks and played only *Pinafore*. (Philip Potter and Ken Sandford were not required for this opera and they flew back to London.) The accommodation was at Mountside serviced flats, which were fairly basic, with no telephone and only a black and white TV. This didn't please some people who immediately started to look for something else, although I can't remember if anyone found anything. Once again I shared with Gordon MacKenzie. There was no available theatre in Perth and we performed at the Concert Hall. This wasn't really suitable as it had no proscenium arch or tabs and little in the way of facilities. The cast had to walk on at the beginning and walk off at the end of each act in blackout, and this rather spoiled the marvellous effect of the curtain rising in Act I on the sailors going about their duties on deck (which often occasioned a round of applause). There was another TV spot on the morning of the 27th, which Fraser played for, and an orchestral rehearsal in the afternoon. Bob Ingram, who had led for us earlier, was with us again, and we were pleased to see him. In the evening we gave our first performance, which again went well, This was followed by another reception at which I met Western Australia's premier, Sir Charles Court, and his wife.

Next morning I was walking along St George's Terrace, heading towards the Concert Hall for a *Gondoliers* rehearsal, when I was literally stopped in my tracks by a newspaper headline: "Lord Mountbatten assassinated". I bought a paper to find out what had happened. Other members of Mountbatten's family had also been killed, and shortly after this eighteen British soldiers had been killed at Warrenpoint. Sadly we have become all too used to acts of violence, but events of this kind were still comparatively rare in 1979. (This, of course, was all part of 'the Troubles'.) It was hard to concentrate on the *Gondoliers* rehearsal, or, indeed, the evening performance of *Pinafore*. I wondered what it would be like when we got home, envisaging tightened security and possibly armed police at the airport. (Again, sadly, this is now commonplace.) Next day I conducted the matinee - my first performance here. During the opening of Act I a terrible buzzing noise started; it turned out to be from the microphone that Ken Robertson was using for his announcements. Mercifully it was quickly traced and silenced.

Much of my social life in Perth was with members of my own family. My cousin Muriel, daughter of my father's eldest brother, was married to a doctor and they had emigrated to Australia in the early 1950s, which involved a long sea voyage in those days, settling first in Perth before moving to Wagin, a small town about one hundred and fifty miles to the south-east. Muriel's daughter Wilma and her husband Arthur lived at Carine, just north of Perth, and I saw them and their daughter Catherine (their son John was at a school camp) on Thursday August 30 which, for some reason, had been designated a free day for the Company. Arthur had a small boat and we sailed from his yacht club down to Fremantle. It was beautiful day, but quite breezy, and partly due to this we had a minor collision with another boat. Luckily there was little damage done to either. In the evening we had a meal in a revolving restaurant – Hilite 33 – at the top of the tallest building in Perth. Unfortunately much of the city was blacked out due to a State Electricity workers' strike, but more lights came on from time to time which enabled us to see more than when we had arrived.

Another month was gone and there was just one more week to go. My cousins, Muriel and Jimmy, arrived from Wagin in the afternoon, and we had a quick meal before the show. There were only five performances in the first week. We had already had one free day and the Saturday was also free, which meant that I could go to Wagin for a long weekend, returning on the Monday. I spent a pleasant two days there. They had recently moved into a new home, their former house being retained as Jimmy's surgery. We talked much about family matters and looked at old photographs. There were even some tape recordings of my late uncle and aunt, the latter singing Haydn Wood's 'A Brown Bird Singing'. Muriel had always loved horses and she now had a small stud that was just a few hundred yards from the new house. On the day after my arrival we discovered that someone had stolen a rug from the back of one of the horses. As there was a local hunt that afternoon we suspected that the rug might turn up there. After informing the police we went to the returning point of the hunt to see if we could find anything. Perhaps not surprisingly we didn't, but it was still an interesting afternoon.

On Monday I said goodbye to Jimmy, who then had to go to the surgery. Muriel drove me back to Perth in the afternoon. With such a long journey she had decided to stay overnight and do some shopping next morning before driving back to Wagin. After saying goodbye to her I went into the Concert Hall, and discovered that we would give our last performance the following day, Tuesday September 4. We were not due to fly back until the Friday and now found ourselves with yet more free time ("too much happiness!"), although originally these two days had been marked as 'tentative' and could well have seen performances. On that last working day I bought some opals, and also the sheet music of 'Waltzing Matilda' and the patriotic song 'Advance Australia Fair', which I had often heard at the end of a day's TV broadcasts. It became the official national anthem in 1984.

In the evening we gave our last *Pinafore*. As it was to be John Reed's last performance – no one at the time had any idea what was to happen just a few years later and that John would return for guest appearances – there was a small change to one of the encores in 'Never mind the why and wherefore'. Normally, at about the fourth or fifth encore, chorister Guy Matthews would come on with a glass of water on a salver after John, feigning exhaustion, had managed to gasp out the single word "... water... " from his line "And a lord who rules the water " in the refrain. On this occasion a small bottle of champagne was substituted – a gesture that was probably lost on the audience. The performance was not marred by any silliness such as we had seen during the last *Mikado* in Adelaide and it went very well. We had drinks with the orchestra afterwards, and said our goodbyes to Bob Ingram and the others. As far as work was concerned the tour was now over.

This extra free time was becoming an embarrassment. We had had a week at the beginning of the tour, admittedly to let everyone get used to the time difference, and had already had two free days in Perth. Now we were to have another two (and no jet lag to worry about). Once again I could hear Freddie Lloyd's words from 1976 – "more like a paid holiday" – but we had the time, and we made good use of it. On the Wednesday a number of the Company went to Rottnest Island, which lies about twelve miles west of Fremantle. Like Sark in the Channel Islands it has no motorised transport, apart from a few necessary vehicles, and the way to get around is to hire bicycles; this we did. The island is home to the quokka, a small marsupial that looks like a large rat but is friendly and harmless. We came across one on the road. It was surrounded by an "admiring crowd of sisters, cousins and aunts" who were feeding it with orange peel. It was a delightful day.

Cycling on Rottnest Island, off Perth, Western Australia, September 1979. L-r: Caroline Hudson, Alexandra Hann, Hélène Witcombe, Alan Rice.

Back in Perth we went to the Concert Hall in the evening, this time as audience, to hear the West Australian Symphony Orchestra, conducted by David Measham, playing Berlioz, Haydn and Respighi – something of a change from G&S. The soloist was the Australian mezzo-soprano Yvonne Minton who sang some Mahler songs and the rarely heard *Cleopatra – Lyric Scene* by Berlioz. Fraser had noticed that two of the orchestral players had recently been students at London's Guildhall School of Music, and the leader of the second violins was a friend of my cousins Muriel and Jimmy. We met all three of them at the interval and had a meal afterwards with the two Guildhall students.

On our last full day, September 6, I bought some more souvenirs and did as much packing as I could. My cousin Wilma then arrived to take Caroline Hudson and me back to their house at Carine where we had a meal and talked for about two hours. Next morning our luggage was collected at noon. Despite being able to send some of my purchases, mainly books and music, back to the UK with our orchestral parts, I still had a quantity of material which was crammed into three tightly packed canvas bags. We were only supposed to have one piece of hand luggage on the plane and I had to do some rearranging to enable me to get it all back home. We weren't leaving until the evening and our little dining club went to a very nice fish restaurant for a final outing.

My cousins Wilma, Arthur, Catherine and John all turned up to see us off. They had brought photographs taken at the revolving restaurant the previous Thursday – even more souvenirs. We finally took off at about 11pm, and travelled throughout September 8, stopping again at Bombay where the temperature was 79 degrees Fahrenheit. I didn't go out. We landed at Heathrow on the morning of September 9 after a flight of some 21 hours. After saying goodbye to those who were leaving the Company, Gordon MacKenzie and I caught the shuttle flight to Glasgow. We were met by Gordon's daughter Michelle who drove us back to Greenock – along with twelve items of luggage.

We now had four weeks' holiday. I spent the first one in Greenock and managed to persuade our local paper, the *Greenock Telegraph*, to print a short account of my visit to 'the other Greenock' in South Australia – along with a photograph of its post office. I also changed my car for a second-hand, but still fairly new Renault 16. Having been fully employed for four years, and particularly with the two foreign tours, which were very lucrative, I was able to write out a cheque for £3,000. I felt like a millionaire. Then, as if I hadn't had enough travelling and sightseeing, I had a two-week holiday in Portugal with Caroline Hudson and her family.

There had been quite an exodus after the tour and the new choristers were Pamela Baxter, Janet Henderson, Michelle Shipley, Clive Birch, Alistair Donkin, Bruce Graham, who had been a pupil of Muriel Dickson, and Michael Lessiter. The principals were Evette Davis (soprano, replacing Vivian Tierney who had left to have a baby), Harold Sharples (tenor) and

Clive Harré (baritone). I had played for most of them at their auditions. We also had a new principal comedian in James Conroy-Ward who was taking over from John Reed – a hard act to follow. Music rehearsals had started for the new choristers on September 3. Paul Seeley had been available to play for some of these, but as Fraser and I were still in Australia the London office had to find someone else as well, and my predecessor Glyn Hale was called in for the week of September 10–14. Production rehearsals started on September 24, but I was still on holiday in Portugal. I had one more week's holiday (October 1–7), and that was the end of my fourth year with D'Oyly Carte.

Chapter 5: 1979–1980

I

My fifth year began on Monday October 8 when the Company reassembled for another year's touring. With so many new choristers and principals there were two weeks of rehearsals. The second week was given over to a run-through of the operas we were taking out on tour, starting with *Iolanthe* on the Monday, then *Pirates*, *Yeomen*, *Mikado*, and ending with *Gondoliers* on the Friday. In the middle of this rehearsal period our former principals Julia Goss, Jane Metcalfe, Geoffrey Shovelton, Michael Rayner and Jon Ellison (Gilbert and Sullivan Unlimited) gave another concert for the Tradescant Trust at St Mary's Church, Lambeth, but I wasn't involved in this one. They were accompanied by the Sullivan String Quartet, our players from the orchestra.

At the beginning of the Australasian tour I had received a letter from Freddie Lloyd offering me a further year's work at a salary of £72 per week, with a subsistence allowance of £55 per week until March 15, 1980 when it was going to rise to £58.20. Towards the end of the tour I received another letter to say that my salary would now be £80 per week, but that wasn't the end of the story. To my astonishment I received a third letter, dated 5th October, to say that my salary was to be upped again, this time to £90 per week. If they could afford to do this then perhaps the Company's finances were not as bad as we had been led to believe. (The annual dress allowance remained unchanged at £65.) We were now ready for another year of touring.

The Australasian tour was the last major event during my time in D'Oyly Carte, apart from the last day and final Last Night in 1982 ("a most painful scene, my Lords – most painful!") So far, for me, it had been a succession of steps up the ladder: joining the Company as repetiteur, then promotion to chorus master and associate conductor, and then two wonderful foreign tours. What could possibly follow that? There was no immediate prospect of another foreign tour, although at this stage we were still unaware of the short time left to the Company. For the moment it was simply back to the old routine of touring around the UK.

We began with a week at a new venue for me, the King's Theatre in Southsea (October 22–27). Designed by Frank Matcham, it had been purchased in 1964 by Commander and Mrs Cooper. It had a very nice auditorium, but the backstage facilities were among the worst I had yet encountered. There was no proper band room and the players simply had to make do with whatever space they could find under the stage, this area being littered with theatrical detritus of all sorts. We had the usual orchestral seating call on the first day and I went in early to get this organised. While I was standing in the pit I saw a huge cockroach, the largest one I had ever seen outside the United States. The theatre was near the sea and there was a cistern under the stage that would start working (even during a performance) if there was any flooding. It could certainly be heard if you were in the pit, although I don't know that the sound would have penetrated much beyond the front row of the stalls. A more pleasant aspect of being in Hampshire was the close proximity of more relatives, June and Ron Millar. June was the younger sister of my cousin Muriel in Australia and I spent a pleasant afternoon at their home at Liss, near Petersfield, telling them about our recent tour 'down under' and my visits to the family in Perth and Wagin. The programme for Southsea was rather unusual, being almost entirely devoted to *Mikado* (four performances) and *Pirates* (three performances), with just one performance of *Yeomen* on Tuesday 23rd. *Pinafore* and

Iolanthe were, of course, still in transit from Australia. The matinee here was again on Thursday.

On Sunday October 28 it was time to move on again. We now faced a very long journey from Southsea to Sunderland where we played for two weeks (October 29–November 10). The Empire at Sunderland, another new venue for me, had a rather unusual balcony whose sides, known as slippers, swept down almost to stage level. It was the largest theatre in the north-east, with a capacity of around two thousand, and was, again, really too big for us. There was also much unemployment in the area at that time and the town itself looked somewhat down at heel. We wondered if two weeks in Sunderland might just be 'a week too far'. There was another Barclays reception after the opening performance of *Mikado* on October 29, held this time in the circle vestibule in the theatre. Our rehearsals were in a variety of venues including the Tyne and Wear Theatre Rehearsal Rooms and a Leisure Centre that was just opposite the theatre. On the Friday of the first week we had a full rehearsal onstage, with the orchestra, for *Iolanthe*, the set and costumes having arrived back from Australia. Somewhat unusually, on Sunday November 4, there was a D'Oyly Carte in Concert in Sunderland itself. I conducted *Iolanthe* on the Monday, and also *Mikado* on the Tuesday. On the second Friday there was a nominated dress rehearsal for *Gondoliers*.

A highlight of our time in Tyne and Wear was a midnight beach barbecue at Marsden Grotto, a few miles up the coast at South Shields, after the first performance of *Gondoliers*. John Ayldon was able to organise this as he didn't appear in *Gondoliers*. The descent to the beach, via a zigzag staircase from the clifftop, was quite hair-raising – and the ascent after much alcohol was even worse! It was certainly an unusual event, at a particularly unusual venue, and luckily it didn't rain. Being in Sunderland for two weeks we performed all five operas, but the number of performances of each was typical of what we had to do to get maximum audiences: *Mikado* (five); *Pirates* (four); *Iolanthe* (three); *Gondoliers* (three) and *Yeomen* – just once on

Friday November 2. It would not have been financially viable to perform *Yeomen* twice on one of the matinee days, but all of the other four did have matinee performances here. Several of us, including Gordon MacKenzie, stayed on a caravan site, which was located somewhere between Sunderland and Newcastle.

After Sunderland we moved to the Opera House, Blackpool for a week. Once again we were in a huge theatre – with its awkward pit that the conductor had to slide into over the catwalk – that we could never fill. We played four operas here: *Pirates*, *Iolanthe*, *Mikado* and *Gondoliers*, with, not surprisingly, *Pirates* and *Mikado* on matinee days. There wasn't much to do in Blackpool out of season, apart from visiting Blackpool Tower or taking a tram to Fleetwood, but there was always Yates's Wine Lodge in which to while away an idle hour. Another round of auditions on November 16 didn't produce anyone for the Company. The following day Fraser gave me a provisional list of the performances I would be conducting up to and including the London season. Apart from the matinees there were many more evening ones than I had done under Royston, but I had already done more of these since Fraser took over, including the week in Christchurch in New Zealand. We then had two weeks at the Theatre Royal, Nottingham. Many of the old theatres that I had first known in my early days with the Company were at last being modernised, and the Theatre Royal now had splendid new dressing-room accommodation. Our room, which was quite large, had office-type chairs with castors and it was great fun propelling them around like demented dodgem cars. (In the film *Witness*, with Harrison Ford, there is a scene where the Amish family are having a meal, and the father is sitting in one of these chairs. He then has to pick up something from the other side of the room, and without getting out of the chair he propels himself across the room and back again - just as we used to do at Nottingham.) There were more auditions on November 22 (the anniversary of Sullivan's death), but, as so often, we never found places for any of the five hopefuls who turned up. We also held a number of orchestral auditions in Nottingham.

A few days later I received a letter from James Lawrie, the editor of *The Savoyard*. I had written to him suggesting that he might like to have an article on the Australasian tour and possibly also something on the 1978 tour of North America as I had kept diaries throughout each of these. I had also suggested that he might like to consider a series of articles on Sullivan's style, although I did wonder if any deeper probing into the use of triads, repeated notes and other musical devices might prove to be too complicated for some readers. In his reply he said that he had not received any material about the Australasian tour, but had somehow managed to compile a complete *Savoyard*. Referring to my other suggestion he also said, with characteristic turns of phrase, that while he wasn't too concerned about articles on Sullivan's style being above the heads of some *Savoyard* readers he wouldn't welcome copious music extracts. The magazine's printers didn't have any music type and music examples had to be photographed and then sometimes enlarged or reduced to make them fit the pages. Despite all of this he finished by saying that he was delighted to hear from me with these ideas – "It's the best news the editor has had for some time!" In the second week, as well as the Wednesday matinee of *Mikado*, I had to conduct *Gondoliers* on the Monday and *Iolanthe* on the Friday. The set and costumes for *Pinafore* were also now back from Australia, and there was a nominated dress rehearsal on November 27 followed by a performance that evening; there were two more performances on our last day, Saturday December 1. The matinees here were at 2pm – another potential trap when everyone was used to the more normal 2.30pm.

On December 2 we moved to Norwich for two weeks for the third successive year. Once again we could do our Christmas shopping in a comparatively leisurely way. The theatre, as before, looked very festive and inviting, with the coloured lights round the main entrance and general manager Dick Condon dispensing Irish blarney along with pints of 'Chateau Liffey'. The following week Michael Heyland, our former production director, came to the theatre to give a talk about his production of *The Sorcerer* which we would be giving during the London season. I had seen it in Birmingham in July 1975, when the Company had no less than ten operas with them, including *Trial* with *Pinafore*, and was looking forward to seeing it again and eventually conducting it.

An unusual event here was a concert on Sunday December 9 at St Margaret's Church, Sprowston on the north-eastern edge of Norwich. It was given by principal soprano Evette Davis and several members of the chorus, who appeared "by kind permission of Bridget D'Oyly Carte". This had come about through one of our ex-choristers, Richard Mitchell, who had been born in Norwich. The first half was given over to G&S, but the second half consisted of a wide range of items, from Handel and Mozart to Ivor Novello and Andrew Lloyd Webber. I played for some items and Richard Braebrook, who also sang, played for others; a third accompanist was John Coe-Roper. John also sang Warlock's 'Yarmouth Fair' and played Rachmaninov's famous *Prelude* in C sharp minor. We even had a member of the orchestra, trumpeter Tim Hawes, playing the obbligato in 'The trumpet shall sound' (*Messiah*), which was sung by Alan Rice. The concert finished, appropriately, with a number of Christmas carols, including Cornelius's delightful 'Three Kings From Persian Lands Afar'. It was a rare event in the annals of D'Oyly Carte, matched only in my time by the concert at Severna Park, Maryland (for Richard Mitchell's cousin) and the cabaret in Boston, during the 1978 tour of North America. It was a chance for the chorus to show what they could do and to sing items other than G&S.

There were more auditions the following day, this time at the Savoy Theatre. Among some twenty-five auditionees we heard Caroline Tatlow (alto) who joined the Company the following March. Back in Norwich the Company was again invited to the Traffords' lovely home at Wroxham after the evening performance of *Pinafore* on December 12. We finished our season that week with two performances of *Pirates* on December 15, at both of which Major-General Stanley was played by Alistair Donkin who eventually took over the role, as James Conroy-Ward had previously taken it over from John Reed. After this we moved back to London. We didn't open on the Monday because of a lighting rehearsal, and I took the opportunity to pay a visit to the Nationwide Building Society to discuss my plan to purchase a property in Eastbourne. Our London season was shorter this year, just nine weeks, and again in association with Barclays Bank. During the season a further grant was made by the Ellerman Charitable Trusts [sic] to cover operating costs. Members of the orchestra, led by Geoff Short, were now listed individually in the programmes.

We opened our London season with *Gondoliers* on December 18 at Sadler's Wells. While the show was running I went with John Ayldon to the Berkeley Hotel where, with the Gilbert and Sullivan Unlimited group (John was replacing Jon Ellison), we performed at a party given by Sir James Hanson. Hanson Trust had been one of the sponsors of the North American tour in 1978. There was another performance of *Gondoliers* the following evening (no Wednesday matinee), and this was followed by a half-week of *Mikado* (December 20–22). On the morning of December 20 there was another full Company rehearsal, this time for *Pirates*. Christmas Day this year was on a Tuesday and to save opening the theatre for one day on the Monday we had the luxury of a four-day break. But to make up for the long break there were now six performances of *Pirates* over three days – a test of stamina for everyone, and particularly for our new principal soprano Evette Davis as Mabel. (There may also have been a performance by her understudy Jane Stanford.)

On December 31 we gave one more performance of *Pirates*. It had been deliberately arranged that we play *Pirates* on this date, as it was the opera's centenary, the premiere having taken place in New York on New Year's Eve, 1879. There had been a performance of sorts at the Royal Bijou Theatre in Paignton, Devon on December 30, 1879 to secure the British copyright, but we couldn't acknowledge this in the theatre, as December 30, 1979 was a Sunday. But some celebration was clearly in order and a centenary cake was brought on to the stage after the performance on the 29th. After the singing of 'Happy birthday', it was cut by Meston Reid, still in his costume as Frederic. We had had a spectacular centenary celebration of *Pinafore* in San Francisco the previous year and it was felt that the centenary performance of *Pirates* on December 31 should also be special in some way. Accordingly, while Fraser conducted Act I, Act II was conducted by no less than Sir Charles Mackerras, well known as a lover of Sullivan's music. The orchestra had not been told that Sir Charles was coming, and it was something of a shock for them when he walked into the pit after the interval. After this performance a similar procedure was followed, and another very large cake was brought on, cut this time by Sir Charles. We gave three cheers, followed by the traditional 'Auld Lang Syne', with those members of the Company nearest the front moving down the aprons to link hands with the audience. Those who did this then moved back to the stage, and we sang the national anthem. And so ended 1979.

There was no performance on New Year's Day, but we were back on January 2, 1980 with two more performances of *Pirates*, followed by eight performances of *Iolanthe* split in the usual way: Thursday, Friday, Saturday - Monday, Tuesday, Wednesday. On Monday, January 7, I went down to Eastbourne by train to see an estate agent, an indication that we still had no idea of how little time the Company had left to run. I was told that it should be quite easy to find a first-floor flat there. With so many elderly inhabitants, it was ground-floor properties that were in short supply. Back in London a week of *Pinafore* followed *Iolanthe*, and this was followed by a half-week each of *Yeomen*, *Mikado*, *Pirates* and *Pinafore*, and then a full week of *Mikado,* which took us into February. There was another concert at Bray on Sunday February 3 – now established as an annual event.

Many of our rehearsals, from December 20, had been for *The Sorcerer*, and in January there were costume fittings for the entire cast held at the Company's wardrobe department in Walworth. One of the reasons that the Company enjoyed *Sorcerer* was that they were cast as individuals representing a rural community in bygone days: an old man, a farmer, old ladies, maids, flunkies, smart villagers, the town band (serpent, cornet and drum), and even 'yokels' and a 'village idiot'. (Would the latter be acceptable in today's politically correct world?) There was a nominated dress rehearsal on Tuesday February 5, a second one on Wednesday 6th, and *Sorcerer* opened on Thursday February 7 for a run of six performances: Thursday, Friday, Saturday (2), and the following Monday and Tuesday. It was good to see it again, and to be able to conduct it. For these performances the small role of the Notary was taken by John Broad, standing in for Bryan Secombe who was ill. John had played this part during his years with the Company from 1969–75. I was to meet him again in 1981. There were more auditions on February 8, and again on the 11th. We heard forty people on each day. From the first batch we took Margaret Williams (later Lynn-Williams), and from the second we took Peter Robinson (later James-Robinson whom we had heard before) and Richard Wales. We then returned to *Gondoliers* for five performances (this time with a Wednesday matinee on February 13) before the Last Night on February 16. In this season we hadn't performed *Patience*, *Ida* or *Ruddigore*.

The last week in London was also interesting in other ways. On the Sunday I met up with an old college friend, clarinettist Kenneth McAllister. Ken had played in D'Oyly Carte before I joined in 1975, and had married Susan Minshull, one of our choristers. Their wedding photograph had appeared in the May 1972 edition of *The Savoyard*. As the January 1980 edition went to press, it was announced that the editor, James Lawrie, who had written to me so recently, had died. There was a musical tribute to him at the Lyric Theatre, Hammersmith on Tuesday February 12. His interests had been wide and varied, and among those taking part were Sir Peter Pears and the accompanist Roger Vignoles, who also played some solos. D'Oyly Carte was represented by Julia Goss, who had left the Company by this time, John Ayldon, James Conroy-Ward, Meston Reid and myself. Julia sang the 'Ave Maria' from Verdi's *Otello*, the men sang the trio 'If you go in' from *Iolanthe*, and Julia, James and John sang 'Never mind the why and wherefore' from *Pinafore*; I played for all of these. Dame Bridget, Freddie Lloyd and Albert Truelove were among those who attended. Along with other Company members I had received an invitation to attend a buffet lunch that day at Barclays Bank in Gracechurch Street, but this was now impossible as we were at Hammersmith. The invitations were from Sir Anthony Tuke, chairman of Barclays Bank, who as plain Mr Anthony Tuke had become a D'Oyly Carte trustee the previous year. His father A.W. Tuke, a former chairman of Barclays, had been the first chairman of the D'Oyly Carte Opera Trust Limited.

And so we came to another eagerly awaited Last Night which, as always, didn't disappoint those who managed to get tickets in the ballot – and the Last Nights were as much fun for the Company as for the audience. One of this year's highlights was a splendid arrangement by Paul Seeley of the Peers' Chorus (*Iolanthe*) in which the noble lords became American marines. This number had the addition of a saxophone played by one of our clarinettists Michael Penny. Another showstopper was a decidedly saucy rendition of 'If somebody there chanced to be' (*Ruddigore*), sung by Evette Davis sitting provocatively on a chair. Patricia Leonard appeared as both Carol Channing, complete with hat, and Shirley Temple, and Lorraine Daniels appeared as her Cockney namesake Lorraine Chase. As we had been 'down under' in 1979 there was a Maori version of 'Braid the raven hair' (*Mikado*) with more help from the orchestra. This included a bass guitar played by Lesley Drury, one of the extra London players, and a vigorous percussion backing from Peter Hamburger who had succeeded Harry Smaile as our resident timpanist. Ken Sandford also made an appearance in his prizewinning Dame Edna Everage costume from the fancy dress party in Sydney. The excellent choreography was, as usual, by Alan Spencer.

In keeping with the Company's policy of adding other music by Sullivan to some of its recent recordings I conducted Charles Godfrey's selection of items from *The Rose of Persia* (1899) – Sullivan's last completed opera – using a set of band parts kindly loaned to us by David Eden of the recently formed (1977) Sir Arthur Sullivan Society. It was a particularly good evening and Freddie Lloyd was moved to write letters thanking us for the hard work that had resulted in what he called "a brilliant occasion". We sometimes wished that we could perform these Last Nights in other towns and cities, but that wasn't really a serious option. They would have meant very little to general audiences who were not familiar with the G&S repertoire, our own productions, or the individual performers. They were just a very special part of the London season. And now another provincial tour was about to begin.

II

We opened with two weeks at the Pavilion in Bournemouth. In common with most of the older theatres the Pavilion had no air conditioning. It could be stifling in hot weather, but it was quite cosy at other times of the year. On the Friday of the first week a number of us paid another visit to Mrs Yorke Batley at Kit's Close for more card games, sherry and boiled eggs – a treat not to be missed. As 1980 was a leap year, and with the *Pirates* centenary just behind us, it was appropriate that Frederic should celebrate his thirty-first birthday on February 29.

We then had another week in Eastbourne; this was very useful for me as I met a lady at the estate agent's office who was selling a first-floor flat. Before we left I had agreed to purchase the flat, although I didn't complete the sale until we were further north, and didn't move in until much later. Eastbourne was followed by two weeks in Bristol. On Friday March 14 there was a staff meeting where we heard that it seemed quite certain that there would be another North American tour in 1982. This was excellent news, and a good excuse for another visit to the Rajdoot.

I had already visited all of the first three cities on this tour, but the order in which we played them was slightly erratic. A better order would have been Eastbourne, Bournemouth and Bristol, but the Company was now less able to plan a logical progression around the country in the way that it was once able to do; this was just another indication that all was not well. Playing the three dates in this order meant that more driving was involved, but driving was already part of the job, and my new car, the Renault 16 – one of the last production models, if not *the* last, with a column gear change – was very comfortable and took all the extra mileage in its stride. It was also a bigger car than my previous one and was ideal for touring as I could pack much more into it. Some people travelled around the country with a mountain of luggage. Beti Lloyd-Jones, for instance, always carried a selection of pots, pans and other utensils, almost everything but the proverbial kitchen sink, rather than trust to what might be available in self-catering apartments.

On our free Sunday in Bristol (March 16) there was a D'Oyly Carte in Concert in Plymouth. Luckily there were no Monday morning rehearsals after the long drive back, but there was a staff meeting at lunchtime on the Monday; this was held in the Royal Hotel. Among various things discussed were the general state of the Company, the recent Field Day, and covers for the comedy roles, which were to be divided between Alistair Donkin and Clive Birch. We also discussed two of the operas, *Patience* and *Gondoliers*. *Patience* was currently out of the repertoire, but it would be the next opera to celebrate its centenary (in 1981), and we surely couldn't "let that pass". But we were aware that October 1981 would also see the centenary of the Savoy Theatre and perhaps that would be the time, if a little late, to mark the *Patience* centenary. The *Gondoliers* set needed replacing, and wigs and costumes needed some attention, so we had to decide if it should come out of the repertoire to enable all of this to be done. It did eventually come out and, like *Patience* and *Princess Ida*, was never performed again by the Company. We had more auditions when we heard another dozen hopefuls, not one of whom we took on.

Bristol was followed by another new venue for most of us, the Tameside Theatre in Ashton-under-Lyne. This had been a cinema, and consequently had very little dressing room space. Portacabins had to be hired to make up the deficiency and these sat in the street outside the stage door. It was far from ideal, particularly if it happened to be raining – and we were there for two weeks. Some of our rehearsals were held in the theatre bar. Being reasonably close to Manchester, several of the fans there, including members of the Manchester G&S Society, came to the theatre. Norman Beckett, the secretary, actually wrote to me to say that he and his wife had never been to Tameside, had no idea what the facilities were like, and hoped that they might be able to see us afterwards in our dressing room as they used to do at the Opera House. We were sharing our portacabin with other members of the staff, and it wasn't really possible to entertain anyone, and so on this occasion we had to make do with a quick chat at the door. On the plus side the town also possessed a Yates's Wine Lodge, which was always worth a visit for a session of people watching. On April 3 there was another 'sing for your supper' concert, this one at Denton Golf Club just south of Ashton-under-Lyne; our choristers sang most of the items.

The next venue was the Alexandra Theatre in Birmingham where we played for another two weeks; once again I stayed with the Oakleys in Appleby Magna. One room in the Old Rectory was a small study cum library, which Hazel called 'the snuggery', and when I got back from Birmingham, or wherever, we would relax there by the fire with a glass of Southern Comfort, a drink that Hazel had introduced me to. Harold usually sat apart at a table, dealing with correspondence, but Hazel had followed the Company for many years and was always keen to hear the latest news and gossip. It was a pleasant way to end a busy day.

Best digs ever - The Old Rectory, Appleby Magna, October 1978.

After Birmingham there was another new venue for me, the Alhambra Theatre in Bradford, hometown of our repetiteur Paul Seeley. We were there for two weeks. During this time Paul's parents kindly invited a number of us to their home. I also managed to visit the famous Brontë Parsonage in Haworth, just a few miles from the city. Seeing all these interesting places was one of the great delights of touring. While we were in Bradford I completed the purchase of my flat in Eastbourne with some difficulty, as much of it had to be done by phone calls to the estate agent from a public phone box. No mobile phones or computers in those days. Rehearsals in Bradford were held in the usual variety of places, including the German Church, the YMCA and even one of the theatre's dressing rooms.

The pit in the Alhambra was similar, in one respect, to the one in the Opera House in Manchester. Here too, the conductor had to go out through the pass door, stage left, into the auditorium, walk along the front row and go into the pit through a little gate. At one mid-week matinee, which I was due to conduct, the audience (mainly pensioners) was very sparse, and they were scattered throughout the various levels of the theatre – a handful here, and a handful there. Shortly before we were due to begin it was decided that it would be better if everyone was brought down to the front two or three rows; this duly happened. I was then sent out through the pass door, and went along by the front row to enter the pit. To my embarrassment, right in the middle of the front row, there was a lady who had a calliper on one leg (something one rarely sees nowadays). She had to be on the front row as her leg stuck out when she was seated, and she needed some space in front of her, and so, as there was no alternative, I had to step over her leg to get to the gate into the pit – in an otherwise virtually empty theatre! The absurdity of the situation was not lost on me.

Peter Riley, who had been with the Company since 1964, had held various positions including technical and stage director. In April 1980 he became deputy general manager and would cease to tour with the Company. He would now be based in the London office at the new location of Rooms 261–263, The Savoy Hotel. To save printing yet more notepaper, a rubber stamp was used to update the old address; it seemed just a further drift away from the magic of 1 Savoy Hill.

There had been a number of staff changes the previous year when Bert Newby had died suddenly at the beginning of 1979.

Gordon MacKenzie had succeeded him as business manager and Peter Riley became company manager and technical director. Ken Robertson, who had been assistant stage manager, now became stage manager, and we had a new assistant stage manager in Alan Riches. With Peter's departure for London Gordon MacKenzie became the new company manager on tour. It may seem that many of these changes were somewhat unnecessary, given the short time left to the Company, but even at that stage it was far from clear what the future would hold, and there were yet further changes before we closed in 1982. For various reasons these designated positions in the Company did not always accurately reflect the work done by the individuals who held them. After Bert Newby's stroke, for instance, it was agreed that he would remain with the Company as a figurehead, with Peter Riley effectively in charge. Bert was also listed in both the 1976 and 1978 tours of North America as company manager, the term business manager not being recognised in USA theatrical parlance.

The May 1980 edition of *The Savoyard – The Pirates of Penzance Centenary Issue* now appeared. It had a new editor in Brian Jones and a slightly different look. There was also an announcement that the size of the magazine was going to be altered, although in the end this didn't happen. It carried obituaries of James Lawrie, the former editor, and Bruce Worsley, the Company's former business manager from 1950–67, but much of it was devoted to *Pirates*. There was an article by Paul Seeley on the underlying themes of love and duty in the opera and one by me, the first of several that I produced for the magazine, on the provenance of the line "From Marathon to Waterloo in order categorical" (sung by Major-General Stanley) which I suggested had come from the title of a book by Sir Edward Creasy called *The Fifteen Decisive Battles of the World from Marathon to Waterloo*, first published in 1851. With only the first part of the lengthy title printed on the book's spine – sometimes just *Fifteen Decisive Battles* – this possible source for Gilbert's line was not immediately obvious. To my knowledge the connection had not been noted before. I had previously had a letter from Brian Jones concerning a technical point that was new to me, namely the use of crossheads in my article. He had inserted them and I wasn't too happy about it. He agreed to remove them, at the same time hoping to convince me to use them in any future articles.

After Bradford we had a week at the New Theatre, Hull (also a 'new' venue for most of us). The theatre occupied one side of a square. There were rows of small terraced houses on two of the other sides, the fourth side being open to a main road. Jimmie Marsland said that several of the houses had been digs in former days – very handy for the theatre. Rehearsals here were in the Co-op Hall. Several of us stayed in nearby Beverley where, among other things, we took riding lessons. I also visited the impressive Minster. The New Theatre, Hull was followed by two weeks at the New Theatre, Oxford which had been my introduction to touring in 1975. This was now my fifth visit. We rehearsed here in the Old Fire Station; on previous visits we had used the Clarendon Press Institute. The variety of rehearsal venues that we used was astonishing, and the sheer number of them was well in excess of the number of theatres that we played. After the performance of *Pinafore* on May 16 we had yet another 'sing for your supper' evening. This one was at North Oxford Golf Club, one of many clubs around the country used by members of the Company in return for a concert. Next day I met Dr Percy Young and his wife who were coming to the matinee of *Mikado*. Percy was working on the critical edition of *Pinafore* for Broude Brothers and I was able to give him information about the Company's production, which had changed little over the years. On Friday May 23 I had to go to London to play for more auditions. There were only four people this time, but one of them was Jill Washington who would soon be joining us.

From Oxford we moved to Liverpool for a week (May 26–31). Once again we were at the Empire, another vast space that we could never fill. On my first visit to Liverpool in 1975 we had played at the Royal Court Theatre, but it had not been available on my second visit in 1976. Now, although we were at the Empire, the Royal Court was again available, and our ladies' chorus and two of the 'three little maids' (*Mikado*) – Lorraine Daniels as Pitti-Sing and Roberta Morrell as Peep-Bo – went there one day to make a contribution to the film *Chariots of Fire*, which tells the stories of the athletes Harold Abrahams and Eric Liddell, and their participation in the 1924 Paris Olympics. In 1936 Harold Abrahams had married Sybil Evers, a D'Oyly Carte chorister who played a number of small parts including Peep-Bo. This connection with the Company became part of the film, although Harold and Sybil did not meet until after the Paris Olympics, and, with the usual dramatic licence, Sybil had to be the principal soprano rather than a chorister and small-part player. In the film she was even confused with another chorister and small-part player, Sybil Gordon, who was in the Company at the same time. They both left in 1931. Harold Abrahams is shown as being a great lover of G&S, and he goes to a performance of *The Mikado* where he is captivated by Sybil (as Yum-Yum) in the 'three little maids from school' scene. The female lead in *Chariots of Fire* was Alice Krige. She naturally had to be seen as Yum-Yum and this meant that Barbara Lilley missed out on an appearance in the film, although Lorraine and Roberta were allowed to retain their roles. Alice Krige had to be instructed in all the moves, including the use of fans, to enable her to take part in the scene exactly as we performed it, and the ladies spent a good part of the day filming at the Royal Court Theatre. Ken Robertson, as a member of Equity, was drafted in to appear as the conductor, and he is seen briefly, but the performance used in the soundtrack was from a separate recording.

The other main character in *Chariots of Fire*, Eric Liddell, was a Scot, and many of the scenes of his earlier life were filmed in Scotland. The scenes purporting to be at Cambridge were filmed at Eton College. For the 'three little maids' scene

Twentieth Century Fox had to choose not just any one of the cities in which we were appearing, but one that also had another suitable theatre that could be used for filming. With the availability of the Royal Court Theatre, Liverpool was now one such city, and the film unit made the most of the location with other scenes being filmed there too. The Town Hall, where we had assisted at the Lord Mayor's Christmas party in 1975, became the British Embassy in Paris where Eric Liddell appeared before the committee to defend his decision not to run on a Sunday. As a coastal city Liverpool was also ideal for filming scenes that represented the English Channel, and Woodside Landing Stage at Birkenhead was used to represent Dover's Admiralty Pier. Two of the Isle of Man steamers, the near-sisters *Mona's Isle* of 1951 and *Manxman* of 1955, were also seen in the film as they both looked traditional enough to the casual observer to represent cross-channel steamers of the 1920s. Much of this only became apparent when the film appeared, of which more later. The filming session had been an interesting, if tiring, experience for the ladies – and they still had to give a performance in the evening.

We moved from Liverpool to Llandudno, again for just a week (June 2–7), playing at the Astra Theatre – yet another new venue for most of us. Originally called the Winter Gardens it had been built in 1935 in Art Deco style as, unusually, a dual-purpose cinema/theatre, which meant that it did have dressing-room accommodation. It also had a Christie cinema organ, which was still working, and the man who looked after it was always willing to give a demonstration of its capabilities. I went in one morning to see it in action; it was fascinating. While we were at the Astra a number of us met the famous tenor Webster Booth, then in his late seventies, who had been in D'Oyly Carte in the 1920s (billed as Leslie W. Booth). Like many another before and after him he had not progressed very far in the Company, playing only First Yeoman (*Yeomen*) and Francesco (*Gondoliers*), and he had left to make his name elsewhere. Much of his later success was with his wife, the soprano Anne Ziegler. They had retired to Llandudno, and had been invited to come in to the theatre one morning, although Webster came without Anne. I had often heard them on 'the wireless' when I was growing up, but I hadn't known until much later that Webster had been in the Company. He died in 1984. In 1989 I did a series of interval talks for BBC Radio 2's presentation of the G&S operas and in one of them I played Webster's recording of 'Take a pair of sparkling eyes' (*Gondoliers*). Shortly afterwards I received a very nice letter from Anne Ziegler thanking me for including it. I was sorry that I hadn't met her at Llandudno.

Elizabeth Denham, one of the two choristers who had given joint birthday parties in San Francisco in 1978 and Sydney in 1979 (the fancy dress one), had now left the Company, but Susan Cochrane celebrated hers with a 'between shows' party on Saturday June 7. On a hand-written invitation card, with a reference to my Groucho Marx costume at the Sydney party, she had written "Fancy dress *not* required, but bring your cigar".

Around this time I received a copy of a letter, which had been sent to the office. People were always writing in about something or other, and if these were on musical topics, such as "Where can I hire band parts for *The Zoo*?", they would eventually come to the music department. This letter, dated 28th May 1980, was in response to one in the latest edition of *The Savoyard* (May 1980) from a man who said that he had seen his first G&S opera in 1915, and could anyone beat that record? The writer of the second letter was a lady who said that she was now ninety-two, and thought that she might have seen her first G&S opera in 1907. But she also said that she remembered being a bridesmaid at her cousin's wedding in 1910, the cousin being no less a person than Bertha Lewis, the famous D'Oyly Carte contralto. Bertha Lewis was tragically killed when a car driven by her fellow principal, the recently knighted Sir Henry Lytton, in which she was a passenger, was involved in an accident in 1931. The writer also quoted from a newspaper cutting, which said that the wedding took place at the early time of 10.30am, and that while the guests were waiting in the church they were treated to an organ recital by the well-known English pianist and composer York Bowen. This was all much more interesting than simply knowing that the lady had seen her first G&S opera in 1907.

Another letter that came from the office at this time was a memo from Peter Riley, which said that in each new theatre we should always check the house rules regarding the use of the pass door that enabled us to come from backstage into the auditorium during performances. Although it was often necessary to use the pass door, this could be distracting to the audience, and some theatre managers might not like it being used at all during performances. We were also reminded that if we were out front at any time we were representing the Company and should always wear a jacket, collar and tie. This, of course, was written to a virtually all-male staff – another indication of former times. There were internal memos too, informing us of principals' nights off and the understudies who would be performing – often Alistair Donkin or Clive Birch for James Conroy-Ward, or Jill Pert for Patricia Leonard.

If I had thought that this provincial tour would seem very routine, after the foreign tours of North America and Australasia, my interest was constantly maintained by the number of new venues, to me at least, that we played. It was like a re-run of my first tour in 1975 when all the theatres, even the Scottish ones, were new to me. I had not been to North Wales before, and at Llandudno we were very close to Conwy with its mighty castle that was well worth a visit. Conwy also boasted a tiny little house, sandwiched between two others, which claimed to be "the smallest house in Great Britain" – a contrast to the many 'tallest' and 'largest' buildings we had seen in the United States and Canada. It was also a fairly short drive from Llandudno to the Isle of Anglesey, with another great castle at Beaumaris. I remember buying three traditional raffia wastepaper baskets in Beaumaris for my new flat in Eastbourne, which I hadn't yet visited. I still have all three.

After Llandudno we moved to the newly restored Opera House in Buxton (another wonderful Frank Matcham theatre) where we played for a week from June 9. On the last night, there was a Gala performance of *Mikado* in aid of the Opera House Restoration Fund and the Buxton Festival. Ticket prices were doubled for this and it was followed by a "grand oriental dinner" at the Palace Hotel. The performance was given in the presence of the Duke and Duchess of Rutland, and Dame Bridget and Albert Truelove also attended. The Opera House was not just another new venue for me – it was the first time that the Company had played there since 1926, and our visit attracted virtually full houses. We performed just three operas: *Pinafore*, *Pirates* and *Mikado*; rehearsals were held in the Railway Hotel. (The International G&S Festival, which was set up some time after D'Oyly Carte closed, was, for many years, held in this lovely little Derbyshire town, and I came back, both as a visitor and a performer, on a number of occasions.)

From Buxton, incredibly, we moved to yet another new venue, this time in Coventry, and once again we were in a converted cinema, now called the Coventry Theatre. We were there for just one week. I don't remember much about the theatre except that it was very large, which was more than could be said for the audiences, particularly after Buxton. We had yet more auditions on Thursday June 19, and out of some half dozen we heard Christine George who later joined the Company; rather unusually we also had orchestral auditions here. On the Friday there was another unusual event – a G&S Buffet at the College of Food. Performing in Coventry meant that I could stay with the Oakleys at Appleby Magna. They had said that they were equidistant from no less than five cities, but up until now we had only played two of them – Birmingham and Nottingham. For the first time we were in one of the other three and if the audiences were on the small side a glass or two of Southern Comfort in the snuggery at Appleby Magna more than made up for that.

Around the middle of June I received a letter from the new editor of *The Savoyard*, Brian Jones, who was keen to develop musical points of view in the magazine. I had recently produced my first article for it and he wondered if I might submit another for the next edition in September. Having written to James Lawrie the previous year with some suggestions for articles this seemed to be a green light to start writing. I wrote to Brian to say that I would be happy to produce something. In his reply he told me that it was now easier to reproduce music examples (the format of the magazine would also change slightly). I then started to think about what I might write.

From Coventry we moved to the New Theatre, Cardiff – yet another 'New' but not 'new' venue – for two weeks from June 23 to July 5. It was a pleasure to be back in Cardiff and to hear those robust Welsh voices singing the national anthem and their own 'Land of My Fathers'. In my free time I further explored Cardiff itself and the surrounding country, visiting Cardiff Castle and the nearby Castell Coch. Much of the former, and virtually all of the latter, had been rebuilt in the late nineteenth century (contemporary with most of the Savoy operas) to the Gothic Revival designs of the architect William Burges, and financed by the enormous wealth of the third Marquess of Bute, John Crichton-Stuart. Castell Coch had also been used for filming, and would have made a splendid Castle Adamant (*Princess Ida*). On the middle Sunday, June 29, there was another D'Oyly Carte in Concert, once again in Devizes. This was our third visit following the concerts in 1977 and 1978. In the second week I met up with an old friend from Greenock who was now living in Cardiff. He and his wife came to *Iolanthe,* which I conducted on July 1. We gave just one performance of *Sorcerer* in Cardiff. Although originally scheduled for the second week, it was moved to the first week, switching with a performance of *Iolanthe*.

A letter from Freddie Lloyd, dated June 26, 1980, reached me while we were in Cardiff. It was a contract for another year's work. My salary was now to be £98 per week and the subsistence had been fixed at £65 per week. Again this was very positive and it was easy to think that if the Company could afford it – both my salary and the subsistence were over three times what they had been when I joined the Company just five years earlier – then all must be right financially. But this was to ignore the fact that these increases were not just for me, and they were draining the Company's resources. Our continuance was almost certainly the result of further sponsorship by Barclays Bank to the tune of £150,000 over a three-year period, although we weren't to last for another three years. There was a press conference at the Savoy Hotel on July 1 to announce the sponsorship, and a photograph showed Dame Bridget, Freddie Lloyd and Ken Sandford raising their glasses in celebration. The toast was not only to Barclays. It also happened to be Freddie's birthday and the twenty-third anniversary of Ken Sandford's first performance with the Company in 1957 as Pooh-Bah (*Mikado*) in Southsea.

We did not receive public funding and without support from Barclays we would almost certainly have closed sooner than we did. But despite trying to look at it objectively, we could not bring ourselves to believe that the Company's days were numbered. We had, after all, recently heard that another North American tour was being planned for 1982. I had joined D'Oyly Carte amid the euphoria of its centenary; we were now five years into 'the next hundred years', which had been so confidently predicted and toasted at receptions in 1975, and I had just bought a property. I had to convince myself that my job was secure for the foreseeable future. Outwardly, there were even signs that the Company was trying to respond to criticism. We now had, at least by D'Oyly Carte standards, three more modern productions (*Sorcerer, Iolanthe* and *Gondoliers*) and our publicity had been updated. The little cards with each town's or city's programmes had recently been changed, and now looked less like cards advertising boxing matches to which they had previously been compared. These too, as with our more recent publicity, now read "D'Oyly Carte in association with Barclays Bank present Gilbert & Sullivan". With all of this, and with at least one further year's work, we could only be optimistic.

After Cardiff there was one more date – a four-week summer season in London. I always had to be reminded that London was part of the tour. My home was now in Eastbourne, but being in London still felt like coming home after touring in the provinces. This may be partly explained by the fact that the Company office was in London and I had worked there in 1976 while the Company was in North America. But I had also grown fond of the old Sadler's Wells (it was to have a revamp some years later), and the regular long seasons over Christmas and the New Year always gave us a settled feeling rarely felt elsewhere, with the possible exception of Manchester. We opened this short season on Tuesday, July 8, and gave two performances of *Pinafore*, the second of which I conducted, followed by four of *Mikado* from July 10 and four of *Gondoliers* from July 14. During the first week we also had more orchestral auditions.

I had to go up to Scotland on July 11 as my father was very ill; he died on Sunday July 13. I had to register the death on Monday and attend to various other things, but I had to come back to London on Tuesday. Fraser was going to be away and I had to conduct the last two performances of *Gondoliers* (July 16). Although it could not have been foreseen at the time, these were the last performances of *Gondoliers* that the Company gave, and, by default, it fell to me to conduct them. I also had to conduct the next four performances of *Mikado* as Fraser was still away. On the Friday evening, July 18, we had understudies Alistair Donkin and Pamela Baxter as Ko-Ko and Pitti-Sing.

While we were on tour, Fraser had compiled a list of the music department's duties during the London season and our respective availability afterwards. By chance, as I was going to be required to play during the holiday period, it had been decided that I would take a week's holiday so I was able to be in Greenock during the week of my father's funeral. (On the way up to Scotland I stopped off at Cambridge to meet Gerald Hendrie and his wife Dinah Barsham who were both working on Broude Brothers' critical edition of *Iolanthe*.) On my return to London, we had four performances of *Sorcerer*, and I conducted the Wednesday matinee. I eventually conducted over five hundred performances with the Company, but these were mainly of the top three favourites, *Pinafore*, *Pirates* and *Mikado*. It was always a pleasure, if slightly more daunting, to be conducting the less often performed works such as *Sorcerer*, *Patience*, *Ida* and *Ruddigore*. The Company also enjoyed these too, particularly *Sorcerer* in which, contrary to the general disposition of the chorus in groups (as pirates, dragoon guards, fairies or schoolgirls), everyone was an individual character.

Many of our rehearsals on the recent tour had been for *Yeomen*. There was a further run-through with piano on July 29 followed by a nominated dress rehearsal on the morning of the 31st in full costume and make-up, with the orchestra. Photographs were taken throughout by Reg Wilson. We then ended this London season with four performances of *Yeomen* (July 31–August 2). I conducted the Saturday matinee. For a company whose repertoire consisted primarily of "innocent merriment" it was something of a departure to end a season on a sombre note, particularly in London where the audiences were used to even more "precious nonsense" on the Last Nights of the annual winter seasons, with the collapse of the jester Jack Point. In retrospect it might even be seen as an omen, foreshadowing the collapse of the Company itself less than two years later. At the time, however, such thoughts were still far from our minds. It was simply the end of another year.

Among those leaving was Leonard Osborn who had originally joined the Company in 1937. His years as production director (from 1977) had not been as happy as those as a principal tenor (1946–59), but his experience had still been invaluable, particularly in the tenor roles. He had played most of them except Alexis (*Sorcerer*), Ralph Rackstraw (*Pinafore*), Hilarion (*Ida*) and Luiz (*Gondoliers*). He had been an outstanding Richard Dauntless (*Ruddigore*) and was able to pass on his interpretation of the hornpipe to Meston Reid. A photograph of them rehearsing this appeared in the May 1977 edition of *The Savoyard*. Leonard's position as production director was to be filled by Wilfred Judd, his assistant since 1979. We also lost principal soprano Evette Davis, principal tenor Harold Sharples and choristers Jillian Mascall, Richard Braebrook, John Coe-Roper, Robert Eshelby and Paul Weakley. Alan Spencer, who had contributed so much to the Last Nights and other functions, was also leaving the chorus, but not the Company. Like Billy Morgan, Bert Newby, Jimmie Marsland and Gordon MacKenzie before him, he was offered a staff position – the newly created post of production assistant and choreographer.

The Company was now on holiday and I had to play for the new intake of choristers at the Church of the Holy Redeemer in Exmouth Market, concentrating, in the first week, on Richard Wales. But this was nine-to-five work, and I now had free evenings in which to do some socialising. One evening I went to see the cellist Eldon Fox, brother of Ivan (our former leader) and of Colin and Joan whom I had met in Australia. There were also two Company weddings at this time, firstly of choristers Alexandra Hann and Alan Rice at St Paul's, Covent Garden on August 9, followed by that of choristers Bob Crowe and Janet Henderson in Perth on August 16. Bob sported a beard at his wedding. He had grown stubble for his role as the 'village idiot' in *Sorcerer*, and had been allowed to let this grow for his appearance as a warder in *Yeomen* in the final performances of the season.

Christine George, whom we had auditioned in Coventry, started on Monday August 11, but Richard Wales wasn't available that week. He was at Glyndebourne and would not be joining the Company until November. Before the beginning of a new season it was sometimes difficult, owing to other commitments, to get new choristers together for preliminary rehearsals. Another chorister, Tom Marandola, turned up at the beginning of the third week. The other new choristers for 1980–81 were Margaret Lynn-Williams, Michael Hamlett, Alexander Platts and Neil Thompson (later Braithwaite). Jill Washington replaced Evette Davis as principal soprano and Geoffrey Shovelton returned as principal tenor in place of Harold Sharples. His return had been advocated by, among others, Gordon MacKenzie, and I was very pleased to see him again.

My fifth year with D'Oyly Carte was now over and I had a week's holiday. I went down to Eastbourne, with my three wastepaper baskets, to start to make my new flat into a home. My mother had sent down some items from Greenock and as my upstairs neighbour, Mrs Dorothy Walden, was buying a new three-piece suite she kindly donated the old one – "It might as well stay in the building", she said. Dorothy was an interesting lady who had in her youth taken part as a dancer in many of the performances of Coleridge-Taylor's once immensely popular trilogy of cantatas *The Song of Hiawatha*, which had been staged annually in London from 1924 until the outbreak of World War Two. Her father had been a captain in the merchant navy and his ship, the Houlder liner *Dunster Grange*, had been in Montevideo harbour when the German pocket battleship *Admiral Graf Spee* had sought refuge there in December 1939. Dorothy later gave me a fascinating photograph showing the two ships in the outer harbour, and photographs of both her father, Captain R.A. Smiles of the *Dunster Grange,* and Captain Hans Langsdorff of the *Graf Spee*. Unusually, the *Dunster Grange* was then embarking ammunition while the *Graf Spee* was simply embarking provisions. These photographic items (for once *not* associated with G&S!) are also treasured possessions.

I spent much of my week in Eastbourne looking for additional furniture, crockery and cutlery for the flat, and I also acquired an upright piano – a Squire and Longson, a make

I hadn't come across before. By way of relaxation I could always walk down to the promenade and listen to the bands, which still played there almost every day during the summer months. I didn't get very much work done during that week, but I had made a start. Despite the recent gloomy prognosis of the Company's future we were still in business – for at least one more year. My sixth year with D'Oyly Carte was about to begin.

Chapter 6: 1980–1981

I

The next year began with two weeks of rehearsals at the beginning of September for the full Company, after which we set off on another tour. Just before we left London I received my dress allowance – still the same at £65. The September 1980 edition of *The Savoyard* appeared and included an article I had written on Sullivan's style – the first, I hoped, of many. When I joined the Company in 1975 my immediate concern was to get to know the repertoire thoroughly. Now that I was familiar with it, and had also had several years' experience of conducting, I could go back to the research I had begun at university, concentrating on the operas rather than on Sullivan's songs, and could publish the results in *The Savoyard*.

The first stop on our autumn tour was at Sunderland, some two hundred and seventy miles north of London, where we again played at the Empire. We were there for just one week. I don't recall another midnight visit to Marsden Grotto, but we didn't have *Gondoliers* with us, and John Ayldon would have been performing every night in the five operas that we played: *Sorcerer*, *Pinafore*, *Pirates*, *Iolanthe* and *Mikado*. It would have been impossible for him, this time, to organise such an unusual event during an evening show. We then began the Scottish leg of the tour, which took up almost all of our time before we were back in London in December. Although we were playing in both Glasgow and Edinburgh these dates were not until later, and we first had to drive from Sunderland to Aberdeen – almost exactly the same distance as from London to Sunderland.

We were in Aberdeen for two weeks, from September 22 until October 4. With regard to auditions on tour, Fraser had previously asked the office to send singers only to certain theatres; we heard one on September 24. As well as the five operas that we had with us on this tour we were also rehearsing other repertoire and there was a full run-through of *Yeomen* onstage, with the orchestra. Understudy calls for the operas continued as usual. An oboe deputy was required for the second Monday, and as oboists are hard to find we had to get one from Edinburgh. On the social side I managed to see an elderly aunt. I also saw an old college friend, Sandy Leiper, who, having worked in education since leaving the RSAMD, was now running a music shop in Aberdeen (his home town). His Majesty's Theatre was due to close shortly for renovation and it was decided that we should end our season there, as we traditionally did on New Year's Eve in London, with 'Auld Lang Syne'. We only heard about this when we got to Aberdeen, and unfortunately I didn't have the score and band parts of my arrangement with me. Like Sullivan in New York in 1879, when he realised that he had left his sketches for the first act of *Pirates* in London, I had to write it out again, trying to recall exactly what I had done before. The revised arrangement had its premiere after the evening performance on October 4.

From Aberdeen we moved to the Eden Court Theatre in Inverness for two weeks. At one matinee of *Iolanthe*, during his second song 'When I went to the Bar as a very young man', which has four verses, James Conroy-Ward suddenly exited stage left after the second verse for no discernibly obvious reason. It certainly took me by surprise, and I immediately tried to get the orchestra, which couldn't always see, or hear, the singers on stage, to stop playing. They probably wondered what I was doing, waving my hands in the middle of a number and muttering, not too loudly lest I disturb the audience, "Stop! Stop!" Several of them, who may have been on automatic pilot anyway, kept going for a few bars until they realised that I had stopped conducting. This was still early days in James's tenure of the comedy roles and he may simply have forgotten his words and panicked. I can't recall that I ever found out what occasioned his premature departure. Of a somewhat nervous disposition, his frequent absences meant that his understudy, Alistair Donkin, aside from his legitimate appearances as Major-General Stanley (*Pirates*), appeared in many of the roles much more often than was usual for an understudy. While we were in Inverness we had a visit from Freddie Lloyd. He spoke to us about the Company's current position and the possibility of closure in the not-too-distant future unless its finances could be put on a more secure footing. Jimmie Marsland said that he had heard it all before, but this time it really sounded serious.

After Eden Court we were at another new venue, the MacRobert Arts Centre in Stirling. I particularly remember the drive south from Inverness. On this occasion, as my previous travelling companion, Andrea Phillips, had now left the Company, one of our new choristers, Margaret Lynn-Williams, was with me. Margaret hadn't been in this part of Scotland before and was glad of the opportunity to see it. The drive down the Great Glen – by Loch Ness, Loch Oich, Loch Lochy and Loch Linnhe – is spectacular at any time, but on this Sunday we were blessed with one of those perfect late autumn days which bring out the colours of the landscape so well. Even Glen Coe and Rannoch Moor were sunny and peaceful – a change from the gloomy and forbidding aspect which they so often present. It was well worth the extra mileage to see such magnificent scenery at its best.

The MacRobert Arts Centre was part of the campus of the University of Stirling and had been opened less than ten years before in 1971. It was a much smaller venue than some of the huge theatres we had played and was more suited to our productions. We were there for just one week before moving to the King's Theatre in Edinburgh for three weeks from October 27 to November 15. I had also received another letter from Brian Jones asking me if I would consider writing an article specifically on *Patience* as we would be celebrating its centenary in 1981, and I said that I would try to do this. *The Savoyard* would now appear just twice each year in March and September.

Shortly after arriving in Edinburgh I received a letter from Elizabeth Meldrum who was the editor of *The College Courant*, the journal of the Glasgow University Graduates' Association. I had been in touch with her about the possibility of an article for the journal about D'Oyly Carte. Elizabeth particularly wanted me to say something about our traditional productions and the problems of continuing to present these now that the copyright had expired. I had already made preliminary notes for an article and soon began work on it. I managed to complete it before the December deadline. I was on holiday during the second week and spent this time in Greenock, going back to Edinburgh for the third week.

We then moved to Glasgow, playing at the Theatre Royal for two weeks at the end of November. While we were there I caught up with a former chorister, Jane Guy, herself a Scot, who was now with Scottish Opera. Jane had been with us for one year, 1976–77. We had more auditions on November 26. While we heard some good voices among the dozen or so who turned up, we were not in a position to offer any work at that time. We did, however, have Richard Wales with us now that he had finished at Glyndebourne and there were numerous rehearsals to slot him in to the performances.

While we were in Scotland the current *Scottish Opera News* (number 4, October 1980) carried an article about the Company. It mentioned not only the sponsorship by Barclays Bank, which had made the ten-week Scottish tour possible, but also further financial assistance from the Scottish Arts Council, Strathclyde Regional Council and Glasgow District

Council. The article also highlighted the careers of both Freddie Lloyd and Ken Sandford, and while it was no surprise to read that the latter had appeared in no less than two and a half thousand performances of *Mikado* I didn't know that he had previously appeared in Scotland's famous *Half Past Eight* show (later known as *Five Past Eight)* with comedians Stanley Baxter and Jack Radcliffe. But it was even more of a surprise to learn that Freddie Lloyd played the cello and that he had conducted amateur productions. It also said that he would soon be travelling to America to make advance arrangements for the 1982 tour of North America, which we had recently heard about. Later we were even given provisional dates of April 12–July 24, but in the end it never happened.

On November 28 I went to see Muriel 'Poppy' Dickson. We talked first about the RSAMD. I had been a student there in the early 1960s when she was on the staff. She then told me about her time in the Company (1928–35), and said that I could use anything that I wanted in the forthcoming article. She had, of course, been with D'Oyly Carte at the same time as Bertha Lewis and Sir Henry Lytton. This was a fascinating link to the Company's past, a time when she could recall ticket queues stretching literally round the block, even for large theatres like the Bristol Hippodrome. But that period was also part of J.M. Gordon's time as stage director (1907–39). He had worked with Gilbert, and had a reputation for exactitude in all matters relating to the operas. Poppy remembered him always being at the back of the theatre during performances, taking notes that would be passed round to the performers afterwards. This is perfectly normal, of course, but Gordon's insistence on certain moves, and even inflections of speech, being rigidly adhered to has always been seen by some commentators as bordering on the pedantic. But despite the flak that we constantly received from some quarters concerning our too traditional performances, it is clear that with J.M. Gordon at the helm the operas in the 1920s and 1930s were much closer to Gilbert's productions than our own. Poppy also said that Gordon taught her a great deal about stagecraft, an important element in the production of the Savoy Operas in which artists are required not only to sing and act, and usually do at least some dancing, but also to deliver dialogue convincingly. I was grateful to her for talking about her days in the Company, and for giving me a more balanced view of J.M. Gordon. In another letter from Brian Jones, pressing me again for something on *Patience*, he also said that he was very interested to hear that I had met Muriel Dickson – a famous name in D'Oyly Carte's history.

Glasgow was the last stop on the Scottish leg of this provincial tour, which was now nearing its end. There was one more stop before London – the Grand Theatre, Leeds. We opened there on Monday December 1 for a run of two weeks. Leeds was one of those rare places where we had a Tuesday matinee. I seem to recall at least one instance of an understudy being hurriedly prepared for a performance when a principal failed to turn up. There were more individual rehearsals for Richard Wales, one of them being held in the band room; another rehearsal (an understudy call for Clive Birch on *Pinafore*) was held in the local Deaf and Dumb Institute. It was not only the variety of rehearsal venues that was interesting – we were once offered a private house in Norwich – but the unexpected things that were often associated with them, the venues being remembered for all the wrong reasons. One place that was used for a chorus call had no chairs, and I remember an occasion when the lady who was supposed to open a hall (possibly the one without chairs) didn't turn up, and we had to wait outside for an hour.

On the middle Sunday, December 7, there was a D'Oyly Carte in Concert in Norwich. This meant another long drive; we met at the stage door, and set off at 9am. It was also during this visit to Leeds that we were invited to attend a late-night cabaret in the theatre given by Victor Borge (we were allocated seats in the upper circle). This took place after a performance of *Pinafore*. There was no time to strike the set, and a grand piano was simply wheeled on to it. It looked rather incongruous. The ship's name, in white lettering, was on a scroll fixed to the railing above the deckhouse, and when Victor Borge walked on to the set he turned to the audience and said, pointing to the scroll, "How appropriate – HMS Pianoforte". When he came onstage he was wearing a lifebelt which was used by John Reed in the last encore to 'Never mind the why and wherefore'. Having supposedly jumped overboard in the penultimate encore, John then appeared with the lifebelt round his waist. Victor Borge, having spotted it in the wings, decided to use it himself.

The week beginning December 15 had originally been scheduled as a rehearsal week, possibly because we couldn't find a performing venue, but in the end there were no rehearsals, and so we had an unexpected holiday. One of our choristers, Caroline Tatlow, was married to someone outside the Company at the end of that week on Saturday December 20. We then began what would prove to be our last London season at Sadler's Wells. As well as the performance details, our attractive new publicity contained a short history of the Company, which ended "For any theatrical foundation to have lasted more than one hundred years is no ordinary achievement. To have given constant pleasure throughout that time is truly remarkable". This did sound as if the end was near.

Emboldened by the success of the early G&S collaborations, Richard D'Oyly Carte had built the Savoy Theatre. It opened in 1881 during the run of *Patience*, and was the first in the world to be lit by electric light. The operas became known collectively as the Savoy Operas and those who performed in them were known as Savoyards. Further emboldened by the success of the operas in the United States, and with an eye for the increasing number of American tourists coming to Europe, who might attend performances at his theatre, Carte embarked on a more ambitious project, namely to build, on an adjacent site, a hotel that would come up to the standards of the superior hotels he had found on his visits to the United States. This was, of course, the Savoy Hotel, which opened in 1889 during the run of *Yeomen*. The hotel had 'ascending rooms' (lifts) and no less than seventy bathrooms – a recently-opened London rival had just four! Despite the fact that the Company office was in the hotel (at 1 Savoy Hill) when I joined, it was often felt that although it had continued to perform the operas, and keep them alive for a hundred years, the Company had latterly become the poor relation to the large business empire of which this world-famous hotel was now a part, and as if to compound this feeling the office had moved yet again. It was now out of the hotel altogether, and located in Tabard House, a building in Southwark Street on the other side of the Thames.

The London season opened on Monday December 22 with *Sorcerer*, which we also played on the 23rd. We then had a two-day break over Christmas, but had to make up for this by having another two performances on Boxing Day and two more on the Saturday. This was followed by a half-week of the ever-popular *Mikado*. On New Year's Eve a news item in *The Times* stated that the Arts Council had refused to give the Company a grant. Consequently, the evening performance of Ko-Ko's 'little list' song included "the Arts Council-ist" (to great laughter) in its list of people who "never would be missed". There were now serious doubts about the future, and no guarantee that the Company would continue after the 1980–81 season. For the moment, we could only sing 'Auld Lang Syne', welcome in the New Year, and hope for a miracle in 1981.

We didn't perform on New Year's Day, but started again on January 2 with a run of seven performances of *Pinafore*. On January 6 (Twelfth Night) there was the first of several interesting events that involved the Company in one way or another, namely a revue to celebrate the fiftieth anniversary of Sadler's Wells. The theatre had opened on Twelfth Night in 1931 as a home for opera and ballet, thanks almost exclusively to the determination of the legendary and eccentric Lilian Baylis. At a Royal visit to the Wells she is reputed to have said to Queen Mary, during the national anthem, "We always play your husband's tune here, right through". An evening of Twelfth Night Revels had been organised to celebrate the Golden Jubilee, and this was given after *Pinafore* – luckily one of the shortest operas in our repertoire.

There were contributions from many well-known figures in the world of opera and ballet, along with items from the Company and even contributions from former Company members. Two of these, Cynthia Morey and John Fryatt, wrote several short pieces for the evening, one of which, News from the Wells, was performed by John Ayldon and Meston Reid. Tom Round, another well-known former D'Oyly Carte tenor, also sang in a couple of numbers, and several former D'Oyly Carte choristers, now at English National Opera, were involved in a piece written by Arthur Jacobs. Fraser Goulding, Paul Seeley and I all took part, and Paul's arrangement of the March of the Peers (*Iolanthe*), which involved almost everyone in the chorus, was staged by Alan Spencer. There was also a Vic-Wells Glory Song, which had been written by the conductor Alexander Faris. I knew his name, but didn't realise even then that I would be seeing more of him in the not-too-distant future. As usual on such occasions a glossy programme had been produced for the evening. It included a full-page advertisement in colour for Barclays Bank in the form of a parody of Captain Corcoran's song 'I am the Captain of the *Pinafore*!', which began "We are the sponsors of the D'Oyly Carte!" – useful publicity. This also appeared on the back cover of the Company's own souvenir brochure. The evening ended with a cake-cutting ceremony followed by the finale which involved everyone, including Dame Ninette de Valois.

After this fascinating event it was back to the normal routine. We followed *Pinafore* with a week each of *Yeomen*, *Mikado*, *Iolanthe* and *Pirates*, although we only gave seven performances of each; there were no Wednesday matinees. On the Wednesday of the *Yeomen* run we had more auditions, which were held in the opera rehearsal room. Towards the end of the *Iolanthe* run there was another Barclays lunch at Gracechurch Street. I hadn't been able to attend the one that they had organised the previous year as I was playing at the memorial service for James Lawrie, but I was able to go to this one. In our parlous financial state it was comforting to know that we did have some real money behind us, but how long would *that* last? For the moment, those of us who went to the event were happy to indulge ourselves with drinks and canapes. Shortly afterwards, a round-robin letter came from Stephen Remington, the director of Sadler's Wells, thanking the participants for taking part in the Twelfth Night Revels (it must have taken him a long time to sign all of them). Many people had written to him to say how much they had enjoyed it and he thought that the show had been "a model of its kind, with just the right combination of humour and nostalgia". As usual in London, I tried to catch up with old friends and relations. A number of them also came to performances.

After the week's run of *Pirates* we had three half weeks – of *Iolanthe*, *Pinafore* and again *Pirates* – before finishing the season with seven performances of *Ruddigore*; there were matinees on the final two Wednesdays. Ken Sandford, as Sir Despard Murgatroyd, altered his "I will give them all to the Nation" dialogue to "I will give them all to the Arts Council, and nobody shall ever look upon their faces again!" – to rapturous applause. We had not played *Patience*, *Ida* or *Gondoliers* in this season. The first two were not our greatest earners, but *Gondoliers* would almost certainly have been played if it had not been taken out for refurbishing. On February 18, during the run of *Ruddigore*, there was a Schools' Special concert on the stage at 10.30am. Geoffrey Shovelton introduced the programme, but most of the work was done by members of the chorus. After the introduction and welcome Alistair Donkin, sitting at the side of the stage, demonstrated how to put on stage make-up, followed by an illustrated talk on lighting using the set of *Ruddigore*. A short concert was then given in front of the tabs. On the following evening, after the performance, we went again to the Arts Club in Dover Street, and the matinee of *Ruddigore* on Saturday February 21 was followed by the customary Last Night.

In January 1981 the Arts Council's long-awaited report of its enquiry into the state of light opera, operetta and musicals in Great Britain had been published (they had started to discuss the subject in July 1979). It began with what amounted to an 'erratum slip' which said, despite statements to the contrary in the report itself, that there had been, as yet, no formal application from D'Oyly Carte for financial assistance, although it was expected that one would be made in the near future. The Company had applied unsuccessfully for a grant some twelve years before this, and a second application had, in fact, been made some eighteen months previously, but, as we had learned on New Year's Eve, it too had been unsuccessful.

The enquiry was in two parts. The first concentrated on operetta and musicals, suggesting that the former, along with audiences for it, was dying out, while the continuing popularity of the latter was not in question. The Council itself had even funded touring revivals of *My Fair Lady* and *Oklahoma!* It was pointed out that while a London production could make money, a touring one rarely did. The second part of the enquiry was devoted to D'Oyly Carte. This was a curious mixture of admiration for what the Company had achieved in a century of existence and, in the Council's own words, a "carping list" of criticisms: technically unsophisticated productions, old-fashioned marketing techniques, musically variable performances (including a "thin sound" from our small orchestra), the much quoted "tired" and "wooden" performances, and even a comment that some of the older members of the Company were "due for a rest". Despite this, however, it was felt that it would be a great loss if the Company closed, given its unique contribution to the musical and theatrical life of the country – whatever its currently perceived shortcomings – although several members of the committee had said, rather drily, that the Gilbert and Sullivan operas would survive without D'Oyly Carte and its management tradition rooted in the nineteenth century.

It was admitted that the Company had managed its affairs very well, and even at the present moment was able to generate about 80 per cent of its required income from the box office, whereas the major opera companies could only count on approximately 25 per cent. Private sponsorship, as from Barclays, helped to make up the deficiency, but the costs of touring were rising, and without further support we would probably not be able to carry on. With regard to our sponsorship from Barclays, it was suggested that we were well placed to seek further commercial sponsorship. If this was forthcoming we might survive without any help from the Arts Council. Having considered the pros and cons the recommendation was that the Council should be sympathetic to any application from the Company. There was, however, a proviso that the application should be for specific expenditure – such as extra musicians, guest directors, or a new production – and not simply to make up any annual deficit. With regard to new productions it had previously been suggested that the Company might try to widen its repertoire by performing other light operas such as André Messager's *Véronique*, but this idea had already been turned down by the D'Oyly Carte trustees. The Arts Council also wondered if a new production of *Véronique*, or whatever, would be enough in itself to regenerate what were deemed to be diminishing audiences – in reference to a comment by Lord Harewood, the managing director of English National Opera, that ENO's production of *Patience* had attracted much smaller audiences than had been expected.

Despite its own recommendations, no money was ever made available to us by the Arts Council. There was a general assumption that the Company had always had funding of some sort, and the press also sometimes got it wrong: an article in *The Daily Telegraph* had the headline "D'Oyly Carte facing last curtain call after losing grant". Shortly after this the February 18, 1981 edition of *Punch* printed some very clever and germane verses by David Taylor on our current situation, parodying 'When a felon's not engaged in his employment' (*Pirates*), and 'As some day it may happen' and 'A wandering minstrel I' (*Mikado*). One line in the latter parody actually stated that we would be closing in July, which was not very reassuring. Three days later, on February 21, we had our Last Night – the last traditional one, and our last ever at Sadler's Wells.

The Arts Council's report was, naturally, a rich source of material for the Last Night and among the inevitable departures from the norm, which included a performance of 'Little Maid of Arcadee' from *Thespis* (1871), the first G&S opera, there were innumerable references to our inability to get a grant, to our "tired" and "wooden" performances, and so on. The Act I dialogue in *Mikado* was rewritten to read "I am the bearer of a letter from the Arts Council", to the effect that "the D'Oyly Carte shall be abolished". Patricia Leonard and John Ayldon, dressed as a marmalade jar and an orange, sang a rewritten version of the duet 'Now wouldn't you like to rule the roast' (*Princess Ida*) in which there was a reference to the fact that the Company was in a "jam" and ought to be "preserved". It was, as ever, a wonderful evening, although it ended on a slightly sombre note with Ken Sandford standing alone on a darkened stage holding a red-covered document (the Arts Council's report) as the lights went out. What was to happen now? Would we indeed close in July? Or could we somehow be saved? For the moment, we now had another provincial tour.

II

The tour started with a week at the Royal Shakespeare Theatre in Stratford-upon-Avon; the mid-week matinee was again on Thursday. Moreen Moss, chairman of the Birmingham branch of the G&S Society, of which I was now a vice-president, came to the Saturday matinee. The Society's programme of events for 1980-81 had included, the previous September, an evening with Anne Ziegler and Webster Booth. After Stratford, we were back at the Congress Theatre, Eastbourne for a further week; once again we had a Thursday matinee. I could now stay at home, and although there was still much to do to the house I was able to have some of the Company round after one of the shows. While we were in Eastbourne, I received another round-robin letter from Stephen Remington at Sadler's Wells thanking us for the Schools' Special concert on February 18. He said that it had been greatly enjoyed and had helped to introduce a new generation to the delights of G&S. Well aware of our current predicament, he ended by hoping that all would be well for the Company, and that we might be back at Sadler's Wells in the summer – something else that wasn't to be.

From Eastbourne we moved west to the King's Theatre in Southsea for two weeks. The backstage facilities hadn't improved, particularly for the orchestra, but at least I didn't see any more large cockroaches. For the third consecutive date we again had mid-week matinees on Thursdays; this was very unusual. On, of all days, Friday March 13 the latest edition of *Private Eye* (number 502) had something to say about the Company, but it wasn't about our current situation, merely some scurrilous gossip about the orchestra. They had previously printed a leaked memorandum by the deputy secretary-general of the Arts Council, Richard Pulford, on a visit he had made to a performance of *Pirates;* it had been very damning, and was the last thing that we needed.

With the Company performing a strict diet of G&S there had often been suggestions that we might try to establish some sort of opera workshop to rehearse scenes and ensembles from the standard operatic repertoire. The problems with this were finding both time and suitable venues, but at the beginning of the tour I had put up a notice suggesting that we might be able to use St Simon's Hall in Southsea. This was just five minutes' walk from the theatre, and in these less security-conscious days a key could be obtained from the chemist just across the road. I had left space on the notice for anyone who would be interested in coaching sessions to sign up, and there were eventually about twenty signatures. Requests of this type invariably produce a few joke names – Donald Duck, Mickey Mouse, and so on (although those two were missing) – and the last name on this list was Placido Domingo! For various reasons we didn't manage to have very many sessions, but it had been a good idea, and might have been developed if the Company had survived.

From Southsea we moved to the New Theatre, Oxford (yet again) for one week; we were now back to the usual Wednesday matinee. We then moved to the Tameside Theatre at Ashton-under-Lyne for two weeks (March 30–April 11). I wasn't in the theatre on the opening night as that was the occasion of the second event that again involved at least some members of the Company, namely an evening party after the Royal Film Performance of *Chariots of Fire* at the Odeon Leicester Square in the presence of Her Majesty Queen Elizabeth the Queen Mother. Earlier in the day there had been a press showing at the Odeon Haymarket, and those of us who were performing in the evening had been invited to that. It was good to see the film as the Company had been involved in the making of it in Liverpool. The party, hosted by Twentieth Century Fox, was held in the ballroom of the Dorchester Hotel in Park Lane. Some three hundred people attended, and entertainment was provided by various groups and individuals including Charles Grant doing a Noel Coward turn, a band (Midnight Follies), the Cambridge Footlights with Hugh Laurie, and D'Oyly Carte: Jill Washington, Lorraine Daniels, Geoffrey Shovelton, Peter Lyon and myself. We were the first to perform, starting at around 10.40pm as the guests began to arrive; later we were given dinner in the Crystal Room.

Among many well-known people from the entertainment world who were at the Dorchester that evening I saw Colin Welland, who had produced the screenplay, and Jenny Agutter who had been at the Queen Elizabeth Birthday Ball in Los Angeles in 1978. The executive producer for the film was Dodi Fayed, a name that was not then well-known to the public. In retrospect, however, it was ironic that the film should have come out in the same year as the Royal Wedding. The evening was certainly a glittering occasion – according to press reports it cost somewhere in the region of £30,000 – and it served to take our minds off the gloom occasioned by the Arts Council's refusal to help us. Next day we were back in Ashton-under-Lyne in the more mundane surroundings of a portacabin outside the Tameside Theatre – the ups and downs of 'showbiz'. Later that week I received a letter from Muriel Dickson thanking me for sending her a copy of the article that I had written for *The College Courant* (No. 66, March 1981) which included her reminiscences. She was aware of our situation, and wished us all the very best for the future.

While we were in Ashton-under-Lyne I played for Geoffrey Shovelton at a concert in Leigh, west of Manchester, and near Geoffrey's hometown of Atherton, on April 4; earlier in the week I had done my share of conducting: *Mikado* on Wednesday (both performances) and *Iolanthe* on Thursday. Being near Manchester it was inevitable that there would be some contact with the G&S Society, and on Tuesday April 7 there was a G&S lunch at the Café Royal. Next day we held some auditions in the local Conservative Club. I met my cousin Norma for a meal on Thursday 9th, and she came to *Yeomen* in the evening. On Friday, after *Iolanthe,* we had a second 'sing for your supper' at Denton Golf Club. It had been an interesting two weeks, the various events making up for our less-than-perfect dressing-room accommodation at the Tameside Theatre.

The March 1981 edition of *The Savoyard – Patience Centenary Issue* was now out. There was, naturally, some coverage of the Arts Council's decision not to award us a grant, along with press and public reaction, much of the latter couched in terms of righteous indignation that something described as "irreplaceable" was in danger of closing down after more than a hundred years. Peter Riley had been interviewed on the BBC Radio 4 *Kaleidoscope* programme, and *Savoyard* readers were now encouraged to try to help by writing to Kenneth Robinson, the chairman of the Arts Council, or Paul Channon, the minister for the arts. But it was not all doom and gloom; the magazine contained several articles on *Patience*, including one by Jane Stedman, an American academic and authority on Victorian literature, who was working on a biography of Gilbert. At Brian Jones's request I had also contributed an article in which I said that I thought that it was in this opera that author and composer finally arrived at a true equilibrium of words and music, and also that I thought that Grosvenor's song 'A magnet hung in a hardware shop' – a tale with a moral, told in a few short lines (with some of Gilbert's trademark puns), set to the most beguiling and enchanting of tunes, and sung by the velvet-clad poet to an admiring circle of love-sick maidens – seemed to encapsulate the quintessential charm of G&S, a view I still hold.

After Ashton-under-Lyne we were at the Alexandra Theatre, Birmingham for a week. Once again I was at Appleby Magna with the Oakleys, and enjoying a nightly glass of Southern Comfort. We only gave seven performances there, with no performance on April 17, which was Good Friday. But before we had even opened this short season there was another interesting event – an appearance by the Company on the TV show *Pebble Mill at One* on Monday April 13. It was hosted by Marian Foster, and was geared to the fact that we needed £200,000 or we would have to close on July 18. Peter Riley was interviewed and gave a succinct account of the Company's current financial position. He said that it was a common misconception that our grant had been stopped. We had never had a grant and had made up any financial shortcomings from existing funds. But the rising costs of touring meant that these funds had now been used up and without help from the Arts Council we would indeed close on July 18.

An appeal had been launched, with flyers inviting contributors to Save D'Oyly Carte (hopefully the first phase in a world-wide appeal to raise £1,000,000), and Friends of D'Oyly Carte had also been set up, members receiving *The Savoyard* to keep them in touch with what was happening. Peter Riley quoted attendance figures at between two hundred thousand and three hundred thousand per annum, but said that as it took us approximately three years to cover all our venues around the country the overall attendance could be measured at around one million. In reply to a question about the possibility of new productions, he said that while the Company would be quite happy to have new productions it also had to satisfy the demands of its followers for the traditional productions that they were used to – and they were the people who kept us going. He also said, in relation to certain criticisms, that the Company was being penalised for good housekeeping. New productions, a larger orchestra or, indeed, any changes all required money that we did not have. We were now asking for the money and it had been refused. Without it we could not begin to counter any criticisms, and we seemed to be in a no-win situation – the classic catch-22.

We had some members of the orchestra with us at Pebble Mill and I rescored three numbers for our reduced forces: the last part of the Act I finale of *Pirates* (from 'Pray observe the magnanimity'), 'Take a pair of sparkling eyes' (*Gondoliers*), which was sung by Meston Reid, and 'Once more gondolieri' from the Act II finale of *Gondoliers*. Jill Washington was also interviewed briefly, and after this there was a performance of 'Three little maids from school' (*Mikado*). I didn't rescore that number. The Act II finale of *Gondoliers* ends, of course, with the appropriate line "We leave you with feelings of pleasure!" – this was a number which invariably ended our D'Oyly Carte in Concert programmes, and almost every G&S concert that I have ever been involved in. I received a fee from the BBC for the Pebble Mill programme and donated it to the Save D'Oyly Carte appeal. The following day I was interviewed by Christine Oakley on Radio WM in a programme called *Good Company*. Christine was Harold and Hazel Oakley's daughter.

She had started work at Radio WM as a reporter, but by 1981 was presenting programmes. Two days later I was able to get complimentary tickets for Hazel and Christine to come to *Ruddigore*, which I conducted.

After Birmingham we had a week at the Alhambra Theatre in Bradford (April 20–25). Fraser was away all week (I think he was conducting Wagner's *Lohengrin* for Northern Opera in Newcastle upon Tyne), and I conducted every performance: *Pinafore, Iolanthe*, *Mikado* (twice), *Pinafore*, *Ruddigore* and *Pirates* (twice). The end of that week brought the coldest spell of weather that the country had experienced at that time of year for at least thirty years, and there was a thick blanket of snow across much of Yorkshire and elsewhere. It was difficult to get to the theatre, particularly if you were coming in by car, but luckily we didn't have to cancel any performances. It was also while we were in Bradford that a little problem was solved. The music stand that we had was the right height for Fraser, but he was several inches taller than I, and I often wished that I could be a little bit higher when I was conducting. Our stage crew had noticed that in the green room there was a dartboard in a frame. They found that by putting it on the podium it gave me the desired extra height; so they bought it from the Alhambra crew, strengthened the frame and painted it black. I used it from then on, and it made all the difference.

Bradford was followed by a week at the New Theatre, Hull. On this occasion I stayed in Hull itself with two sisters whose house was full of books and cats. I like both, and the cats were not a problem. One of them had given itself a nasty shock by jumping onto a hot cooker, but at least it had survived, although it always seemed wary of everyone and everything. Then, even at this late stage, there was another new venue – the Haymarket Theatre in Leicester, one of the five cities that the Oakleys had said were equidistant from Appleby Magna. We had already been to Birmingham, Nottingham and Coventry and this was the fourth; we never did get to Derby. We were at Leicester for a week, and despite having been at Appleby Magna recently for our week in Birmingham I was back for more Southern Comfort in the little study cum library. The Haymarket was a curiously shaped red-brick building on a main road. In previous years the Company had played at the De Montfort Hall, an older and more traditional building that stood in own grounds. As a hall, rather than a proper theatre, its facilities were far from ideal for the Company and, according to those who had played there, the Haymarket was a great improvement, despite its unusual external appearance. With the prospect of closure just a matter of months away, we still held auditions on Tuesday May 5. We heard seven people, but we never used any of them.

From Leicester we moved to Blackpool for two weeks. At this time of year it was more difficult to find digs, but people with their own transport were able to find accommodation out of town, sometimes in the pleasant surroundings of neighbouring Lytham St Anne's. But the interesting thing about this visit was that we were now in a new venue, the Grand Theatre (another lovely Frank Matcham building), which was smaller than the Opera House and much better for us. While we were in Blackpool I purchased a Henry Lytton autograph from a private source. It had been offered for sale at £10, with the proviso that the seller would retain £5 and donate the other £5 to the Save D'Oyly Carte appeal. I was more than happy to go along with that. I had contributed again to the Fund and also had an interesting autograph for my expanding collection. We then moved on to a more familiar venue, the Theatre Royal, Norwich, for another two weeks.

On the travel Sunday, May 24, there was a concert in Market Drayton, organised by Alistair Donkin. It clearly involved quite a lot of travelling – Blackpool to Market Drayton and on to Norwich – but we took it all in our stride. It was just part of being on the road all the time and living out of a suitcase.

On May 30 the Gilbert and Sullivan Society held a convention (its seventh) at the Law Society Hall in Chancery Lane, London. I travelled down from Norwich to attend this, as I had been asked to contribute a couple of short sessions on Sullivan's style along the lines of the article I had published in the September 1980 edition of *The Savoyard*. They were introduced by Norman Beckett of the Manchester G&S Society. There were numerous sessions throughout the day, ending with an entertainment arranged by Albert Truelove and former principal soprano Cynthia Morey, which involved seven former members of the Company, some of whom (Julia Goss, Lyndsie Holland, John Reed and Billy Strachan) I already knew. But it was interesting to meet the other three: Jennifer Toye, Michael Wakeham and Adrian Lawson, all of whom I worked with after the Company had closed. Jennifer Toye was a niece of Geoffrey Toye who had been a guest conductor with the Company during the years 1919–24, had written a new overture for *Ruddigore*, which we still used, and had produced and conducted the 1939 film of *The Mikado*. As well as the expected G&S numbers there were Victorian music hall songs and some of Gilbert's *Bab Ballads*, the latter entertainingly delivered by Adrian Lawson; I particularly remember his rendition of 'Hongree and Mahry'. Then it was back up to Norwich for another week before travelling south again, this time to Brighton for three weeks from June 8–27. Unusually, during this time, we gave another concert in Bray on June 14.

Brighton is just over twenty miles from Eastbourne and I was able to stay at home, driving in to the theatre every day along the coast road. It was very pleasant at that time of year. We already knew that the wedding of His Royal Highness Prince Charles and Lady Diana Spencer was to take place on July 29, and one particular memory of that Brighton season was a competition to see who could find the tackiest souvenir (of which there were many) of the couple. I submitted a lapel badge showing a photograph of Charles and Diana in which Charles's hair had been removed, the caption on the badge reading 'The King and Di', a reference not only to Rodgers and Hammerstein's *The King and I*, but to the follically-challenged Yul Brynner. Several people submitted this one, but it wasn't a winner as it wasn't the tackiest by a long shot. There were more auditions in London on June 26, although at this stage it was doubtful if we would ever be able to employ any of those who attended.

The Save D'Oyly Carte campaign was now under way, but we didn't know how much money was coming in, or if there would be any further work after July 18. In the meantime we had two more dates and, surprisingly, both were new venues. The first of these was the Cliffs Pavilion at Southend-on-Sea, more precisely at Westcliff-on-Sea, where we played for a week. Although I had never been there I knew that Westcliff was the home of my accountant John Kennedy Melling who had several Company members as his clients. Thankful as we were to have a week's work, the Pavilion itself was another less than satisfactory venue. It had a very strange acoustic. The sound seemed to take longer than usual to come off the stage, but you had to keep conducting or the performance would grind to a halt. This was similar to the old tracker action organs where the sound came shortly after you depressed the keys, and woe betide you if you inadvertently slowed up to wait for it; you just had to keep going. It was a bit like that at Westcliff-on-Sea. There was a Barclays reception in the Pavilion itself after the opening performance on Monday June 29, something we hadn't had for some time.

And so we came to the last stop on the tour – Cambridge, where the season was being presented jointly by Cambridge City Council and ourselves in association with Barclays Bank. An attractive programme, giving all the operas being performed, cast lists and Freddie Lloyd's opera synopses, also contained another Barclays advertisement, based this time on 'When Britain really ruled the waves' (*Iolanthe*). Would this be the last-ever venue for D'Oyly Carte? The programme actually suggested that the performances here might be among our last. We still didn't know for sure. But the uncertainty was offset by the venue itself, certainly the most unusual one that I had yet encountered, even including some of those on the North

American and Australasian tours, namely the Big Top Theatre on Jesus Green. The city's Arts Theatre was not large enough to take major touring companies and Cambridge had for some years been deprived of performances by, for instance, the Royal Ballet and ourselves. Other towns were in the same position and someone had come up with the idea of using a circus-type 'big top' that could, like the various companies, tour around the country. This was certainly better than no venue at all, but it was very unsatisfactory in some ways.

On July 6 the full Company and orchestra assembled for what was called an acoustic clarity test. Duckboards had been put down to facilitate one's movements to and from the dressing rooms (marquees again), but if it rained these still didn't stop the costumes or our conducting clothes from getting wet. We expected warm sunny days, but we didn't always get them. Mid-week matinees in Cambridge were again on Thursdays, and I will never forget the matinee of the second week, July 16, when we were doing *Iolanthe*. This was the day of the great storm. The performance started normally, but during the interval the heavens opened and you could hardly hear anything above the rain pounding on the canvas. The rain was followed by thunder and lightning, but the Company somehow kept going although most of the dialogue was totally lost. The conductor's stand also happened to be directly under the opening in the roof for the tent pole and water dripped relentlessly onto my score. It was a very difficult afternoon. I was reminded of Her Majesty's Theatre in Brisbane, which had a corrugated iron roof, making it almost impossible to hear the dialogue when it rained, as it did one matinee day when I had to do both shows. At least at Her Majesty's there was no hole in the roof to let the rain in.

It didn't rain all the time, of course, and on other days we were able to see something of Cambridge. We hired a boat on the Cam and tried to cope with punting. I also managed to see my old professor from Glasgow University, Frederick Rimmer, a Cambridge graduate himself, who had retired there. On the day before our last performances, I had lunch with him and his wife at their home in Grantchester on the edge of the city. We were there for two weeks, from July 6–18. During our stay some of us were allowed to use a staff and artists' car park, but we had to have passes, and as early as April we had had to submit details of our cars – make, type and registration number. The car passes had been printed for the Royal Ballet and ourselves. Peter Hamburger, our timpanist, didn't have a pass, but he required access for his van on the first and last days.

We had already heard that if the appeal had not raised enough money we would close on July 18, but just before we reached that deadline I received a contract from Freddie Lloyd, dated July 15, offering me work for another year, or at least for part of the year. The engagement was to commence on August 24, 1981, but was to terminate in February 1982. It appeared, then, that the £200,000 spoken of in *Pebble Mill at One* had not materialised. In fact, only some £70,000 was eventually raised. Ironically, the contract was printed on new yellow notepaper with an attractive logo consisting of five of the principal G&S characters dancing on top of the name D'Oyly Carte. This was all part of the Company's recent efforts to brighten up its publicity – sadly, to no avail. I often wondered if the Company really ought to have closed on July 18, assuming that the money had indeed run out, but that some extra sponsorship and private money, along with the £70,000 raised by the Save D'Oyly Carte appeal, had enabled us to stagger on into another London season. If it really was to be the end after one hundred and seven years, better to give our last performances, and particularly our final Last Night, in more dignified surroundings than a soggy circus tent.

My salary for this final half-year was to be £107.80 per week, more than three times what it had been just six years previously – £32 per week – although that was as the repetiteur. My subsistence allowance of £78.43 per week had risen from £18 to almost £80, and I was also to get my usual dress allowance of £65. But I was just one member of the Company, and despite being able to get some 80 per cent of what we needed from the box office, these increases in salaries and subsistence could not be sustained. With no public funding, it was hardly surprising that the Company's own funds had now dried up, and the cupboard seemed well and truly bare. I think that many of us would have been prepared to forego salary increases in order to help the Company survive. We, after all, were the ones who would be losing our jobs. Even our orchestra had said that they would be prepared to do this, but both Equity and the Musicians' Union insisted that increases were negotiated for *all* their members and these increases had to be paid. And so there was no saving there. In truth, any such savings would have been a drop in the ocean compared to what we required. The end was now clearly in sight.

I can't remember when I first heard that Alexander 'Sandy' Faris was to join the Company as musical director, but I remember thinking that it was rather strange that at a time of financial crisis we should be taking on one more member of staff. There was also the question of how this would affect all of us in the music department and it was never really made clear. At first I was led to believe that we now had two equal musical directors, although their respective titles suggested otherwise. In our programmes, and in the fourth supplement to Rollins and Witts' *The D'Oyly Carte Opera Company in Gilbert and Sullivan Operas*, Sandy Faris was listed as musical director and Fraser was listed as associate musical director, although an earlier internal memo had informed us that he was to be "Resident Conductor with responsibility for music preparation". Altogether it was an awkward situation. My own new (and final) contract said that it was understood that I accepted the position of assistant [sic] conductor, with no mention of my previous role as chorus master. Reading between the lines it seemed to me that both Fraser and I had effectively been demoted. Perhaps Fraser was really now the chorus master and associate conductor and I, even if I continued to conduct some performances, was once again the repetiteur. And where would that leave Paul Seeley? Would he simply be the orchestral manager? Or would this post eventually go, leaving the music department with just three people as before?

With all this doubt and uncertainty in my mind I drafted a long letter to Freddie Lloyd asking what had happened to the position of chorus master and, if we were to have three conductors, was I going to lose some performances, even although I was now to be 'assistant' conductor? I eventually had a meeting with him and he said that I wasn't to worry. The changes were only at the top and my job would be more or less the same. Nevertheless the post of chorus master had effectively vanished, although Fraser eventually persuaded the management that I should, as before, be 'associate' conductor. There was also the possibility of another North American tour in 1982 (if we survived that long). If a tour *should* materialise would I still be able to go? Or would I be left behind as I was in 1976, and as Paul was left behind in 1978 and 1979? There surely wouldn't be room for three conductors. The job of orchestral manager was taken on by Alan Franks and Charles Norton, two colleagues of Sandy Faris who were never listed as part of our music department, and Paul now became the assistant to the company manager, Gordon MacKenzie.

The 1980–81 tour ended in Cambridge on July 18 and I went back to Eastbourne for a week. Our relative positions in the music department were now clearer in my mind and we knew that there would be some work until at least February 1982. Despite the future uncertainty we were still performing, and we even had to take on seven new choristers – Linda Darnell, Riona Faram, Ann-Louise Straker, Philip Creasy, Robert Gibbs, Peter James-Robinson and Sean Osborne. While I was at home, I received a letter from the office asking me to remind them to make appointments with the wardrobe department. There were two weeks of music calls with the new intake, beginning on Monday July 27, at the Church of the Holy Redeemer in Exmouth Market, a venue we had often used. Another letter from Tabard House, dated August 5, asked me to remind one chorister to submit a biography and another to supply a photograph. Having purchased a season ticket, I travelled up and down by train every day from Eastbourne for the music calls. On the face of it things seemed no different to my earlier sessions with new choristers just a few years before. It was hard to accept that this was almost certainly the last time I would be thus gainfully employed.

The Royal Wedding took place at St Paul's Cathedral on the Wednesday of the first week, July 29, and we had a holiday that day. At the end of the two-week rehearsal period I was instructed to leave the *Mikado* fans for Jimmie Marsland as there would be production rehearsals for the new choristers the following week. I then set off for Scotland on August 8, stopping overnight with the Oakleys in Appleby Magna. Hazel was anxious to hear the latest news on the Company's future. I was back in Eastbourne by August 12 and on the following day I went to a Prom where my old friend Sandy Oliver was singing in a performance of Richard Strauss's *Ariadne auf Naxos*. On the Saturday he sang again, this time in Johann Strauss II's *Der Zigeunerbaron*. I was to have been on holiday for the last week of the new choristers' rehearsals (August 17–21), as Fraser was going to play for these, but he was later tied up with various Company meetings, and he asked me if I could step in and so, having acquired another season ticket, I travelled again every day from Eastbourne for a further week. Chorus rehearsals were at Islington Town Hall and there were some principals' rehearsals at the Church of the Holy Redeemer, and that ended my sixth year – my last full year - with D'Oyly Carte.

Chapter 7: 1981–1982

I

The last year began, as always, with full Company rehearsals for the operas we were taking out on tour. These were held in Islington Town Hall during the week of August 24–28, and consisted of *Mikado* (Monday afternoon), *Mikado* and *Pinafore* (Tuesday), *Pirates* and *Yeomen* (Wednesday), *Yeomen* again (Thursday), *Iolanthe* (Friday morning) and *Ruddigore* (Friday afternoon) – six this time. On Saturday the 29th we had a D'Oyly Carte in Concert at the Maltings, Snape, one of the more interesting venues for these concerts. Monday August 31 was a holiday, but there were more rehearsals during the rest of the week. There was a wine and cheese party at Tabard House on Wednesday September 2, from 6pm onwards, to open the new premises. This was an unusual event in itself, but it was also interesting to see the building. It was pleasant enough, but for all its amenities it certainly lacked the ambience of 1 Savoy Hill where I had worked just five short years before; being away from the Savoy Hotel complex, and with the apparent demise of the Company imminent, it was hard not to think of the biblical words "How are the mighty fallen". On the Thursday I had to go to the store in Walworth (run by James 'Jim' Murray, another Company character) to see about our music skip; finally, on the Sunday, I set off to drive north for our last provincial tour.

The tour began with two weeks in Manchester (September 7–19); this time we were at a new venue, the Palace Theatre in

Oxford Street. Sandy Faris was now at the helm. He obviously wanted to make some changes, but found that with limited rehearsal time at his disposal, and the fact that we were a repertory company used to doing things in a certain way, he didn't always get the performances that he wanted – certainly not at the beginning of his short tenure. I particularly remember one *Pinafore* (it may have been his very first performance with the Company) that was singularly lacking in co-ordination; this was mainly because the orchestra followed him more or less implicitly while the Company performed as they usually did, whatever was happening in the pit. It did latterly come together as everyone got used to him, but Fraser and I also had to accept any changes that he wanted to make, and modify our performances accordingly.

Sandy Faris was a graduate of Oxford University and his musical pedigree was certainly not in doubt. He had once been chorus master of the Carl Rosa Opera Company, but much of his working life was in musicals and operetta. He had been involved in Sadler's Wells Opera's revivals of Offenbach's operettas and had conducted *Iolanthe* for them in 1962 (the first production after the expiry of Gilbert's copyright). He had also conducted *Mikado* at the Wells, *Yeomen* at the Tower of London in 1978 and had made several recordings. To the general public he was probably better known as the composer of the theme tunes to the TV series *Upstairs, Downstairs* (1971–75) and *The Duchess of Duke Street* (1976–77). All of this experience might eventually have made some appreciable difference to our performances, but, like the choristers who joined for this last season, he didn't even complete one full year. He maintained a somewhat aloof position, perhaps deliberately, and never seemed to be part of the family atmosphere of D'Oyly Carte. I hardly got to know him at all, although I heard that he had seen one of my performances before he joined us and had passed some favourable comment on my conducting.

Despite having a new conductor, our rehearsal schedule seemed thinner than before; perhaps this was a sign that we really were winding down. In the first week there was a full chorus rehearsal for *Iolanthe* and *Ruddigore* on the Tuesday (September 8) and another *Iolanthe* rehearsal on the Friday, this time for chorus and principals. These were held at the Royal Northern College of Music in Oxford Road; there were no understudy calls that week. Barbara Lilley had now left the Company and had been replaced by former principal soprano Vivian Tierney who had left the Company in 1979. Although born in London, Vivian had been brought up in Manchester and it was appropriate that her first reappearance with the Company should be in what she regarded as her home town. On Wednesday September 9 I played for Geoffrey Shovelton at a concert for the disabled held in the Radcliffe Civic Centre in Bury. This was the International Year of Disabled People and the event had been organised by the Community Contact Department at Bury Police Station; the band of the Greater Manchester Police also performed. I can't remember how we got involved in this.

On the middle Sunday of our stay in Manchester (September 13), Geoffrey, Jill Pert and I, along with several former Company members and the Rugby Operatic Society with their conductor Martin Jackson, took part in an afternoon concert held in the Temple Speech Room at Rugby School. This was presented by a local G&S enthusiast, Malcolm Lax (who had become a Friend of D'Oyly Carte), and was in aid of the Save D'Oyly Carte appeal. Malcolm had assembled quite a galaxy of former Company members, including Michael Rayner and Gareth Jones who had both recently left us, John Broad whom I had met when he came back to play the Notary (*Sorcerer*) in 1980, and John's wife, former chorister Rosalind Griffiths, who had left the Company with John in 1975. But Malcolm had also managed to persuade two of the biggest names in recent D'Oyly Carte history, Tom Round and Donald Adams, to take part. I had previously met Donald at a function in Bristol and had met Tom earlier in the year at the Twelfth Night Revels at Sadler's Wells in January. The first half of the programme was devoted to performances of *Cox and Box* and *Trial by Jury*, and the second half consisted of excerpts from the operas along with other items. Donald sang the Mikado's Act II entrance song 'A more humane Mikado never/Did in Japan exist' (with his idiosyncratic and electrifying laugh – more of a shriek – halfway through each verse) and Geoffrey sang Sullivan's famous song 'The Lost Chord'. I hadn't known until then that Donald Adams had worked with the variety star Arthur Lucan, better known as Old Mother Riley: from that, via G&S, to grand opera his was indeed a varied career in the theatre.

At the beginning of the following week I received my last dress allowance cheque: still just £65. Later that week I had a session playing bridge with several members of the Company, including Bruce Graham who had introduced me to the game. During the Australasian tour Caroline Hudson and I had sometimes played Scrabble with Patrick and Jackie Wilkes, and that was fairly straightforward (although it sometimes led to heated arguments over obscure words), but bridge was something I found rather difficult, although I had often played various forms of whist. I never mastered it and didn't play it again after the Company had closed. The rehearsal schedule that week was slightly fuller and consisted of a *Ruddigore* run-through for the new choristers on Tuesday the 15th (held this time in the Quaker Church in Mount Street), a full cast rehearsal for *Iolanthe* (onstage and with the orchestra) on Wednesday and a similar rehearsal for *Ruddigore* on the Friday. My cousin Norma came to *Ruddigore* that evening, having seen *Pirates* on our last visit in 1979 and *Yeomen* when we were in Ashton-under-Lyne earlier in the year. She and her brother Ron had been brought up surrounded by light opera. Their father, Arthur Millar, had been the conductor of the Dundee Operatic Society, and he eventually became president of NODA – the National Operatic and Dramatic Association – which I had joined while still at school.

After Manchester we had two weeks at the Theatre Royal, Nottingham (September 21–October 3) and yet again I stayed with Harold and Hazel Oakley. I had now been there so often that I began to wonder if they were doubting the wisdom of having told me that they were equidistant from five cities, but they seemed to enjoy having company in that very large house, particularly now that their children, Christine and Geoffrey, had left home. On the Tuesday and Friday of the first week there were understudy rehearsals which were held in Central Scout Hall (yet another new venue), and on Thursday, in the theatre and with the orchestra, there was a full cast rehearsal of *Iolanthe* which was taken by Sandy Faris. On the Wednesday morning (matinee day) of the second week there was a Schools' Special which was presented in much the same way as the similar event at Sadler's Wells on February 18. It began at noon with an introduction and welcome by Geoffrey Shovelton. This was followed by details of many aspects of the theatre: front of house, pit, proscenium arch, safety curtain (all two tons of it), lighting, and the stage area itself, eventually shorn of any scenery, which was something of a revelation to most of the young audience. Heather Perkins talked about the problems involved in keeping wigs in good condition and Alistair Donkin again went through the process of 'making up' in front of the children. The Company members who took part were then introduced to the audience and three numbers were performed: 'For the merriest fellows are we' (*Gondoliers*), 'Three little maids from school' (*Mikado*) and 'I shipped, d'ye see' (*Ruddigore*). After this, with the tabs still open, the stage was set for the afternoon performance of *Pinafore* (which the children were going to see after having had a packed lunch), and the Company members appeared in their costumes; 'When I was a lad' and 'Never mind the why and wherefore' were then sung. Geoffrey had explained about encores, and the latter number was sung no less than six times.

It had been a very successful morning, but it wasn't the end of our involvement with the idea of educational programmes. A project, D'Oyly Carte for Schools (financed by Shell UK Ltd), had been initiated, and ex-teacher Geoffrey with his customary enthusiasm prepared a folder with a wide variety of items, many of which he illustrated with his own inimitable drawings and cartoons. There were notes for teachers, brief histories of Gilbert, Sullivan and D'Oyly Carte, and even instructions on how to build a model theatre out of a used cereal packet. The folder also contained numerous items relating specifically to *Pirates*, with backcloths and scenery for each act which could be coloured by the pupils to their own taste, glued onto rigid card and then slotted in to the model theatre. There were also drawings of the individual characters which, again, could be coloured, glued onto card and put on the stage, and even puzzles and games for younger children. It was well thought out and cleverly done. I contributed simplified piano arrangements of 'Poor wandering one!', 'Ah, leave me not to pine/Alone and desolate' and 'Come, friends, who plough the sea'. If the Company had survived and this idea had taken off, I think we might have prepared kits for all, or at least the most popular, of the operas. In retrospect the project should perhaps have been called Gilbert and Sullivan for Schools, but despite the expiry of the copyright some twenty years before, and also numerous new productions (such as those at ENO), it is significant that D'Oyly Carte was still synonymous with G&S. There were several other Schools' Specials in our last London season.

I was with Geoffrey again on October 1, playing for him at a concert in the Albert Hall, Bolton, the nearest large venue to his home town of Atherton. Earlier that day there had been a staff meeting in the theatre. The famous Nottingham Goose Fair had now opened and several of us went along after the performance on the Friday. One of the attractions was an enormous gondola, with multiple seating, which was suspended from a frame. It started by swinging gently forward and back like a pendulum, and this was quite pleasant at the beginning, but with each movement the arc increased until it encompassed one hundred and eighty degrees, with the bow and stern eventually being at right angles to the ground, alternately left and right – but still moving slowly. It was really quite alarming, and certainly not for the squeamish, but we survived. Encouraged by our previous bridge sessions, I bought a book entitled *Contract Bridge for Beginners* while we were in Nottingham, but the closure of the Company put an end to our sessions and I never opened it again.

The September edition of *The Savoyard – The Savoy Theatre 1881-1981* was now out. Reduced to just two issues per annum, this was the last one produced while the Company was still in existence. Several articles were devoted to the Savoy Theatre, as its centenary was about to be celebrated in October, but there was also a report on the current financial crisis. We already knew, from our contracts, that the Company would continue until February 1982, but there was still no word of any extension to that deadline. We now learned that the Save D'Oyly Carte appeal had raised £50,000 by the end of July; this included individual donations which ranged from £1 (the contents of a five-year-old's money box) to a generous £2,000, but that was nowhere near the £200,000 that we needed immediately, let alone the £1,000,000 that it was hoped to raise worldwide. There were still fundraising events, such as Malcolm Lax's concert in Rugby, but it all seemed too little too late, and *The Savoyard*, despite trying to sound optimistic, could only say that the next few months would be decisive in the fight to save the Company – which, of course, we all knew. This issue also contained my second article on Sullivan's style and a tribute to Beti Lloyd-Jones who was celebrating twenty-five years' work with the Company. Beti had been interviewed for this article and she stressed the special family atmosphere that was so much a part of D'Oyly Carte.

We ended this short provincial tour on Saturday October 3 and then had three weeks' holiday. Other dates, in Bristol, Cardiff and Leeds, had originally been planned for the tour, but these had been cancelled, and no less than five weeks had been set aside for a project that we had been led to believe was going to save the Company, namely the filming of five of our productions for American television by Brent Walker Productions which had been founded by the entrepreneur and former boxer George Walker. Unfortunately nothing came of this as Brent Walker decided that a different approach was required for their American audiences. They particularly wanted to have at least one major star in each opera and decided to have studio productions rather than simply videotaping our own performances. And so, in the end, no one from the Company, apart from Sandy Faris and Fraser Goulding, took part. Eventually no less than twelve of the operas (including *Cox and Box*) were filmed; the series was produced by the American Judith de Paul, and a wide variety of well-known artists such as Joel Grey, Frankie Howerd, Keith Michell and Vincent Price appeared in leading roles. The casts did, however, include six former members of the Company: Donald Adams, John Fryatt, Tom Lawlor, Pamela Field, Gillian Knight and Elise MacDougall. My old friend Sandy Oliver and other fellow students from our time at the RSAMD played several roles, as did Sandra Dugdale who would soon be making guest appearances with us. The chorus was provided by the Ambrosian Opera Chorus with their chorus master John McCarthy, and the London Symphony Orchestra was conducted by Sandy Faris; Fraser Goulding also acted as assistant conductor.

When it finally became clear that the Company would not be involved in the project it was too late to find other theatres that would take us. The long break now meant that there would be no revenue for five weeks – the last thing we needed. Brent Walker did, however, cover the Company's costs for this unexpected gap in our schedule, and with the extra free time we were able to arrange rehearsals in London: these started, at the beginning of the fourth week, on October 26. Perhaps the most disappointing aspect of Brent Walker's change of plan was that we were denied having at least some of our productions recorded for posterity. Many individual numbers from the operas have been recorded, often in concert performances by former members of the Company, and there is the 'three little maids' scene in *Chariots of Fire*, but the only complete Company performances are of *Pinafore* and *Mikado*, although much of *Trial* can be seen in the 1953 film *The Story of Gilbert and Sullivan*. D'Oyly Carte's productions, whatever critics might say of them, had style, and they had charm (two qualities singularly lacking in many of today's productions), and it is a pity that they were not recorded so that future generations could see how we performed them.

At the end of the first week's holiday the Company was in the Savoy Theatre for the centenary concert. This was billed as a Savoy Centenary Gala and was held on Sunday October 11, the day after the actual centenary; although I had played for auditions there this was the first time that I had actually performed in the theatre. The programme consisted mainly of items from G&S but not from the early operas, as these had originally been performed elsewhere; consequently there were no numbers from *Thespis*, *Trial*, *Sorcerer*, *Pinafore* or *Pirates*. The concert opened with a short curtain-raiser (William Douglas-Home's *Dramatic Licence*) which had been written for the Company's centenary in 1975. It involved just three characters – Gilbert, Sullivan and Richard D'Oyly Carte. The first musical item was the overture to *Patience*, the first opera seen at the Savoy (although it had been running at the Opéra Comique since April 23, 1881), which Paul Seeley and I played on two pianos. There was no orchestra, and all of the items had piano accompaniment, some of this from two-piano arrangements which the office library had for hire along with the standard sets of orchestral parts. (These had been made some years earlier by Francis Buckley to meet the needs of smaller societies, and were in memory of Stanley Parker, long-time Company secretary and treasurer, who had died in 1960.) The exceptions in this concert were *Ida*, *Ruddigore, Yeomen*, *Utopia Limited* and *The Grand Duke* for which we had to use our ordinary vocal scores. The overture was followed by two excerpts from *Patience* – 'Silvered is the raven hair' and 'It's clear that mediaeval art' – and that was effectively our own centenary tribute: we had been in Bradford on the opera's centenary day, April 23 (St George's Day), and had performed *Pinafore* that evening.

The other G&S numbers were from all the succeeding operas (*Iolanthe* to *The Grand Duke*), but there were also five items from other operas and shows that had been staged at the Savoy: the Prologue from Leoncavallo's opera *Pagliacci* (sung by Peter Lyon), 'The proposal' from the comic opera *Jolly Roger* by Walter Leigh (sung by Vivian Tierney, Patricia Leonard, Meston Reid and Peter Lyon), 'Free to sing' from the musical *Free as Air* (a dance routine with Alan Spencer and Hélène Witcombe), 'Bronxville Derby and Joan' from Noel Coward's *Sail Away* (sung by Patricia Leonard and John Ayldon – it was a number they excelled in and performed at every opportunity) and 'You'd better love me while you may' from the musical *High Spirits* (sung by Lorraine Daniels). Paul and I also played two further pieces which we had arranged for two pianos: a selection from John Gay's ballad opera *Polly* (the sequel to *The Beggar's Opera*) and Sullivan's *Princess of Wales's March*. The concert ended, as so often, with the finale from Act II of *The Gondoliers* with its so appropriate final words "We leave you with feelings of pleasure!" We then had another two weeks' holiday.

It was pleasant enough having some time to ourselves, but with the approaching demise of the Company, and the general uncertainty of what would happen after February, it was something of a relief to be back in harness; we started rehearsing again on Monday October 26. For this final season we were at the Royal Adelphi Theatre in the Strand and so we could not use the excellent rehearsal facilities at Sadler's Wells. At first our rehearsals were held in the Old Vic Theatre in Waterloo Road and we all received a memo suggesting that artists should wear "practical rehearsal clothes – i.e. clothes you don't mind getting dirty", although I don't recall that this rehearsal venue was any worse than many another that we had used. We had had fewer rehearsals during our recent provincial tour, but the schedule was now fully back on course. As there were no shows in these weeks we made full use of the sessions we were allowed and there were rehearsals every morning and afternoon for chorus, principals or understudies; there were even rehearsals on the morning of Saturday October 31 – a rare event. All the rehearsals in the first week, and most of those in the second, were devoted to Wilfred Judd's new production of *Mikado*, and on the Monday and Thursday of each week there were staff and production meetings at the end of the afternoon sessions. It was a busy time for everyone, but we were about to open what would probably be our last season, and as we were now performing in the heart of London, and hoping to attract even more people than our regular audiences, we had to be on top form. The Company was also determined to give of its best and to refute any suggestions of being "tired" and "wooden".

There were *Ruddigore* rehearsals on Monday November 16, this time in the Adelphi. On the Tuesday there was a publicity event in the Piazza, Covent Garden to draw attention to our plight. We had secured the services of London's Town Crier, Peter Moore (whom we got to know quite well during the season), and Courage Brewery had provided a dray, a coachman and two horses, which had been renamed 'Gilbert' and 'Sullivan' for the day. (In 1962, when the St Martin's Tavern in London's John Adam Street had become the Gilbert and Sullivan pub, Whitbread had also provided a dray, a coachman and two horses which had been similarly renamed for the occasion.) Several of the Company were aboard the dray in costume, and with Peter Moore walking in front with his bell (Oyez! Oyez! Oyez!), there was a short procession from the Adelphi Theatre to the Piazza where a press call had been organised by John Watt, the Company's press representative. Numerous photographs were taken, and members of the Company then gave a concert of some dozen items. Orchestral calls also began that day and a list of these, which had been sent out earlier, introduced many of us to a new word, sitzprobe (literally a seated rehearsal with singers and orchestra), which was in common use in opera houses and elsewhere: yet another change, if a small one. The *Ruddigore* sitzprobe was held on Tuesday afternoon at the Adelphi. Afterwards Freddie Lloyd spoke to the Company; he outlined the current position which was, to say the least, depressing. On the following day (the day on which we opened) he sent a letter to everyone stating why he had spoken to us. He had particularly wanted us to know the facts prior to a forthcoming BBC broadcast and to be fully aware of what the position might be at the end of February; he could only hope (as we all hoped) that help might be forthcoming and that 1982 might be a better year for all of us.

While Freddie Lloyd's letter expressed a faint hope that something positive might just happen to save the Company, another letter, this time from Dame Bridget herself (dated simply November 1981), said that even if the end didn't come in 1982 some radical reorganisation, in whatever form, was clearly necessary. Although quite shy and retiring by nature, she began by saying how close she felt to everyone in these "testing times" and how much she appreciated everything that we had done to keep the Company alive. Having been responsible for the operas since her father's death in 1948, she had been in a position to close the Company when the copyright ran out at the end of 1961, or again in the centenary year, 1975, but had not done so as all was going well on each of those occasions. She also said that any changes need not be the end of a tradition but the beginning of a continuously developing one. It was, however, for the trustees to decide how best this might be achieved. This all seemed to imply that even if the Company could somehow survive after February 1982 (which seemed doubtful) it would not be in the form that we had known it, and, more to the point, would we all be able to retain our jobs if it *did* survive? Neither letter was really very encouraging, particularly as we were about to start performing again.

II

And so we came to our last London season, the longest one that I had yet experienced: fifteen weeks with a total of one hundred and fifteen performances – not counting the final Last Night which was very different from the ones everyone had been used to. Once again we had a larger orchestra, led now by Carmel Hakendorf. There was a nominated dress rehearsal of *Ruddigore* on the morning of Wednesday November 18 and we opened the season that evening with the first of five performances of it (we did a further week in January); next day we were back at the Old Vic for more *Mikado* rehearsals, and on Friday morning, November 20, there was a run-through of *Pinafore*. Before each performance at the Adelphi one or other of the principals would go out in front of the tabs to draw the audience's attention to our plight and to inform them that receptacles were available in the foyer for donations to help the cause. It was all rather embarrassing to be resorting to the begging bowl, but we had to make every effort to raise more money, despite still being supported by Barclays Bank, in the hope that even at this late stage there might be an eleventh hour reprieve – changes or no changes.

On Sunday November 22, having had digs elsewhere, I moved in to Sandy Oliver's temporary accommodation in Hamilton Terrace in St John's Wood. This was essentially one large room in a flat that was owned by the actress Beryl Cooke (not to be confused with the artist Beryl Cook – with no 'e') who was seldom there. Sandy himself was working abroad. On the Monday we began a half-week of *Pinafore*. Earlier in the day we gave another lunchtime concert in the Piazza and this was followed by a second one on the Tuesday. On the Thursday we began a full week of *Iolanthe* and on the Friday there was a meeting about the forthcoming Schools' Specials – one each in the months of December and January, and two in February. On Tuesday December 1 we had rehearsals in the Portcullis Theatre in Monck Street near the Houses of

Parliament: it was a rather dingy building. As we now had three conductors in the Company I didn't conduct as many performances as I had done under Fraser (just eighteen in this London season), and these were mainly matinees; my first one was the Wednesday matinee of *Iolanthe* on December 2.

Iolanthe was followed by a week of *Pirates* from Thursday December 3; on the last day, December 9, we had the first London Schools' Special. We had now evolved a programme for these. They all began with 'For the merriest fellows are we' and ended with 'Once more *gondolieri*' (both from *Gondoliers*), the latter number always being referred to by the Company as 'Feelings of pleasure' from the text of its last line. After 'The merriest fellows' there would be one or two numbers from other operas, but before 'Feelings of pleasure' there would be two or three numbers from the particular opera that the children would be seeing that day at the matinee, in this case *Pirates*, which I conducted. Next day we began a week's run of Wilfred Judd's new production of *Mikado*. Sandy Faris had written a new, and shorter, overture (orchestrated by David Redston) which began and ended with two strokes on a tam-tam – a gong of indefinite pitch. (The 1939 film of the opera begins with a stroke on a gong after the fashion of the J. Arthur Rank Organisation, or, indeed, of the many instances of gleeful dismissal in *The Gong Show*.) On the Friday I played for Geoffrey Shovelton again, this time at his church in Harrow Weald.

On Monday December 14, the day on which we were originally scheduled to be in London for the start of an eleven-week season, a number of us took part in a lunchtime session of Christmas carols, again in the Piazza, Covent Garden. We had a piano for these concerts, but some members of the orchestra also took part in this one, adding a touch of instrumental colour to the proceedings. We sang about a dozen of the best-known carols, including an arrangement of 'Good King Wenceslas' that I had originally made during my brief period as a schoolteacher. We repeated this on Thursday the

17th, but on that occasion we dropped two of the carols, began with 'Hail, Poetry' (*Pirates*) and ended with 'Feelings of pleasure' (*Gondoliers*): these were both D'Oyly Carte 'trademarks', and they helped to draw attention to our predicament. We then went to a nearby hostelry, the Peacock, for refreshments; this all helped to take our minds off the Company's approaching demise.

A very welcome feature of our performances in this last season was the inclusion of a number of guest artists. Several of these (John Reed, Valerie Masterson and Pamela Field) were former principals, but we also had Sandra Dugdale (soon to be involved in four of the Brent Walker productions) as Phyllis (*Iolanthe)*, and Laureen Livingstone (another fellow student from the RSAMD) as Elsie Maynard (*Yeomen*). Laureen had played Elsie in the City of London Festival production in 1978, conducted by Sandy Faris, and with Tommy Steele as Jack Point. There was also a guest appearance by Sir Charles Mackerras. These guest rehearsals started at the Old Vic on November 23 with Pamela Field in *Iolanthe* (she too was playing Phyllis). John Reed, as the Lord Chancellor, joined on the 24th and, following the dress rehearsal in the morning of the 26th, *Iolanthe* opened that evening. Pamela also played Josephine in the short run of *Pinafore* (December 16–19).

Next to appear was Valerie Masterson who made two guest appearances as Mabel (December 21 and 22) in the second run of *Pirates* (December 21–26); the evening performance on December 23 was conducted by Sir Charles Mackerras. Christmas Day was on Friday that year, but we were back on Saturday for the last two performances of *Pirates* before having a further two-day break, starting again on December 29 with another seven performances of *Iolanthe*; this time Sandra Dugdale (as Phyllis) was the guest artist. On December 31 we sang 'Auld Lang Syne' for the last time. There was another break on New Year's Day, but, as in previous years (and despite being just weeks from closure), we had to make up for these breaks by having extra matinees; there were two performances each day on December 30 and 31, and two more on Saturday January 2. This was followed by a half-week of *Pinafore* (January 4–6), this time with Vivian Tierney as Josephine, and a full week of *Mikado* (January 7–13). Rehearsals during the first week were back at the Adelphi.

If anyone was still in any doubt as to what would happen at the end of February it was finally made clear in a letter from Peter Riley, dated January 12, which stated that the Company would close down after the last performance on Saturday February 27, 1982. Contracts would terminate on that date, and the Company was not in a position to offer any more work. He said that the decision to close had not been taken lightly, but was the result of insufficient funds being raised to enable us to continue. He ended by saying that our service with the Company was much appreciated and wished us every success for the future. And so that was that: no eleventh-hour reprieve; all we could do now was to enjoy the last few weeks of the Company's existence.

We then had a week of *Yeomen* (January 14–20), being joined this time by Laureen Livingstone as Elsie. Although credited in the advance publicity with only one appearance (December 23) it was thought at one time that Sir Charles Mackerras might also conduct a performance of *Yeomen* (an opera he later recorded with Welsh National Opera), but this didn't happen. *Yeomen* was followed by a week of *Ruddigore* (January 21–27) and on the last day we had the second of our Schools' Specials; once again I conducted the matinee. On Tuesday the 26th I went down to Sussex to play for Geoffrey Shovelton at a concert at the Beacon School in Crowborough. With exactly one month to go, we followed *Ruddigore* with a week of *Iolanthe* (January 28–February 3); Sandra Dugdale again played Phyllis. In one unusual performance the overture was conducted by Fraser, Act I was conducted by Sandy Faris and Act II by Sir Charles Mackerras (although this was not credited). This was followed by a week of *Sorcerer* (February 4–10); Pamela Field was again the guest artist, this time playing Aline. On Monday February 1 there had been a run-through of *Sorcerer* with the orchestra. There was an understudy call on the Tuesday and the dress rehearsal was on the Thursday morning before we opened that evening – and these were the Company's last proper opera rehearsals. All rehearsals in the next three weeks were devoted entirely to the Last Night.

On Sunday February 7 we gave a concert at the army base at Aldershot, organised by one of the chaplains, Father Paul Lenihan, who was a great fan of the Company. Security was, of course, very tight, and it was slightly alarming to be faced with armed guards at the entrance to the base where we had to show our authorisation. Those taking part were Vivian Tierney, Lorraine Daniels, Jill Pert, Roberta Morrell, Jane Stanford, Geoffrey Shovelton, Alistair Donkin and Michael Buchan, with myself at the piano. Paul Lenihan, another larger-than-life character, sadly died at too early an age some years later.

After the show the following evening, we paid our final visit to the Arts Club in Dover Street. Knowing that it was our last season, they had laid on an extra-special three-course meal for us, each course loosely based on one of the operas. The menu itself ('menu gastronomique d'Oyly [sic] Carte') had been written out in exquisite calligraphy with little drawings to accompany each course; it too must surely be a collector's item. The first course was 'Three little maids' (smoked trout in profiteroles), the main course was 'Rondelle de veau des Gondoliers' (loin of veal with a sauce Martini) and for dessert we had a 'Tutti-Frutti Mikado' (a multicoloured open fruit tart). There were also excellent wines to accompany the first two courses. It was another splendid occasion.

Two days later we had the third of our Schools' Specials. I conducted the matinee (*Sorcerer*), but I also had to conduct the evening performance. We followed *Sorcerer* with a third week of *Mikado* (February 11–17), our number-one crowd-puller. During this run, on Sunday 14, there was a return visit to Norwich for a D'Oyly Carte in Concert, the last one we gave while the Company was still performing. On this occasion we ended with the Act 11 finale of *HMS Pinafore*. With its patriotic sentiment ("For he is an Englishman") this seemed just as appropriate as 'Feelings of pleasure', and *Pinafore* was also the opera that would shortly be our swan song. (These G&S concerts continued after the Company closed but, as the name D'Oyly Carte could no longer be used, they were marketed under different titles – An Evening of Gilbert & Sullivan, or Gilbert & Sullivan in Concert – eventually becoming The Magic of Gilbert and Sullivan.) During this last London season I went to Bristol with Meston Reid and Vivian Tierney to take part in yet another television programme; once again they sang 'Refrain, audacious tar' (*Pinafore*). We were just one item among several, and one thing I remember is that there was an owl in the studio. It sat on a perch and seemed to be able to swivel its head almost completely independently of its body, following the progress of anyone who walked past it; this was very amusing to watch. After the session we were put up in a hotel before returning to London the following morning.

In the week after the Norwich concert we received another letter, dated February 16, from Peter Riley. Acknowledging that it was a sad time for all of us, he emphasised that there was no way in which we could continue after February 27. At the end of the current financial year, on March 31, the Company would be faced with a trading deficit of over £250,000. Our box-office income, even with current sponsorship, simply wasn't enough to enable us to keep going. He also paid tribute to Barclays Bank which had been our main sponsor for just under four years. In that time they had helped us to the tune of some £300,000, had paid the rent and rates on Tabard House, and had covered a large proportion of our publicity and marketing costs. Thanks were also due to the Hanson Trust and the Ellerman Charitable Trusts whose contributions had helped us to stay afloat.

There had been much talk about the future of the Company and the possibility of updated versions of the operas after the style of the Broadway *Pirates* (which had been an undoubted success, and which D'Oyly Carte would support when it came to London three months later), but as usual much of the talk (and the press coverage) had been inaccurate. Lord Forte, the hotelier and caterer, had earlier offered financial assistance, but he was currently involved in a takeover bid for the Savoy group and this brought him into acrimonious conflict with Sir Hugh Wontner who was also one of the D'Oyly Carte trustees. It was believed, rightly or wrongly, that Forte's offer of assistance had been dependent on his gaining control of the Savoy, although it was never made clear if his business dealings did in fact cause the trustees to reject his offer. He had now become involved in a campaign for a new D'Oyly Carte, although it remained to be seen if anything would come of this. But the days of retaining a company, staff and orchestra for a full year, and touring continually for forty-eight weeks of the year, were definitely over. (It is perhaps only circuses and funfairs that are now on the road all the year round.) If anything came of the campaign it might be possible to offer work for anything between twenty-four to thirty weeks every year, and this could even include further tours of North America, Australasia and perhaps Japan – but it was very much a question of 'if' and not 'when'. Despite this somewhat doubtful possibility we were all encouraged to keep in touch in the hope of a positive outcome, but now it really did feel like the end. The office too was affected by all of this uncertainty. It would continue after February 27, but on a reduced basis.

After *Mikado* we had four more performances of *Sorcerer* (February 18–20). On the Thursday afternoon there was a short concert at Moor Park Golf Club, although I can't remember how this came about. Company members were now exploring every opportunity for further employment, and on the Friday I played for Alistair Donkin who was auditioning at English National Opera; as usual I conducted the matinee on Saturday. I had now conducted all three *Sorcerer* matinees and at the end of one of them (possibly this last one) I had an interesting encounter. I had put down my baton, but was still standing inside the barrier that separated the pit from the auditorium. I was then aware of a little lady, dressed fairly inconspicuously and wearing a woolly hat, who had come up to the barrier. She said that she had very much enjoyed the performance and, as I thought I detected an Australian accent, I wondered if she might have seen one of our performances on the 1979 Australasian tour. She kept on talking, still being very complimentary, and then said, "I know what I'm talking about, you know. I'm in the business myself". My ears pricked up immediately, and I said, "Oh, what's your name?" "You won't have heard of me", she said. "My name's Joy Nichols". Well, I *had* heard of her. She had been the original female lead in a famous radio show, *Take It From Here* with Jimmy Edwards and her fellow Australian, Dick Bentley. I had heard the show often in the later 1950s, but by that time her role had been taken over by June Whitfield and I couldn't honestly say that I remembered hearing her when I was younger. But it was still fascinating to have met her.

On Sunday February 21 I took part in a rather different event: an eightieth birthday celebration for Henry Havergal who had been principal of the Royal Scottish Academy of Music and Drama when I was a student there in the early 1960s. Billed as 'A Music-Making with Henry', it had been arranged by his friends and was held at the Royal College of Music. It took the form of an afternoon choral concert which Henry conducted; those of us who turned up (mainly former RSAMD students and pupils from the various public schools at which he had taught) formed the choir. We rehearsed in the morning and then had a lunch break from 1pm–3pm before starting the concert which consisted of the first eleven numbers of Bach's *Mass in B Minor* followed by Parry's *Blest Pair of Sirens*. We had sung both of these works at the RSAM, and I particularly remembered *Blest Pair of Sirens*, as we had sung it for Her

Majesty Queen Elizabeth the Queen Mother who had come to the College in her capacity as Patron: it was supposedly one of her favourite pieces of music. At the rehearsal I found myself sitting beside a tall distinguished-looking gentleman who turned out to be Robert Washington Shirley, 13th Earl Ferrers, who at that time was deputy leader of the House of Lords. He had been educated at Winchester when Henry (who had previously been director of Music at Fettes, Haileybury and Harrow) had been Master of Music [sic] there. It was all quite a change from our world of G&S, but it served to take my mind off the fast-approaching end of D'Oyly Carte.

There had been much press coverage of our plight throughout the previous year and this had gathered momentum as we came into London. One article, written by Martin Haldane, appeared in the *Scottish Opera News* of February 1982; it suggested that in refusing to give the Company a grant the Arts Council was running the risk of discrediting the system of public funding for the arts, and pointed out that the Scottish Arts Council had supported the Company on its last tour of Scotland (this had been mentioned in the October 1980 issue of *Scottish Opera News* which also highlighted the careers of Freddie Lloyd and Ken Sandford). Another article, by Janet Watts in the *Observer Review*, said that the Company was a much-loved institution, despite any shortcomings, but also drew attention to the fact that in refusing to give the Company a grant the Arts Council had actually rejected the advice of its own advisers. There was clearly a great deal of sympathy from many quarters and not just from die-hard fans. Martin Haldane's article concluded with an apposite quotation from *Utopia Limited* – "With fury deep we burn".

In addition to the numerous press articles, the short procession to the Piazza (with Peter Moore, the dray and horses) and our subsequent concert performances had all helped to draw attention to our imminent closure. The current prime minister, Margaret Thatcher, showed no obvious interest in G&S, but former prime minister Sir Harold Wilson was a lifelong fan.

On one publicity stunt, when members of the Company, in costume, travelled around Westminster in an old open-topped London bus, Sir Harold and a former Lord Chancellor, Lord Elwyn-Jones, both came to lend their support; this turned into a welcome photo opportunity. Their support, sadly, was in vain, but they were not the only people to make an effort to save us: there were also leading lights in the theatrical world. During our last week a delegation consisting of Richard Todd, Sir Geraint Evans, Joanna Lumley, Derren Nesbit, Roy Dotrice and Gordon Jackson handed in a petition to 10 Downing Street – a protest at the failure of the Arts Council to give the Company a grant – which was received by the MP Ian Gow who was then Margaret Thatcher's parliamentary private secretary. Peter Riley and a researcher were also present. The petition had been devised and organised by Janet Reeve, a Friend of D'Oyly Carte and loyal Company fan. It too had no effect, but we were grateful to Janet for her efforts and also for the moral support of these distinguished thespians.

The last week (February 22–27) was devoted entirely to *HMS Pinafore* – seven performances in all. The tension mounted as the week progressed and the emotion became more palpable. The end of the Company would be more than just the loss of a job: for many of us it would be the end of a way of life. Jimmie Marsland had been there since 1949, Gordon MacKenzie since 1954 (although not continuously); Beti Lloyd-Jones had recently celebrated twenty-five years with the Company and, had the Company survived, Kenneth Sandford would have celebrated *his* twenty-five years in July. The Company really was like a family and for those like myself who had stayed for any length of time it was as much the thought of possibly not seeing many people again (certainly not regularly), as much as being made redundant, that was the hardest thing to come to terms with. We had our final Schools' Special on Wednesday the 24th, and again I conducted the matinee. As there would be no more performances after

February 27, and therefore no need to rehearse principals or understudies, the rehearsal time in the last three weeks had been given over to the Last Night (a draft of the programme was marked 'strictly top secret'); the dress rehearsal (the Company's last-ever rehearsal) took place on the morning of Friday the 26th.

And so we came to our last day: February 27, 1982. This followed the general pattern of the last day of a London winter season which consisted of an ordinary matinee followed by something rather different in the evening – what had come to be called a Last Night. *This* Last Night was clearly going to be something very special, but even the matinee that day was no ordinary one: it was the last complete performance of an opera given by the original D'Oyly Carte Opera Company. As this was something of a historic occasion I was surprised that it had not been given any special publicity and I was equally surprised that it had been entrusted to me to conduct it. But as I was not involved in the Last Night (Sandy Faris and Fraser Goulding were conducting), it was perhaps just a way of sharing out the work and I was simply told to conduct the matinee as usual. It was performed absolutely straight, with no gimmicks and nothing out of the ordinary. I had conducted many a lacklustre matinee (often, mid-week, played to a sparse and unreceptive audience), but this time we had a full house and everyone knew that it was the last complete opera performance. Cast and orchestra pulled out the stops and gave of their best; I hope I did too. Recording procedures were in place for the Last Night, and I was sorry that it hadn't been possible for the matinee to be recorded as well. John Reed was the guest artist (as Sir Joseph Porter) for this last *Pinafore* and I was glad that he was there: he had been with D'Oyly Carte for twenty-eight years, from 1951, before leaving after the Australasian tour. *HMS Pinafore* was the first opera that my school had put on in 1958 and it was the opera I had conducted in Australia on the very day that the school was celebrating the twenty-first year of its opera productions;

now, by another "curious coincidence" it was to be my last performance with D'Oyly Carte.

I can still see the curtain coming down for the last time, with the Company waving to the audience: the emotion was obvious on many faces and some may well have been in tears. But it is at such highly charged moments that an element of farce will often creep in – and one did, just then. I must have made a particularly expansive flourish with my baton on the last chord as it caught on the edge of our conductor's stand and flipped out of my hand; I had no idea if it had simply landed on the floor of the pit or had finished up in the auditorium (possibly to be retained by a souvenir hunter). I had previously decided that I would never use this baton again in case it got broken, but would keep it as a very special memento – and now I had lost it! In fact I didn't lose it: luckily it had landed at my feet, and after this near disaster I made sure that it was put away safely. I still have it.

There remained the Company's last actual performance, the final Last Night – this time only for the Friends of D'Oyly Carte. Abandoning the pattern that had been established over a number of years, it had been decided that the evening performance would be a concert of items from all of the surviving G&S operas, starting with *Cox and Box* (Sullivan without Gilbert, but, like *Trial by Jury*, a long-established Company curtain-raiser); there was even a nod to the first G&S collaboration (the chorus 'Climbing over rocky mountain' from *Pirates* had originally been part of *Thespis*). Many of the operas (*Cox*, *Trial*, *Patience*, *Ida* and *Gondoliers*) were currently out of the repertoire and this had necessitated much revision. Luckily the majority of the items from these operas were for principals only, but there were some numbers that were unfamiliar to many choristers, particularly the latest intake, and there were excerpts from *Utopia Limited* and *The Grand Duke* that were known only to those members of the Company who had been in the centenary performances in 1975. (A decade earlier some numbers from *Utopia* had been recorded by the Company and issued with the 1964 recording of *Trial by Jury*.)

In keeping with the element of surprise, as in previous Last Nights, the programme for the evening contained very little apart from a short history of the Royal Adelphi Theatre, a list of the principals, chorus, staff and orchestra, and information about the Friends of D'Oyly Carte: it could not list the pieces to be performed as the audience had to be kept in the dark. Geoffrey Shovelton had designed an extra slip-on cover for it which also listed Company members, the music staff, the orchestra and the Friends' information. It also listed the operas in chronological order and this was the only guide to what the audience might expect to hear, although many of them would have known that order anyway. One further item that it listed was a concert overture, based on themes from the Savoy operas, which had been written by Paul Seeley. This opened the second half of the programme, but it didn't find its way on to the recording that was issued later.

The evening began with an appearance by Peter Moore, the Town Crier (complete with bell), who introduced the Company, thanked the Great British Public for its support throughout the Company's existence and invited everyone to sit back and enjoy the evening. The first item was the overture to *The Yeomen of the Guard* which Fraser conducted; the programme then proceeded more or less chronologically, starting with *Cox and Box*, with items being introduced from time to time by members of the Company. Despite the fact that everyone knew that this really was the last performance, it was still an evening of great fun. The more serious numbers, such as the almost Mozartian 'The world is but a broken toy' (*Princess Ida*), the madrigal 'When the buds are blossoming' (*Ruddigore*) and 'Eagle high' (*Utopia Limited*), were performed straight, but at every opportunity there were ad-libs and asides such as "See you at the Labour Exchange". Towards the end of the evening a number was inserted into the original programme; this was 'Dole queue ladies', essentially the ladies' chorus 'In a doleful train' (*Patience*) with appropriate new words – "In a full dole queue". On a couple of occasions the audience was invited to join in. The first of these was in the encore to 'Poor wandering one' (*Pirates*) when a prompt sheet was dropped from the flies in true pantomime tradition, with just "Ah, ah, ah, ah" written on it; the second occasion was an encore to the trio 'My eyes are fully open' (*Ruddigore*) which was taken at such a breakneck speed that even the principals could barely keep up with it. This was all very much in the Last Night tradition and everyone, including the Company, enjoyed it to the full, although there was, at times, an almost defiant mood from the stage – often alcohol-fuelled which was hardly surprising. After the numbers from *Utopia* and *Grand Duke* there was the Act II finale of *Mikado* followed by the only possible piece to end with: 'Once more *gondolieri*' (*Gondoliers*) with its appropriate words – never more so than on this occasion – "We leave you with feelings of pleasure!"

As I wasn't taking part in the Last Night I stood in the wings, as I had done so often in my first year, and listened to it all for the last time – certainly the last time with D'Oyly Carte. (I had been allocated two Last Night tickets but I gave them to Hazel and Christine Oakley.) I couldn't quite believe that it had all come to an end – not just my seven years with the Company but the entire one hundred and seven years since *Trial by Jury* in 1875. A phrase from *Ruddigore* came to mind: "Can this be possible?" After the performance there was a short speech from Gordon MacKenzie and Freddie Lloyd came onstage to thank the audience (which included the veteran former principal Marjorie Eyre) for its support. Dame Bridget then said a few words of farewell from her box, an effort that must have caused her considerable strain. A flyer, which was available in the theatre, announced that a recording had been made of the performance and would soon be on sale; proceeds would go towards helping to build a future for D'Oyly Carte: many people were working hard to ensure that there *would* be a future. But what sort of future might that be

– *if* it ever happened? I had been privileged to be part of a unique theatrical institution which had just run its course. It had been a wonderful experience, particularly with the foreign tours in 1978 and 1979, and I would be unlikely to find similar employment anywhere else. Despite the ups and downs it really had been "nothing like work". Once again I thought of Freddie Lloyd's words – "a paid holiday"; it had often seemed like that, but it had also been so very much more.

Postscript

There was little celebration after the last performance on February 27 – no normal after-show carousing in some bar or other. Most people still couldn't quite believe that the Company had finally closed, and simply went home, in my case to Eastbourne, hoping that there might soon be a phone call to say that money had magically appeared, and that we would be back on the road again before long. We had been told, in so many words, to go home, sit tight and wait for further developments: hope springs eternal. The Company *did* reform, but not until 1988 following Dame Bridget's death in 1985, although *its* performing life was much shorter than our one hundred and seven years. Dick Condon, from the Theatre Royal, Norwich, became the new general manager, but despite the fact that he had happily welcomed us to Norwich on many occasions it was made quite clear that there was no question of the new Company automatically re-employing anyone from the old Company who wished to join: you had to re-audition. Several Company members *did* appear in the first season: Vivian Tierney and Gareth Jones sang principal roles, as did former choristers Jill Pert and Philip Creasy, with Pamela Baxter and Guy Matthews in the chorus, and there was also former principal contralto Gillian Knight who had been with the Company from 1959 to 1965. I never became part of the New D'Oyly Carte, but by then I had already started out in other directions.

At first, in 1982, I realised the mistake of having purchased a property in Eastbourne. It was very pleasant living there

(I could listen to the army bands during the day, and I did "like to be beside the seaside"), but there was simply no work to be had. I would have to try to teach again, which I had resolutely refused even to consider, to attempt to find similar work, either in another opera company or perhaps in a musical, or simply do something else. But what else could I do? Any career change would require further training. I vaguely considered taking up my childhood idea of becoming an architect, but I soon realised that that wasn't remotely practical. Being now unemployed I had to sign on; I did this every two weeks. We had been given redundancy payments, differing amounts depending on how long you had been with the Company, and mine was enough to last me for a year; that at least was something, but I had recently taken on a mortgage, and would have to find some regular work fairly soon.

I now had time to look for more things for the flat and also to get to know Eastbourne. While exploring the town one Sunday, I came across a second-hand shop. To my amazement there was a small bust of Sullivan in the window, but as it was Sunday the shop was closed. I hastily scribbled a note, which I put through the letter box, asking the owners to keep the item for me. Luckily, when I went back on Monday, I was able to purchase it. Was this serendipity? Or, given my close association with Sullivan's music, was it another "curious coincidence" finding the bust in the very town I had chosen to live in? It took pride of place on my new piano. With unlimited time at my disposal, and a photocopy of the surviving solo part to hand, I then sat down to try to reconstruct Sullivan's unpublished cello concerto, which had been destroyed in a fire. I eventually managed to do this, although it took me a full year. As I sat at the piano, working at the reconstruction, I had the master looking down on me, overseeing my efforts and hopefully providing some inspiration!

One of the biggest problems I now faced was simply being so far from London. This meant that if I was able to find any employment in the city I would have to spend a good part of the day travelling, but although I was quite prepared to go up to London every day there were a great many musicians there – all looking for work – and it was highly unlikely that any potential employer would bother to phone someone in Eastbourne. If I wanted to work in the city I would have to be on hand. Company members had of course returned to their homes, some in London, but others further afield, and it was now even difficult to engage in any socialising, the one exception being with Geoffrey Shovelton who then lived near Heathfield in East Sussex. We spent much time together bemoaning our situation, but we also began to make plans for future collaborations if neither of us could find any permanent work.

The Savoyard survived the Company by two issues, appearing in March and September 1982. The March issue began with a brief introduction, which stated that the Company had stopped performing; it also expressed a hope that it would soon return. There was an account of D'Oyly Carte for Schools by Elaine Draper who had recently joined the Company as its publicity and marketing officer. This included some of Geoffrey Shovelton's illustrations of the characters in *Pirates*. There was also an obituary of Joan Robertson, Freddie Lloyd's former secretary, who had died in November. I didn't contribute anything to this issue. Later, as the Company had now ceased to perform, many of us were free to take part in a week of concerts in July at Pencarrow House in Cornwall, the home of the Molesworth-St Aubyn family. This was to celebrate not only Gilbert and Sullivan generally, but *Iolanthe* specifically, as it was now in its centenary year, and Sullivan, a friend of the family, had actually written part of the opera there. It was also publicity for the house itself. Although already open to the public it was hoped that the concerts would attract even more visitors. Those who took part were Vivian Tierney, Lorraine Daniels, Kenneth Sandford, John Ayldon, Meston Reid, James Conroy-Ward and myself, and we also had a local amateur chorus.

Peter Riley was there too, and Peter and I stayed in the house while the others were accommodated elsewhere.

In September came *The Savoyard–Iolanthe Centenary Issue*. *Iolanthe* was the first opera to have its premiere at the Savoy Theatre and was, strictly speaking, the first of the Savoy Operas – the centenary coming later in the year on November 25, my birthday, and yet another "curious coincidence". My final article appeared in this issue. It concerned the possible provenance of one of the songs in *The Grand Duke*: 'Come, bumpers – aye, ever-so-many', a number that had been taken up by, among others, Patricia Leonard and Lorraine Daniels. There was also an article by Paul Seeley on Helen Lenoir (Helen Couper Black, Dame Bridget's step-grandmother), an account of the final Last Night, and news of various musical activities involving Company members. Peter Riley was the subject of a long-running series – Introducing the Company – in which he expressed a hope that there would still be a future for D'Oyly Carte in some form or other. He also contributed an account of the week's activities at Pencarrow. We didn't know at the time that this would be the last issue of *The Savoyard*.

The end of D'Oyly Carte didn't mean the end of my association with G&S – far from it. G&S was vital in helping me to keep going during the first two or three years after 1982, and there were numerous concerts such as those at Pencarrow. D'Oyly Carte in Concert (at first renamed An Evening of Gilbert and Sullivan) continued to perform. The artists were now all former Company members – principals *and* chorus. On one occasion we gave a concert in Leeds and rather than spend some of my precious fee on a night's lodging I decided to drive back to Eastbourne. The first few hours were not too bad, but by the time I was within striking distance of home I was so tired that it was a miracle that I didn't end up in a ditch. Luckily, at that time of the morning, there was virtually no traffic around. I also became part of a concert party called The Best of Gilbert and Sullivan that toured the United States and Canada annually for almost twenty years. Initially the singers were Vivian Tierney, Lorraine Daniels, Kenneth Sandford, Alistair Donkin and Geoffrey Shovelton, although, apart from Geoffrey and myself, the personnel changed several times over the years; among other artists who joined the group were Patricia Leonard, Sandra Dugdale and John Ayldon.

The eventual reconstruction of Sullivan's cello concerto, latterly in collaboration with Sir Charles Mackerras, received its first performance in 1986 and was later recorded. In 1989 I wrote and presented fourteen interval talks for BBC Radio 2's presentation of the complete G&S operas, and some years later I became musical director for semi-staged performances at Grim's Dyke (Gilbert's former home). In 2000 I conducted a concert at the Royal Albert Hall, with the Royal Philharmonic Orchestra, former Company principals and a chorus of over five hundred, to commemorate the centenary of Sullivan's death. This work was "all very well in its way", but it was still "not enough" to keep body and soul together.

With the closure of the Company, many of us began to broaden our repertoire. Vivian, Lorraine, Geoffrey, Clive Harré and I formed a group called London Airs (specialising in Victorian music) for which I made some arrangements. Some members of the Company found work with other opera companies, and some went into the numerous musicals that were running in London. I applied for jobs with various companies and even managed to contact some well-known individuals in the music business such as Cyril Ornadel, who wrote the music for *Pickwick*, but with no success.

I realised that sooner or later I would have to leave Eastbourne, and I finally moved into London in 1984, where I stayed first of all with some friends while I put my flat on the market, shortly before the first of the tours with The Best of Gilbert and Sullivan. On the advice of Albert Truelove I then joined the Concert Artistes Association where I began to make contacts that were very useful in finding other work. I continued to apply for permanent jobs, but eventually found that I could just about make a living as a freelance accompanist, repetiteur and conductor, and soon realised that I enjoyed the freedom and variety that this entailed. In London there was a wide range of options such as playing for opera companies, children's ballet classes and other groups, and I later conducted two amateur operatic societies. I played in hotels and restaurants, often with singers from the Company, and I also played at masonic functions, many of these held at the Connaught Rooms in Great Queen Street where I again met Andre Eldon-Erdington who had organised D'Oyly Carte's visits to the Arts Club in Dover Street. I began working for the Council for Music in Hospitals, as it was called then, and was the musical director for a number of pantomimes. This variety soon became the pattern for the rest of my working life, but all of that, as they say, is another story.

THE END

Lightning Source UK Ltd.
Milton Keynes UK
UKHW040704020119
334826UK00001B/190/P

9 781786 233165